The

New SCHOOL MANAGEMENT

by

Wandering Around  !

In memory of our good friend and colleague, Larry E. Frase

The New SCHOOL MANAGEMENT by Wandering Around

William A. Streshly
Susan Penny Gray
Larry E. Frase

Foreword by Fenwick W. English

CORWIN
A SAGE Company

CORWIN
A SAGE Company

FOR INFORMATION:

Corwin
A SAGE Company
2455 Teller Road
Thousand Oaks, California 91320
(800) 233-9936
www.corwin.com

SAGE Publications Ltd.
1 Oliver's Yard
55 City Road
London EC1Y 1SP
United Kingdom

SAGE Publications India Pvt. Ltd.
B 1/I 1 Mohan Cooperative Industrial Area
Mathura Road, New Delhi 110 044
India

SAGE Publications Asia-Pacific Pte. Ltd.
3 Church Street
#10-04 Samsung Hub
Singapore 049483

Based on the original book *School Management by Wandering Around*, by Larry E Frase and Robert Hetzel.

Original drawings by David Sullivan.

Printed in the United States of America.

Library of Congress Cataloging-in-Publication Data

Streshly, William A.

The new school management by wandering around / William A. Streshly, Susan Penny Gray, Larry E. Frase.

p. cm.
Includes bibliographical references and index.

ISBN 978-1-4129-9604-4 (pbk. : alk. paper)

1. School management and organization—United States. 2. Educational leadership—United States. I. Gray, Susan Penny. II. Frase, Larry E. III. Title.

LB2805.S8144 2012
371.200973—dc23   2011039965

This book is printed on acid-free paper.

Acquisitions Editor: Arnis Burvikovs
Associate Editor: Desirée A. Bartlett
Editorial Assistant: Kimberly Greenberg
Production Editor: Cassandra Margaret Seibel
Copy Editor: Teresa Herlinger
Typesetter: C&M Digitals (P) Ltd.
Proofreader: Wendy Jo Dymond
Indexer: Sheila Bodell
Cover Designer: Gail Buschman
Permissions Editor: Karen Ehrmann

Certified Chain of Custody
Promoting Sustainable Forestry
www.sfiprogram.org
SFI-01268

SFI label applies to text stock

12 13 14 15 16 10 9 8 7 6 5 4 3 2 1

Contents

Additional materials and resources related to
The New School Management by Wandering Around can be
found at www.corwin.com/wandering.

List of Tables and Figures

Foreword

A Life of Managing by Wandering Around

A Tribute to the "Larry Lens"

M anaging things by wandering around came naturally to Larry Frase, coauthor of the original *School Management by Wandering Around*. After having travelled with Larry and his lovely wife, Maria, on trips to Portugal and New Zealand, and watching how Larry was an itinerant learner, how he let his curiosity about things go where they led him, and how he framed his observations after those incursions, I realized this was a man who was open to being amazed, amused, and absorbed.

In retrospect, I think there was a lot of Larry in that first book, perhaps more than he actually was aware. Also, I think a leader who is successful with the idea of managing by wandering around has to suspend prestructuring everything so that he or she only sees what the structure lets in. Being open means not imposing too many conscious filters and trying to come to understand the unconscious ones that can be attributed to culture, gender, language, and past lived histories.

Successful managing by wandering around is allowing oneself to be playful and supple, fluid, and without too much regard for the system one is in. Managing by Wandering Around is not for compulsive rule followers. It means seeing through your own lens but also seeing around those same lenses. It means allowing yourself to be curious and to avoid the requirement that everything has to have some larger and immediate purpose, or not insisting that meaning must always be known first, before observation.

One good test for the leader doing MBWA is the "Larry lens." The "Larry lens" is to just go with the flow (and flow was one of Larry's favorite academic pursuits) and see the paradoxes, contradictions, and humor in situations. When Larry found such intersections in his travels, he would retain their complexity through humor. He had a natural way of mimicking speech of those he found to be profound and profane. If one can find something to laugh about in the human condition, I think one is beginning to deal with the gray space between all of the blacks and whites framed by theory. Humor is one of the ways we see grey in the world, and it is a way we joke about some of the false blacks and whites of organizational life.

So this is what I remember most about my times with Larry Frase. It was the laughter at the end of the day of wandering around the side streets of little towns on the Douro River of Portugal and driving down such narrow streets in Porto we had to pull in the side-view mirrors or have them sheared off. It was asking for directions and walking the parched dry furrows of the terraced rows of grapevines high above the river and questioning the growers about how and why water was important. It was learning and listening with mind, body, and heart.

I think Bill Streshly and Penny Gray, both of whom knew Larry well, were the right pair to extend "Larry's lens" in this wonderful revision.

Fenwick W. English
R. Wendell Eaves Senior Distinguished
Professor of Educational Leadership
School of Education
University of North Carolina at Chapel Hill

Preface

Being a principal is primarily a thinking, walking, and talking job.

—Neil McNiell and Ray Boyd,
Australian school principals

I n the spring of 1987, Fenwick English asked our mutual friend and colleague Larry Frase if he would be interested in writing a book on Management by Wandering Around (MBWA). As superintendent of a small school district near Tucson, Arizona, he didn't know where he was going to find the time to complete such a project or even if he knew enough to fill a book. He wondered, how much can you say about wandering around? But the offer came at the right time. Larry had been considering hanging up his superintendent spurs and pursuing his original professional goal of joining the faculty at San Diego State University. So Larry decided to accept Fenwick's challenge, and in August of 1987, he went to work on the original best-selling version of this book. It was titled, simply, *School Management by Wandering Around*.

After giving the potential contents of the book much thought, Larry realized that many of the administrative practices he had instituted in his school district—for example, the superintendent being in the schools once a week, the principals spending 40 percent of the school day in classrooms, the teachers maintaining a focus on curriculum and instruction, and the entire leadership team giving sincere attention to the mental health and professional readiness of staff—all were integral to the MBWA philosophy. However, he found the number of actual research studies on MBWA extremely sparse. When he looked for research to support the MBWA idea, he actually found only three studies that analyzed practices resembling MBWA. Consequently, Larry relied heavily on the empirical observations of very successful professional school administrators as well as his own practical experience—a decision that rendered the original book particularly valuable for real-world administrators learning to cope with the myriad problems of the modern school. This book preserves this worthy characteristic while at the same time bringing other aspects of MBWA preparation up to date.

The first edition of *School Management by Wandering Around* was printed in 1990, and much to the publisher's and Larry's surprise, it was a big success. Larry began the task of updating the first edition but passed away suddenly before he could finish the job. We decided to pick up where Larry left off for two reasons: First, Larry was a loyal friend and colleague with a missionary's zeal for reforming the way schools are run. Second, and equally important, the fundamental concepts developed in the book are more important now than ever.

The *good* news is that researchers have now produced numerous well-constructed research studies on MBWA or closely related topics—and all indicate that MBWA promotes desirable outcomes (see Chapter 5). We now have strong evidence that being out and about in classrooms is highly related to such sought-after outcomes as improved student discipline, higher teacher efficacy, higher teacher-perceived effectiveness of the school, higher opinions of teacher evaluation and professional development, and higher student achievement. The list goes on, as you will find in the ensuing chapters.

When Larry was writing the first edition, his coauthor Bob Hetzel asked, "And what are principals supposed to do while wandering?" A darn good question, and we have answered it! We have included a brand-new section on "walk-through" classroom observation techniques, including descriptions of some of the most successful walk-through models. These powerful strategies have caught on nationally and internationally. This book gives principals the tools to get into classrooms and focus their attention on the "right stuff"—the curriculum. School leadership is an art, and we should not apologize for the passion, ardor, and other personal qualities of great school administrators. We believe Aristotle was right when he declared that poetry is truer than history.

The figures and tables from this book are also available online at www.corwin.com/wandering for downloading and use with individuals and school learning teams.

In writing this book, we have made an effort to present practical approaches to the school administrator's job. We do this by guiding the reader through strategies for dealing with the nitty-gritty of school leadership, beginning with a definition of School Management by Wandering Around and a description of its potential for building great leaders and effective school organizations. Building on the strong research and practice base, we provide a well-defined system of "what to do" in classroom walk-throughs. In addition, we present practical discussions of the applications of this powerful leadership style, ranging widely from such topics as developing meeting agenda to supervising instruction, and from dealing with marginal teachers to creating safe campuses. In short, this book presents the best of MBWA research and the related administrative practices that have emerged over the past few decades.

William A. Streshly

Susan Penny Gray

Acknowledgments

We acknowledge here our dear departed friend and colleague, Larry E. Frase, who, along with Robert Hetzel, coauthored the original *School Management by Wandering Around* (1990). Larry's wife, Maria, has supported us throughout our work on this new version of that book.

We especially appreciate the advice and criticism of Larry Marquand, an expert human resources consultant who grounded our discussions of personnel management in real-world experience. We also appreciate and acknowledge Kathy Juline, who helped assure the flow and readability of the book. A special "thank you" goes to our very talented artist, David Sullivan, who drew the cartoons for this book.

Finally, we thank our respective families for their encouragement and assistance. Their unflagging support made the task of writing this book enjoyable.

About the Authors

William A. Streshly is Emeritus Professor of Educational Leadership and former Chair of the Department of Administration, Rehabilitation, and Post-Secondary Education at San Diego State University. Prior to his service at the university, he served for 30 years in K–12 school districts in California, including 5 years as a high school principal and 14 years as superintendent of districts ranging in size from 3,000 to 25,000 students.

As a Senior Lead Curriculum Management Auditor for Phi Delta Kappa International, Dr. Streshly has audited the curriculum and instructional operations of more than 40 school districts in 16 states and the District of Columbia.

Dr. Streshly has authored or coauthored seven books on school law, education reform, school leadership, and educational labor relations; authored or coauthored scores of journal articles; and presented at numerous conferences, including refereed presentations at the National School Boards Association annual conventions and the National Organization on Legal Problems of Education annual conference.

Susan Penny Gray has served for more than 35 years as an instructor and an administrator in Indiana and California. Until 2004, she was the Director of Curriculum Services in the San Marcos Unified School District in San Marcos, California, where she earned a statewide reputation as an expert curriculum leader.

Currently, she is teaching graduate courses in curriculum and educational leadership for San Diego State University and is certified to train administrators and teachers in Conducting Walk-Throughs for Higher Student Achievement. In addition to several journal articles, Dr. Gray has coauthored with William Streshly two other books titled *From Good Schools to Great Schools: What Their Principals Do Well* and *Leading Good Schools to Greatness: Mastering What Great Principals Do Well.*

Dr. Gray received her BA from the University of California at Santa Barbara, her MA from San Diego State University, and her PhD from the Claremont Graduate University–San Diego State University Joint Doctoral Program. She received Phi Kappa Delta International audit training in Burlingame, California, in 1998. She has served on 18 major school district audits in 11 states.

1

Defining the MBWA Leader

Every leader needs to look back once in a while to make sure he has followers.

—Unknown

The first edition of this book was published a few years after Tom Peters and Bob Waterman (1982/2004) noticed that the most successful private sector companies all had CEOs who spent a lot of their time in the field. In their popular book, *In Search of Excellence,* they dubbed this practice "Management by Wandering Around," or "MBWA." In interviews with these outstanding CEOs, they learned that this was the way the leaders stayed abreast of operations, enabling them to anticipate problems before they happen. Really, these superstar execs were not "wandering" at all. Neither were they simply "managing." They were engaged in dynamic leadership of their enterprises—MBWA.

In public schools, the best principals spend a large part of the instructional day in the field (Collins, 2005; S. P. Gray & Streshly, 2010). By "wandering around," the principal becomes the catalyst that brings the individual members of the school community—teachers, instructional aides, parents, students, and administrators—together in the pursuit of excellent schools.

MBWA is an active, person-to-person process that relies on deeds, involvement, and participation to create better schools. It is the school principal's practice of giving up time in the office to be close to the teachers and students on the campus, in classrooms, in the halls, and at school events. Being an MBWA principal means wandering with the purpose in mind of building a better school for students and teachers. It means being close to the people and the action. It means coming out of the protective office and engaging in the day-to-day work of the school at the teacher level. It means searching for ways to better serve teachers so they can do their jobs better.

To be clear, MBWA results in the principal being close to the teachers, but it does not imply micromanagement or "snoopervision." Instead, it allows for informal communication and actually decreases the bureaucratic line of communication. MBWA allows principals to see teachers and staff and talk with them. These short talks have been identified as a powerful change strategy (Downey, Steffy, Poston, & English, 2010).

MBWA principals are out of their chairs and on their feet looking and listening for better ways to do things. They wander
with a purpose.

PERSONAL ATTRIBUTES AND BELIEFS
OF MBWA LEADERS

MBWA leaders know that people are the most important asset
of an organization and that being with them, communicating
with them, and acting on what they say will boost morale.
These leaders learn much more about the heart, soul, and
operation of their organization by being in touch with the
people—other leaders may miss this, and the organization
suffers. General Colin Powell (1995) expressed this very well
when he described his leadership style—"Go where your
flock is" (p. 208).

In schools, student learning is the goal, and people are the
mechanisms for producing and sustaining student achievement. Education is a human relations enterprise. It was no
surprise to us that the highly successful principals we
encountered in an earlier study were all experts in building
relationships (S. P. Gray & Streshly, 2008). The presence of the
MBWA principal and the hands-on approach to problems
genuinely build trust—a critical aspect of healthy professional relationships.

MBWA leaders also know that when given a chance, people speak from their hearts. The words may not be what the
leader wants to hear, but they are what the leader must know
to assess what is going on. The words may sting, and that's
okay. MBWA leaders never punish people for saying what
they believe. Do this once, and likely no one will be honest
with you again. Only yes-men and sycophants will remain in
the organization. When a leader operates with less than 100
percent feedback, the full perspective and the truth are not
knowable. One successful leader told us he rarely finished his
morning rounds without having someone come up to tell him

something of importance that he would not have learned had he not been there in person.

The best MBWA principals boldly confront the "brutal facts" of their current reality. One effective way to identify problems is to regularly survey your community and faculty. Principals who use this proven technique stay ahead of the wave. They use the feedback to support improvement goals and plans. The result is a stronger, more effective campus climate. Resources A and B at the end of this book contain sample parent surveys for elementary and secondary schools.

In his study of private sector CEOs, Collins (2001) described certain critical leadership practices that are necessary for creating this kind of climate in an organization. We found these same practices also apply to MBWA leaders in the school setting, typified by the following:

- They lead with questions, not answers. Earlier we mentioned the importance of creating an environment of trust in building relationships. Leading with questions is a signal to your staff that you want and respect their thoughts above your own concerning the truths of the problem.
- They engage in dialogue and debate, not intimidation.
- They establish protocols to ensure constructive conflict takes place in a trusting atmosphere.

MBWA leaders possess an honest awareness of self and how their day-to-day operations affect everyone in the organization. Their behaviors are consistent with their espoused values. They create, help others create, and help clarify new visions. They encourage and empower others to join in the quest to capture visions and transform them into reality. MBWA leaders are aware of the power, worth, and value of people. They actively pursue the school's mission along with other people because they know that leaders who lock themselves in offices and force their visions on others through power-play memos are seldom successful. Power-play executives scare no one, and no one pays attention. Worse yet, no one is inspired to follow their lead.

Leaders who embrace MBWA do not just spout platitudes describing the value of people; they actually demonstrate that they value people by being with them physically. The best of the great principals also talk about "rolling up their sleeves" and helping with the stuff of curriculum and program development. Simply being with the members of the organization at all levels speaks louder than words. This physical presence with purpose states dramatically, "I'm here because I believe in you. I know that you are key to our success. I want to know what you think—what's good about your work life, what's not so good, and what I can do to make it better."

EXAMPLES OF **MBWA** FROM HISTORY

Throughout the ages, effective leaders have practiced key elements of MBWA. One example from the distant past comes from Alexander the Great. When it was clear that his Macedonians were mutinying against his plans to collaborate with the Persians, Alexander went directly to his men and spoke to them. He did not send a memo or a messenger. As H. G. Wells (1920/1961) describes it, "with some difficulty . . . he brought them to a penitent mood and induced them to take part in a common feast with the Persians" (p. 292).

Donald Phillips (1992) used one of America's most highly esteemed presidents, Abraham Lincoln, to illustrate this style of leadership. Phillips pointed out that President Lincoln believed part of the definition of leadership is to act on behalf of the wants, the goals, and the aspirations of the follower, and he managed to accomplish this directly. No secondhand report for the Civil War president. Lincoln spent much of his time among the troops. They were number one to him; they were the people who were going to get the job done.

EXAMPLES OF MBWA FROM INDUSTRIAL
AND EDUCATIONAL LEADERS

Industry has used MBWA effectively for decades. Early on in the 1940s, Hewlett-Packard began using company-wide MBWA practices when Bill Hewlett and Dave Packard institutionalized them as part of the start-up of their new enterprise. To the wonderment of many in the electronics business, it was alive and well more than 50 years later as evidenced by Lew Platt, then Chief Executive, when he declared MBWA to be a key factor in the company's success. Today, more than 65 years after the management approach was initiated, the company is on a roll. Some say it's stronger than ever, even in precarious national and world financial times.

Joel Slutzky, CEO of Odetics, a high-tech products manufacturer in Anaheim, California, is another example. His public relations manager claimed he ate lunch in the cafeteria every day. He went from table to table—not because he forced himself to, but because he was just that kind of person; it came naturally. He said he has learned that the best interaction results from leveling the playing field in the company. "Optimal communication takes place in the gym— I'm talking to an assembler, a technician, or an engineer, anyone in my organization. . . . The best dialogue I'll ever get is in these kinds of environments" (as quoted in McKenna, 1993, p. 13). But close encounters between executives and the people in the organization are infrequent in most companies. It is as if management took its cue not from Tom Peters, but from the late Greta Garbo—"I want to be alone!" Unfortunately, this characterizes too many industry managers. Yet wouldn't America, let alone Enron or Lehman Brothers, be in much better shape today if the board members had spent more time wandering around? Lack of administrative presence in classrooms also characterizes the management style of many school administrators, as we discuss in subsequent chapters.

Elliot Eisner (2002), one of America's most respected thinkers in pedagogy and one who comes from a nonmanagement leadership background, is in sync with MBWA. Eisner says that in the kind of schools America needs, principals would spend about a third of their time in classrooms, so that they know firsthand what is going on. Is one-third the precise fraction, or is it 40 or 50 percent? We've seen that any percentage between 30 and 80 works. The key is what the administrator does while wandering.

The message is catching on in education. A few years back, Los Angeles Unified School District Superintendent Roy Romer had a surprising, fresh-air message for all 850 of the district's principals—he told them he wanted them to wander around inside their schools (Ritsch, 2001). Romer was on to something good. He knew that people desire a sense of involvement, a sense of importance, a sense that what they do makes a difference. Smart leaders nurture this drive, and principals should know that teachers, possibly more than any other group, possess this drive. What teachers really want is some ability to shape what goes on in the workplace. MBWA embodies this "Count me in; we can do it as a team" spirit. The MBWA school leaders, like their private sector counterparts, regularly walk throughout the facility and in and out of classrooms because they know where education takes place. MBWA school principals are out listening for hints and clues to strengths, weaknesses, problems, and solutions. They know that MBWA is about caring enough about what's going on in the organization to talk to the people who know.

FOR REFLECTION

Consider school leaders you have known who exemplify the MBWA approach described earlier.

- How did the faculty perceive them?
- Were they successful in achieving their objectives?

The Research Base

In 1990, the authors of the original *School Management by Wandering Around* were forced to admit that MBWA was not based on years of research or numerous scientific studies; rather, they concluded that it was an idea based on common sense and hundreds of years of experience. Happily, we can now amend this statement. MBWA *is* based on many high-quality research studies as well as ancient wisdom and common experiences throughout the ages. MBWA is not new, nor is it difficult to understand. But more often than not, it has been forgotten or put aside in favor of seemingly more impressive activities that can be completed only behind closed doors. As one client of Peters and Austin (1984) said, "MBWA is a blinding flash of the obvious" (p. 3). It clarifies the techniques that successful school leaders and leaders of all institutions, groups, and organizations have been practicing for a long time.

Research over the past 21 years has confirmed MBWA's benefits (Downey et al., 2010; Frase, 2001, 2003, 2005; S. P. Gray, 2005). The idea not only sounds great; it also appeals to managers, and it is based on hundreds of years of wisdom. It has been practiced by highly successful business leaders such as McDonald's founder Ray Kroc, automotive industry leader Lee Iacocca, Costco CEO James Sinegal, General Electric CEO Jack Welch, and by many prominent education leaders across the United States. The elite professionals running these organizations understand the value of being with the frontline workers.

Predictably, some leaders simply jumped on board the MBWA bandwagon for the thrill—for the glamour and attention it gave them. They did it without understanding the inherent meaning of the practice, without having it in their hearts. One of our fellow professors tells a story about an executive who had heard of MBWA at a conference and liked the idea. He went to the office the next day to give a power order to all of his management team—an order citing the exact time and day of each week they should wander. He obviously missed the point. He did not have MBWA in his soul. For him, it was just good advice others should heed. Having middle managers practice MBWA is a fine idea, but the people in charge must demonstrate it. They must live it, if the followers are going to follow.

2

School Leadership

What Matters Most

Shoot for the moon. Even if you miss it, you will land among the stars.

—Les Brown, band leader

James Kouzes and Barry Posner (2010) introduce their latest book, *The Truth About Leadership,* with an insightful observation: "Good leadership is good leadership . . . the context of leading may change a lot, but the content of leading changes very little" (p. xvii). So what makes a successful leader?

"Great Man" Theory of Leadership

Throughout history, theories about what constitutes great leaders have been varied. Although they usually had little in common, they were touted as the source of "truth" about leadership and how leaders rise to greatness. Historians and biographers wrote about the great leaders long before the invention of the printing press. It was once widely believed that great leaders were born, not trained, and were attracted to their role in life by a mystic magnetism. This genetic attribution notion was labeled the *"great man" theory* of leadership. The common denominator for becoming a great leader, according to this theory, was an inherited capability that destined certain people to become leaders. Great leaders were believed to be endowed genetically with unique talents that set them apart from the masses.

The Trait Theory

The "great man" theory had virtually no evidence to support it and eventually gave way to the *trait theory.* Great leaders like Julius Caesar, Alexander the Great, and Napoleon were studied to determine what characteristics or personal traits they had in common. In addition to their military feats, historians inform us that each was relatively short in stature, even for his time, and all three were left-handed—hardly qualifying factors for chief executives or commanders-in-chief. The trait theory was based also on the assumption that there are certain personality characteristics or *traits* that could predict success in leadership positions. Leaders in all kinds of settings and organizations were studied, ranging from schools to the military services and from banks to farm machinery companies. Every imaginable trait seems to have been considered, including height, weight, state of health, intelligence, self-confidence, sex, personality type, and many others. Burke (1980) concluded that the leadership trait studies revealed very little, with the exception of a few interesting bits of trivia, such as the following:

- Taller people are more likely to be successful, although they are also more likely to have an opportunity for leadership.
- Successful leaders are more outgoing than their followers in certain situations, through not necessarily in all.
- Successful leaders tend to be more intelligent than the average person, but there is no positive correlation between success and measured IQs above 115.

The study of traits was not limited to leadership studies. For many years, psychologists predicted that certain body types (shapes) also had certain personality types. For instance, it was supposed that chubby people are always happier than thinner people—a fact not supported by the research.

As the study of leadership matured over the years, trait theories lost credibility. Leadership qualities are far too complex to be reduced to simple associations with personal traits or body characteristics.

MODERN LEADERSHIP THEORIES

In the early 20th century, Taylor (1911) founded and popularized the notion of *scientific management.* This theory put forth the idea that the best way to increase output was to improve techniques or methods used by workers and was interpreted to mean that people had to be manipulated and used as instruments by leaders. The concept of scientific management was embodied in the metaphor "man as machine." The assumption was that human beings are basically lazy and need to be prodded or otherwise extrinsically motivated to be productive. McGregor (1960) renamed this philosophy "Theory X." He rejected the view of mankind that people are basically lethargic, lazy, and irresponsible. He felt Theory X was an extremist viewpoint and hardly justifiable. He proposed *Theory Y,* which represents an opposite view of the nature of man as it relates to the workplace. This theory holds that people want to work and find considerable value in doing their work well.

McGregor's work helped to pave the way to a more rational behavioral approach to the study of management. The human relations movement of the 1960s and 1970s led to a focus on individual leaders and what they do. This advent was accompanied by an assumption that successful management behaviors, characteristics, and strategies could be learned. Still, it was not entirely clear what those behaviors, characteristics, and strategies were. Years later, Bennis and Nanus (1985) echoed this stalemate:

> Decades of academic analysis have given us more than 350 definitions of leadership. Literally thousands of empirical investigations of leaders have been conducted in the last seventy-five years alone, but no clear and unequivocal understanding exists as to what distinguishes leaders from non-leaders. (p. 4)

Years before, Bennis (1959) had described the dilemma when he wrote, "More has been written and less known about leadership than about any other topic in the behavioral sciences."

A different approach to the study of leadership was embraced by Peters and Waterman (1982/2004). They focused on learning how the leaders of our most successful companies operated and why they were successful. Their research revealed that our most successful CEOs embraced similar leadership principles, and their companies exhibited similar operational characteristics. These were as follows:

1. A bias for action   5. Hands-on, value driven

2. Close to the customer   6. Sticking to the knitting

3. Autonomy and   7. Simple form, lean staff
   entrepreneurship

4. Productivity through people   8. Simultaneous loose-tight
                                                        properties

It is interesting to note that the concept of *Management by Wandering Around (or MBWA)* was made popular by these authors in this publication, although the term had been used by others previously.

Two decades after Peters and Waterman initially released their findings, Jim Collins (2001) conducted a similar study. He began by identifying great companies and asking, "Why?" The idea in both studies was to examine great operations and determine why they were great. Collins found that the CEO makes all the difference. The details of his study and findings were reported in his best-selling book, *Good to Great: Why Some Companies Make the Leap . . . and Others Don't*. We were not at all surprised that Collins's findings were entirely consistent with the earlier findings by Peters and Waterman.

ASSESSING YOUR LEADERSHIP STYLE

We recognize that a body of well-respected leadership behaviors and strategies is far more likely to predict your success as a leader than your height, weight, facial characteristics, confidence level, and other such notions. The purpose of the remainder of this chapter is to assess your leadership style, a prerequisite to successful mastery of MBWA. Four questions measuring four elements of leadership are provided; each is designed to assess an important aspect of your leadership style and readiness for MBWA. These four elements are embodied in the four questions below:

1. Are you a Theory X or a Theory Y type—do you see people as basically motivated and well-intended or as slothful and non-caring?

2. Do you have a favorable balance between concern for the mission of the school and concern for the faculty and staff?

3. Do you promote trust among the faculty and leaders in your school?

4. Do you exhibit the qualities and characteristics of highly successful school leaders—the "level five" school executive? (Collins, 2001)

In the following paragraphs, we discuss these four elements of leadership in more detail and offer you suggestions for assessing your leadership style.

Leadership Element Number 1: Theory X Versus Theory Y

The first exercise for assessing your leadership style is to read the following characteristics and check those that describe your beliefs. Use your first impressions in selecting your answers.

1. _____ The employees' only interest in the organization is economic gain.

2. _____ People are not by nature passive or resistant to organizational needs.

3. _____ Work is natural for people if the conditions are favorable.

4. _____ Negative consequences are effective in motivating employees.

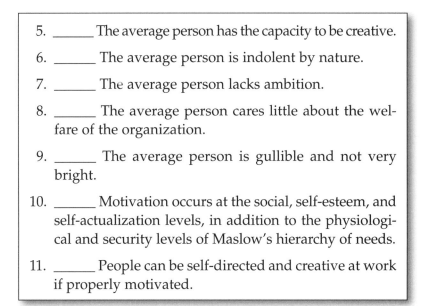

5. _____ The average person has the capacity to be creative.

6. _____ The average person is indolent by nature.

7. _____ The average person lacks ambition.

8. _____ The average person cares little about the welfare of the organization.

9. _____ The average person is gullible and not very bright.

10. _____ Motivation occurs at the social, self-esteem, and self-actualization levels, in addition to the physiological and security levels of Maslow's hierarchy of needs.

11. _____ People can be self-directed and creative at work if properly motivated.

SCORING: The highest score possible is 5, and the lowest is –6. Give yourself one point for each of the following items that you checked: 2, 3, 5, 10, and 11. These items reflect the basic tenets of Theory Y.

Now, consider the downside. Give yourself –1 for each of the Theory X items: 1, 4, 6, 7, 8, and 9. Figure the total for the two sets of items. Example: If the total for the Theory Y set is +5 and the total for Theory X is –1, your score is +4. A higher score indicates a stronger alignment with Theory Y. A score of +3 is the minimum acceptable score for an MBWA leader. The X items are clearly not in keeping with what we know about human nature and work. Scores of less than + 3 reflect Theory X tendencies—be cautious here and analyze why you hold these beliefs. These beliefs and related behaviors are not associated with highly successful leaders, either in schools or in private industry.

Theory Y leaders tend to be people-oriented, and they are the ones who should be out walking around interacting with others—practicing MBWA. Theory Y leaders believe people in general can be self-directed and creative, and they believe people can enjoy work if the conditions are favorable. Moreover, they believe that people are not resistant to change or organizational needs, and that people are intrinsically motivated to achieve goals for themselves and the organization.

Theory X beliefs reflect a negative view of people. We agree. In fact, Theory X types should not practice MBWA. They should stay in their offices and let others do the wandering around. Practicing Theory X will set a school back at least a half-century and shatter any trust that may exist. This description is not entirely tongue-in-cheek. No leadership theory since the early 1900s has favored the Theory X style, and all newer theories are consistent with Theory Y.

FOR REFLECTION

Before moving on to the next assessment, take a few minutes to reflect on your orientation to either Theory X or Theory Y. Consider all of the 11 characteristics listed in the assessment above. Try to be specific about why you hold your core beliefs.

Now that you know where you stand regarding Theories X and Y, take a minute to list a couple of actions you can take to put yourself more in line with Theory Y. Use the space below.

MY THEORY Y PLAN

1. _____

2. _____

3. _____

4. _____

Leadership Element Number 2: Concern for the Faculty and Accomplishing the School's Mission

Crucial to the successful practice of MBWA is the belief in the worth, integrity, intelligence, and work ethic of people. As a next step, let's examine the way in which these core beliefs about people balance with the leader's recognition that the organization has a mission and that the leader's job is to *lead people in the attainment of that mission.* Today, the emphasis in schools is on high-stakes tests and producing learning, and we must attend to both the people and the task. Concern for our faculties and staffs is a prerequisite to successful educational leadership, but concern for people only, the "far left" interpretation of Theory Y, dooms the organization to failure. Under this form of leadership, the organization will fall short of accomplishing the school's long-term vision of what it is striving to become. As a school leader, you must balance these concerns for people against the concern for the mission. To achieve this goal, we recommend you begin by analyzing your conformity with this dimension of leadership.

Blake and Mouton (1989) developed an effective method to help business leaders learn where they stand. It involves plotting leadership practices on a grid to help these leaders analyze their concern for people and their concern for the mission of the organization. It is obvious that both concerns are very important to schools. The current era of high-stakes testing, low teacher morale, and high attrition rates makes both concern for our people and concern for our mission of prime importance. These concerns cannot be isolated from each other. Instead, they must be constantly balanced by leaders.

We have adapted Blake and Mouton's Managerial Grid model to conform to the school setting, providing principals and other educational leaders with a pertinent instrument to analyze their status. Figure 2.1 plots *Concern for Faculty and Staff* on the vertical axis and *Concern for School's Mission* on the horizontal axis.

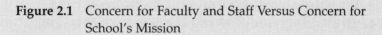

Figure 2.1 Concern for Faculty and Staff Versus Concern for
School's Mission

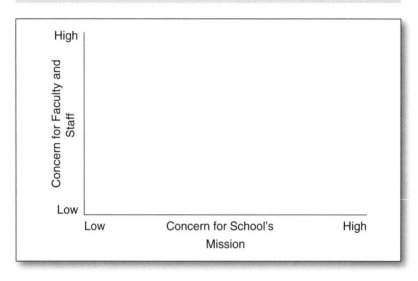

Figure 2.2 shows a grid with the five leadership patterns most often observed in school organizations. The first digit describes the leader's concern for accomplishing the school's mission, while the second describes the concern for faculty and staff.

Each of the five leadership patterns defined by the patterns on the grid is described below:

Pattern 1: Laissez-Faire, Impoverished Management (1,1)

This pattern occupies the 1,1 section of the grid (lower left corner) and describes the type of administrator that simply goes through the motions. These leaders are not really involved in the organization's affairs and contribute little to it. They have little concern for either people or production.

Pattern 2: Task Driven, Authority-Obedience (9,1)

This pattern is in the 9,1 section of the grid (lower right) and depicts the extremely *task-oriented* administrator with little

Figure 2.2 Five School Leadership Patterns

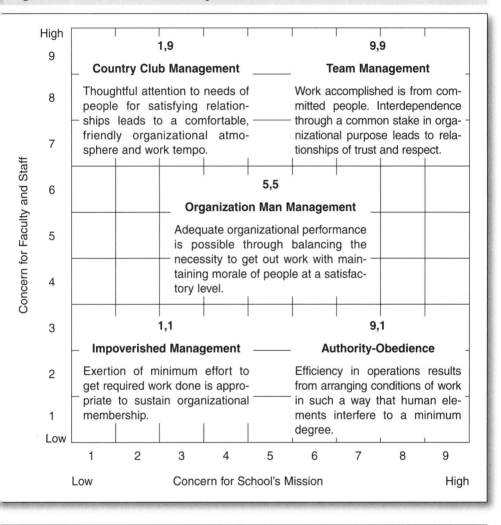

* source* (for Figures 2.1 and 2.2): Blake Mouton Managerial Grid adapted from Mind ~~T~~ools (2011).

concern for subordinates or other people and intense concern for "getting things done." This administrator knows what needs to be done and directs people to accomplish the goals. In this leader's organization, efficiency in operations results from arranging conditions of work in such a way that human elements interfere to a minimum degree. You've seen this principal or superintendent: Directive, hard-hitting memos are common; any talk in the school is business and never personal or for pleasure; teachers are given little autonomy; school is a place for work and is not the place to address personal problems. Even holiday celebrations are directed. An illustrative holiday party announcement might read, "There will be a holiday party and you *will* enjoy yourselves—Cheers!"

Pattern 3: Epitome of Mediocrity,
Organization Man Management (5,5)

This pattern is located in the 5,5 center section of the grid and represents the leader who is moderately concerned with the school's mission and with people. Production is typically adequately high to avoid sanctions and morale is "OK" but nothing more. The principal is not sweetness and light as in the 1,9 style, but is mediocre and ineffective at best. Conventional expectations are met. Test scores are average, morale is average, community opinion is average, and the principal's expectations are average. "Don't rock the boat! We're not getting a whole lot accomplished, but I'm OK and you're OK."

Pattern 4: Let's Party, Country Club Management (1,9)

This pattern is located in the 1,9 section, upper left, of the grid This type represents the "Country Club" atmosphere style where the principals believe happy teachers will get the job done and the solution to the easy life is to not cause trouble. This principal is minimally concerned with the school mission and the community and devotes much attention to maintaining satisfying relationships with the staff by covering up for frequent late arrivals or unexplained absences. This leader also devotes energy to rebuking parents' complaints that teachers are ill-prepared and frequently waste students' time with meaningless seat work. At the same time, this type does as much glad-handing with members of the public as possible. The payoff is that the teachers and parents will say nothing when the principal takes off once or twice a week to play golf and tennis. This leader's goal is to maintain comfortable and friendly relationships in the hope that a comfortable organizational atmosphere and work tempo will result. This style is one of "You protect me, and I'll protect you." The 1,9 administrator's MBWA style is more MBSG, Management by Smilin' and Grinnin.' In this MBWA scenario, the administrator occupies his or her time extolling the virtues of the school, the teachers, the parents, and all others who touch the school, and by ensuring that all people in the organization have a good time.

Pattern 5: Focused on People and
Mission, Team Management (9,9)

This type is the 9,9 leader (upper right of grid) and strongly reflects the Theory Y and MBWA orientation. Teachers can be highly involved and enjoy their work, and the demands of the school's mission can coincide nicely with the needs that teachers have for satisfaction and recognition from their work. The 9,9 leader assumes work is accomplished by committed teachers working in high-quality work environments. Interdependence occurs through a common belief in the school's mission and leads to relationships of trust and respect. The 9,9 style is perfectly suited to the school environment and is supported by an abundance of research. The MBWA principal's job as a 9,9 leader is to help teachers accomplish their goal of helping students learn.

So what is your grid leadership type? To what extent do you emphasize concern for both the mission of the school and concern for the faculty and staff? Let's find out. The following items (see Whitefield, 1981) describe aspects of leadership behavior. Respond to each according to the way you would most likely act if you were the leader of a work group. Circle the response most common for you in each situation.

Response Options: Always (A), Frequently (F), Occasionally (O), Seldom (S), Never (N)

1. Most likely act as a spokesman   A F O S N

2. Allow staff complete freedom
   in work   A F O S N

3. Encourage use of uniform
   procedures   A F O S N

4. Permit staff to exercise
   judgment in solving problems   A F O S N

5. Needle staff to give more effort   A F O S N

6. Let staff work as they think best   A F O S N

7. Keep work moving at a rapid pace   A F O S N

8. Turn staff loose on a job and
   let them go at it   A F O S N

9. Settle conflicts when they occur   A F O S N

10. Be reluctant to allow staff
    freedom of action   A F O S N

11. Decide what to do and how to
    do it   A F O S N

12. Push for increased production   A F O S N

13. Assign staff to particular tasks   A F O S N

14. Schedule the work to be done   A F O S N

15. Be willing to make changes   A F O S N

16. Refuse to explain my actions   A F O S N

17. Persuade others that my ideas
    are to their advantage   A F O S N

18. Permit the staff to set its
    own pace   A F O S N

Now determine your concern for the faculty and staff as well as your concern for the mission of the school by completing the following:

A. Circle the item number for 1, 3, 9, 10, 11, 15, 16, and 17.

B. Write a 1 in front of the circled items to which you responded S or N.

C. Write a 1 in front of the items not circled to which you responded A or F.

D. Circle the 1s you have written in front of the following items: 2, 4, 5, 6, 8, 10, 14, 16, 18.

E. Count the circled 1s. This is your score for concern for faculty and staff.

F. Count the uncircled 1s. This is your score for concern for the mission of the school.

Plot your score on the grid in Figure 2.3. Place your concern for faculty and staff on the horizontal axis and your concern for the mission of the school on the vertical axis.

So how did you do? The average score for administrators is 3 on Concern for the Mission and 5 on Concern for Faculty and Staff. Please take a minute and contemplate your responses. The questions listed below may help.

FOR REFLECTION

- Consider both of your scores. How do you feel about them? Do they reflect how you see yourself as a leader?
- Do you see a pattern in your responses? If so, what?
- How do people react to you when you are in a leadership situation? Do they shun you? Follow you? Question you? Do they participate?
- After considering the first three suggested reflections above, create a few ideas that can move you closer to the 9,9 level.

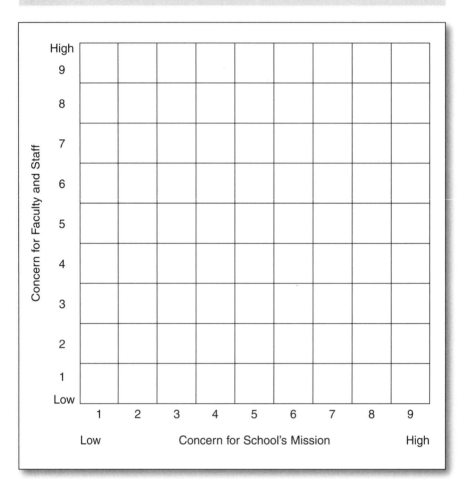

Figure 2.3   Your Concern for Faculty and Staff Versus Your Concern for the Mission of the School

For private sector businesses as well as public schools, the classic Blake Mouton Managerial Grid in its original form remains a very legitimate concept for leaders to use in diagnosing their styles. This time-tested instrument is still widely used in modern-day companies and business schools, and it is commonly accepted that high concern for both people and production is absolutely essential to success in school leadership and the MBWA philosophy. Blase (1987); Andrews and Soder (1987); and Valentine, Clark, Nickerson, and Keefe (1981) all have demonstrated that the principal's concern for production as demonstrated by accessibility, consistency, decisiveness, time management, and problem-solving orientation leads to increases in teachers' feelings of confidence and sense of professionalism while at the same time reducing feelings of tension, uncertainty, and anger. For the student, these characteristics lead to reduction of discipline problems, uncertainty, and wasted time while increasing time on task and acceptance of advice. Both Blase, and Eisner (2002) have also shown that principals' concern for the faculty and staff as demonstrated by confrontation of conflict, recognition, participation, and willingness to delegate authority yields increases in teacher efficiency, professional self-esteem, and satisfaction while decreasing ambivalence, goal uncertainty, competition, defensive clique formation, and nonconstructive conflict (backbiting).

No creditable leadership theory denies the need for concern for production and concern for people, although the proponents of situational leadership (Hersey & Blanchard, 1982) and contingency theory (Fielder, 1967) contend that one must be emphasized more than the other, depending on the situation. The list of leadership theories seems endless— theory Z, contingency theory, chaos theory, total quality management, the *Good to Great* findings by Collins (2001), and more recently our *Good Schools to Great Schools* study (S. P. Gray & Streshly, 2008). All of these theories and management models support the premise that concern for both people and the school's mission is prerequisite to successful leadership, and this forms the foundation of the MBWA leadership philosophy.

We next explore the topic of trust. This subsection gives you the means to judge how much your teachers trust you as a leader—a most important insight.

Leadership Element Number 3: Trust

Trust is a key component of transformational leadership and thus a key component of successful change—this is especially important in these days of high-stakes testing and the stress that so frequently occurs under these conditions. The current emphasis on trust and our purpose for including this topic grow out of a well-documented tendency for teachers and principals to mistrust each other. We do not need research to confirm just how important trust is in all work fields and even in one's personal life with family and friends. Unfortunately, it is too often conspicuously absent in schools these days.

Credibility builds trust, and credibility is requisite to effective leadership. Efforts to increase trust in many fields including education have often failed (S. P. Gray & Streshly, 2010; Kouzes & Posner, 1993). Managers all too frequently do not do as they say they will—the age-old chasm between words and deeds. Not doing what they say they will has disastrous results; teachers no longer follow their lead. Layering this condition over the stringent demands of high-stakes testing spells failure. In order for subordinates to willingly change their ways of teaching to be in line with the goals of the organization, they must first have deep trust in the integrity and credibility of their leaders.

Let's examine how trust is related to behavioral integrity. A formal definition of *behavioral integrity* is the perceived degree of congruence between the values expressed by words and those expressed by actions. It is indeed impossible to build bonds between teachers and the principal when trust regarding words versus deeds is lacking, and without such bonds, implementing successful change is not possible.

Here is a brief, eight-item instrument for assessing your trust level as a leader among teachers. Unlike the previous three instruments, this one is completed by your *teachers* and tallied by you.

Directions: Five responses are possible. Circle the number that matches your perception—5 = strongly agree, 4 = agree, 3 = neither agree nor disagree, 2 = disagree, 1 = strongly disagree.

1. There is a match between my principal's words and actions.   1   2   3   4   5

2. My principal delivers on promises.   1   2   3   4   5

3. My principal practices what he/she preaches.   1   2   3   4   5

4. My principal does what he/she says he/she will do.   1   2   3   4   5

5. My principal conducts himself/herself by the same values he/she talks about.   1   2   3   4   5

6. My principal shows the same priorities that he/she describes.   1   2   3   4   5

7. When my principal promises something, I can be certain that it will happen.   1   2   3   4   5

8. My principal encourages constructive conflict.   1   2   3   4   5

Source: Simons & Peterson (2000).

Trust Scale

Here are some ideas on how to proceed.

- To personalize the instrument, strike "my principal" and insert your name.
- Explain to your faculty and staff exactly what you are doing—getting a reading on their trust level of you.
- Instruct them in how to complete the instrument—it's pretty easy.
- Remind them that responses are anonymous—no one need put his or her name on it, and it will be turned in anonymously.
- Tally the responses and reflect on the results.
- Compile the results and share them with the staff.

- Also share your plans for increasing your trust score. This is very important if you ever want them to take the time to complete another instrument for you. Start bolstering your credibility now.

This is a very important instrument to complete personally and with your faculty and staff.

Leadership Element Number 4: Personal Qualities of Great School Leaders

Although no one research study can define all intricacies of successful leadership, the study by Collins reported in his best-selling book, *Good to Great: Why Some Companies Make the Leap . . . and Others Don't* (2001), offers good insight from the industrial sector and has demonstrated its applicability in schools (Fullan, 2003).

Collins (2001) found that CEOs who led companies from good to great status exhibited the following characteristics and behaviors:

1. Displays a duality of professional will and personal humility—The example from history is Abraham Lincoln. His duty to the enduring nation was always first on his agenda. He put his ego second to the larger cause and the greater good of the people.

2. Displays ambition for the success of the company rather than for one's own personal renown—David Maxwell, CEO of Fannie Mae, is a prime example. He turned the company over to an equally capable successor. He felt that the company would be ill-served if he stayed on too long.

3. Is characterized by compelling modesty—When things go well, they give credit to others; when things go badly, they accept the blame. During interviews with the good-to-great leaders, they would talk about the

company and the contribution of other executives but would deflect discussion about their own contributions. This is much like what Covey (1992) called the *abundance mentality* in contrast to the *scarcity mentality.* In the former, the principal leader believes that there is an abundance of credit, plenty to go around. In the latter, the leader hordes the credit, thinking that this makes him or her look better. The latter is obviously wrong. The reality is that as we give more credit, we receive more.

4. Possesses an unwavering resolve to do what must be done to make the organization successful—CEOs of the good-to-great companies are driven by an incurable need to produce results and do whatever it takes to make the company great.

5. Exhibits the "Hedgehog Concept"—These leaders are passionate about student achievement, know what the school can be best at, and know what will make the difference.

6. Confronts the brutal facts—Successful school leaders analyze student achievement and demographic data, work through challenges, and are not resigned to difficulties.

7. Exudes a culture of discipline—Such leaders have vision focusing on student achievement, are not micromanagers, and promote teacher responsibility.

8. Gets "first who . . . then what"—"Good-to-great" school leaders are doggedly persistent in getting the right faculty and staff on board.

9. Builds relationships—Effective leaders exhibit good people skills, openly communicate with school faculty and staff, and involve staff and community in decision making.

These are definitely characteristics of highly successful MBWA leaders, and they represent the spirit of MBWA. MBWA principals have that unwavering resolve to make the school successful. That is why they are in the classrooms. They know that this is where learning happens, that this is what education is all about. MBWA principals are humble. They *give* credit; they do not grab it. They put themselves second, and they are out and about to help others. Even without considering the research, these four characteristics make a lot of sense.

Where do you rank on the good-to-great criteria? Use the information in the following box to determine your status.

THE GOOD-TO-GREAT DIAGNOSIS

Two scales are provided: one for the principal to complete and one for the teachers and staff.

For the Principal:
Use the following three response choices to determine your status—*3* means "Yes, that is me"; *2* means "That is me in many cases"" and *1* means "No, that is not me."

(a) ____ I am humble. I attribute the school's success to others, not me.

(b) ____ My ambition is to make the school great, not build my reputation.

(c) ____ I am modest. When things go well at my school, I credit others, and when they don't go well, I accept the responsibility.

(d) ____ I have unwavering resolve to do what must be done to make the organization successful.

(e) ____ I am passionate about our mission, and I know what will make a difference.

(f) ____ I face difficult challenges to our school's success and take action to overcome them.

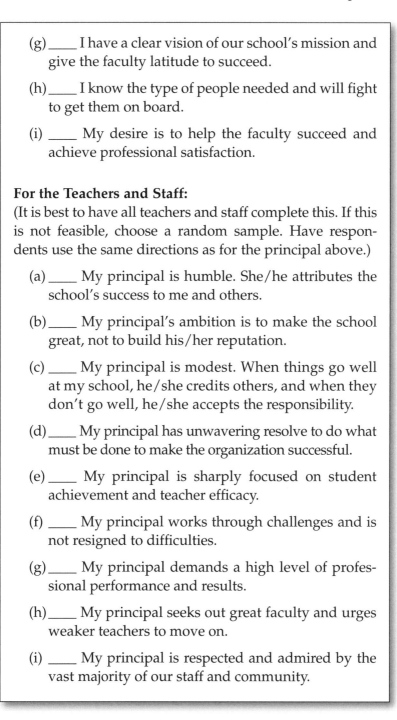

(g) ____ I have a clear vision of our school's mission and give the faculty latitude to succeed.

(h) ____ I know the type of people needed and will fight to get them on board.

(i) ____ My desire is to help the faculty succeed and achieve professional satisfaction.

For the Teachers and Staff:
(It is best to have all teachers and staff complete this. If this is not feasible, choose a random sample. Have respondents use the same directions as for the principal above.)

(a) ____ My principal is humble. She/he attributes the school's success to me and others.

(b) ____ My principal's ambition is to make the school great, not to build his/her reputation.

(c) ____ My principal is modest. When things go well at my school, he/she credits others, and when they don't go well, he/she accepts the responsibility.

(d) ____ My principal has unwavering resolve to do what must be done to make the organization successful.

(e) ____ My principal is sharply focused on student achievement and teacher efficacy.

(f) ____ My principal works through challenges and is not resigned to difficulties.

(g) ____ My principal demands a high level of professional performance and results.

(h) ____ My principal seeks out great faculty and urges weaker teachers to move on.

(i) ____ My principal is respected and admired by the vast majority of our staff and community.

Tally your scores. A score of 25 to 27 on either of the surveys is in the Good-to-Great category. Of course, not everyone is going to score at this level. The key is to move in that direction and attain it.

Match your score on each item with the average score from your teachers and staff. Second, determine which of your responses differ from those of your teachers or staff. This is key and can offer valuable information because a leader's perception is frequently different from that of others in the organization, and their perception is their reality. It is important to remember that the purpose of all of these instruments is to gain information that can be used to improve your performance.

If you scored below 25, list a couple of changes you can make to boost your score and move closer to that of a great leader.

1.
2.

Effective school leaders of yesterday, today, and tomorrow are those who make MBWA an integral part of their management style, and those who mirror the basic tenets of Theory Y and the 9,9 leadership style. They have high trust levels with their staffs and model the good-to-great personal leadership characteristics. All of these practices have been used by highly successful leaders for more than two thousand years. Consider the match of leadership characteristics with the ancient leaders during the entire span of civilized times—the cradle of civilization, the Mediterranean world, the Orient, Europe, and the New World. Also consider some of the great religious leaders—Buddha, Christ, and Gandhi. Humble? You bet. Far more concerned about the cause than themselves? Yes! Focused on the mission? Absolutely. Gave credit to others? No doubt. Were they *with* the people and not isolated from them? In all cases! Were they concerned for people? Abundantly so. Did they collaborate and not dictate? Yes. Did their very presence command great respect from their people? Yes. What extraordinary examples. This is an impressive list, and the characteristics worked for them. We used as many of these characteristics as we could in the administrative positions we held. Did we attain their status? No! But attempting to emulate these characteristics did make us better administrators. We highly recommend them to you.

You have completed four instruments to determine your MBWA status. More importantly, you have listed ideas for further enhancing your status. However, in order for you to employ MBWA as a leadership approach, you must first understand the nature of the people whose energy drives our school enterprises—the faculty and staff. In the next chapter, we examine why teachers teach—and why they leave.

3

Why Teachers Teach and Why They Leave

We know that from the moment students enter a school, the most important factor in their success is not the color of their skin or the income of their parents—it is the teacher standing at the front of the classroom.

—President Barack Obama (2010)

The teacher is the primary customer of the MBWA princi-pals. Management by Wandering Around allows the principal to see and understand firsthand what makes a teacher tick—what guides a teacher's decisions in the class-room. "Wandering" then provides the principal with insights for making decisions in support of the work that the teacher does. In this chapter, we provide our thoughts on the impor-tance of the MBWA principal understanding why teachers teach and what makes them leave.

FOR REFLECTION

Consider your position in the education hierarchy. Who is your primary customer? Is it students, parents, teachers, the community, or others?

We have asked hundreds of school principals to tell us who they thought were their customers, and their response was most often "students." A valuable lesson comes from the late W. Edwards Deming (1986) and what he called the "next in line" customer. Each group of people should serve the people it directly surpervises. When that happens, that is, when assistant superintendents serve principals, principals serve teachers, and teachers serve students, the organization maximizes the power of the people next in line to do their very best for those they serve. The benefit for teachers and students is powerful. Student learning improves, and teacher satisfaction and motivation increase (Chester & Beaudin, 1996; Frase, 2001; Freedman & Lafleur, 2003; Glickman, 2002; P. Gray, 2003; P. Gray & Frase, 2003; Varrati & Smith, 2008). If teachers are not nourished—if they do not receive the training, the feed-back, and the tools they need to do their jobs well—student learning declines, teachers are more likely to depart, and the public schools' reputation further deteriorates. Teachers are leaving at ever-increasing rates, and teacher morale is at an all-time low; however, MBWA leaders can reverse this trend if they spot the problems and act.

Our investigation of the dilemma facing American schools reminds us of the wisdom of Albert Einstein. He conjectured that all of space is bubbling with an invisible form of energy that creates a mutual repulsion between objects normally attracted to each other by gravity—negative gravity. Scientists more recently discovered proof of this theory by viewing exploding stars (Glanz, 2001). We learned in elementary school that gravitational attraction increases as the mass of objects increases, and just as the sun attracts the earth with gravity, we would also think, quite naturally, that teachers and schools would attract each other. Wrong! "Negative gravity" describes the current gravitational status of educators and our public schools. Over the decades, teacher and administrative jobs have attracted high numbers of applicants. These people had a powerful desire to do the job and believed they would be successful and that they would help young people achieve. They found satisfaction in doing do. Enter negative gravity—over the past three decades, teacher and administrator satisfaction has fallen, and recent studies show that teachers' inclination to stay in teaching and their overall satisfaction and morale have dropped dramatically (Bushaw & McNee, 2009; Farkas, Johnson, Foleno, Duffett, & Foley, 2000; MetLife, 2006; Ravitch, 2010). This is what we mean when we speak of negative gravity between schools and teachers, and it must cease. Schools must not repel teachers.

Two questions for MBWA principals are explored in this chapter:

- Why do teachers teach?
- Why do teachers leave teaching?

Let's look first at why teachers choose teaching as a profession.

WHY TEACHERS TEACH

The reasons for entering teaching may be grouped into two categories:

1. Altruistic motives—the desire to serve and work with young people

2. Practical motives—decent salaries, job security, time off in the summer, and the possibility of some upward mobility

Research studies from as early as the beginning of the 1980s support the finding that the most powerful motivational force for attracting teachers is the prospect of working with students (Fruth, Bredeson, & Kasten, 1982; Griffin & Tantiwong, 1989; Joseph & Green, 1986; Kane, 1989; Keller, 2003; L. Olson, 2003). More recently, research conducted and reported by the California State University Center for Teacher Quality (Futernick, 2007) found that 81 percent of the teachers who participated in their survey said they entered the profession because they wanted to make a difference for children and society. This overwhelming number indicates that teachers want above all to be effective teachers.

Teachers tend to be an altruistic lot. Most come into the profession with a strong desire to help young people learn, and they know that they need skill to do so (Kottkamp, Provenzo, & Cohn, 1986). This stimulates their energy, and when they experience success, they are motivated and satisfied. Over the years, we have asked teachers to identify the job factors most important to them. The factors surfacing most often were the chance to use their minds and abilities and the chance to work with young people and see them develop. These answers have remained relatively unchanged for decades and top the list today.

WHY TEACHERS LEAVE

Why do teachers leave? Sarason (1990) answered the question this way: "It is virtually impossible to create and sustain over time conditions for productive learning for students when they do not exist for teachers" (p. 145).

Why is teacher turnover so high? Many assume that retirement is the primary reason for teacher attrition, but when the facts are examined closely, it becomes clear that the number of teachers retiring from the profession is not a leading cause.

Sparks and Keiler (2003) interviewed a sample of teachers who left the teaching profession early in their careers. All of these teachers expressed overall positive feelings about teaching, the joy of working with students and helping them grow and learn, and their accomplishments as teachers. However, when asked about details of negative experiences, light was shed on their reasons for leaving teaching. They described various demoralizing experiences that may have led to their decision to leave the school or change careers altogether. These experiences include the following:

- Lack of principal support
- Rarity of principal visits in classrooms
- Lack of colleague support for new teachers

The lack of collegiality as an impetus for teachers leaving teaching is further supported in a teacher survey conducted in 2008–2009 (Keigher, 2010). Teachers reported they left the profession because opportunities for learning from their colleagues were better in the position they moved to than in teaching. Reasons given for leaving the teaching profession include the following:

- Few occasions where colleagues embraced new ideas and interests
- Belief that low pay reflects lack of community respect

- High stress levels created by
  - Routine paperwork
  - Parental criticism and hostility
  - Student violence
  - Teacher appraisal system

- Administrators not treating teachers as professionals
- Work of teachers lacking creativity, challenge, and intellectual stimulation

Teacher Demoralization

The demoralizing effects of many of the negative experiences listed above were especially apparent in San Diego during the years between 1998 and 2005 while Alan Bersin was superintendent of schools. Work environments that reportedly stifled creativity and intellectual stimulation were very real issues for teachers when Bersin mandated the "Blueprint for Student Success in a Standards-Based System." The Bersin leadership centralized decision making and made no pretense of collaborating with teachers. Many teachers were upset with what they felt was heavy-handedness in implementing the reforms. They felt a lack of respect and were insulted by the leadership's refusal to collaborate with them. Morale among teachers in the district was low, and teachers felt that they were being evaluated not on how well they teach, but on how well they followed district mandates. Diane Ravitch (2010) summed up her thoughts about the state of San Diego teacher morale by asking

Can teachers successfully educate children to think for themselves if teachers are not treated as professionals who think for themselves? Can principals be inspiring leaders if they must follow orders about the most minute details of daily life in classrooms? If a get-tough policy saps educators of their initiative, their craft, and their enthusiasm, then it is hard to believe that the results are worth having. (p. 67)

Ravitch interviewed San Diego educators and heard story after story about stress-related illnesses among teachers, which was coined "Bersinitis." She learned that during Bersin's reign, many San Diego teachers sought medical attention for work-related depression and anxiety due to a hostile work environment. When Bersin left the superintendency, and during the 2 years that Carl Cohn was superintendent, not a single teacher sought medical assistance with a similar problem. Cohn (2007) remarked, "Any genuine school reform is dependent upon empowering those at the bottom, not punishing them from the top" (p. 32).

Lack of Focus on Student Learning

Teachers leave because they feel as though they cannot attain their number one goal of helping young people learn. Educational administrators and pedagogical pundits have not been at a loss for solutions; witness the advent of differentiated staffing, site-based management, poorly designed merit pay systems, restructuring, and block scheduling. Unfortunately, these solutions have only tinkered with fringe factors that have not and could not increase learning and therefore could not better satisfy teachers. We believe that the lack of alignment between student learning outcomes and instruction is, in large measure, the real barrier to student learning. One research study (Newman, Smith, Allensworth, & Bryk, 2001) illustrates this beautifully. The study analyzed the degree of instructional program coherence (the fit between learning outcomes and classroom strategies and resources) in 222 Chicago schools and showed that higher degrees of fit between pre-identified learning outcomes produce significantly greater student achievement than lesser degrees of fit. The side benefit is that teachers then know that their teaching efforts will lead to student learning. Another study (Olson, 2003) covering 39 states found that the most commonly suspected reason for teacher attrition, low pay, was just not true. The study found that many teachers who departed the teaching ranks did so even though they could earn sizable bonuses.

In one case, a nationally certified teacher left her school even though she could make a $20,000 bonus. She said she could not succeed in helping her students learn. She complained that the school lacked focus on high-quality teaching and learning. She offered the following criticisms:

- Teachers were too often assigned to teach the grade levels for which they lacked proper skills.
- Staff development meetings were not focused and were superficial, and teachers just swapped lesson plans rather than focusing on what makes for excellent instruction.

Other studies (Archer, 2003; Buckley, Schneider, & Shang, 2004; Olsen & Anderson, 2007) support the finding that low salary and professional status are not primary reasons for teachers leaving the profession. More prevalent reasons given by teachers were as follows:

- Poor conditions of the work and the work environment
- Heavy workload—increased paperwork and additional nonteaching demands
- Lack of parental support and negativity from parents
- Lack of administrative support

Unfortunately, the poor working conditions in schools have not allowed many new or experienced teachers to maintain their sense of efficacy—the fundamental belief that they can help students learn. The attrition rate for teachers is threatening the quality of public schools. There is an imbalance between positive and negative influences. When the negatives overpower the positives, the teacher has far too few "successes," and the result is a decreased sense of belief in the self. Lacking this, teachers tend to drop out, literally or figuratively.

Deming (1986), who taught the Japanese how to use quality techniques to rebuild their industrial infrastructure and achieve high profitability levels, believed strongly in treating the worker with respect and ensuring that the workplace conditions are adequate so the job could be done well. Without this in the schools, teachers' efficacy and the belief that they can help students learn weaken.

Teachers come to teaching precisely because they want to help young people learn. When "negative gravity" gets the best of them, they leave. Practicing service to the next-in-line customer is enhanced greatly by MBWA. Principals who embrace MBWA are zealots in ensuring that the schoolwide focus is on learning outcomes (curriculum) and high-quality instruction. They understand the fundamental underpinnings to the meaningful work of teachers. (We discuss this emphasis more in Chapter 5.) They are in the classrooms observing and initiating constructive conversations with teachers so as to become fully aware of teaching and learning conditions. They ferret out problems and are zealous about creating an environment where teachers have a better chance to practice their craft with success. The late Sandra Feldman, former president of the American Federation of Teachers (AFT), stated,

> Teachers want to feel safe; they want to feel they have a supportive and pleasant environment . . . and they need to feel they can turn to people for support for their students. . . . You must have the environmental factors, or teachers will look elsewhere. (cited in Keller, 2003, p. 44)

In Chapter 4, we discuss why teachers stay and the effects the MBWA principal has on lessening the conditions that increase teacher attrition.

4

Why Teachers Stay

It is better to lead from behind and to put others in front, especially when you celebrate victory when nice things occur. You take the front line when there is danger. Then people will appreciate your leadership.

—Nelson Mandela

I n Chapter 3, we discussed why people enter the teaching profession and why they leave. Now let's explore the factors that encourage them to stay and the support mechanisms that must be provided by the MBWA principal to ensure teacher retention.

FOR REFLECTION

What factors do you believe encourage teachers to stay in the profession? What support must a principal provide to ensure teacher retention?

SUPPORTIVE LEADERSHIP OF THE MBWA PRINCIPAL

A survey conducted by Scholastic and the Bill & Melinda Gates Foundation (2010) asked 40,000 public school teachers for their thoughts on American education and education reform. When asked about what keeps them in their jobs as educators, nearly all teachers said supportive leadership and collaborative working environments are the most important factors to retaining good teachers. Research on policies that affect teacher recruitment and retention (Guarino, Santibañez, & Daley, 2006) support the Scholastic and Gates findings. Results of research conducted by Olson (2003) show that good working conditions top the list for staying in teaching, particularly for teachers in high-poverty, high-minority, and low-achieving schools. Good working conditions include

- adequate and timely provision of materials;
- ongoing mentoring and support from other teachers and administration, especially for new teachers;
- a safe and orderly environment that is welcoming and respectful;
- principals who are strong instructional leaders; and
- principals who delegate authority and develop the leadership skills of others.

Our research on highly effective principals points to the importance of the school leader in building a school culture where trust, effective interpersonal communication, and critical conversations encourage teachers to jump on the "improvement ethic" bandwagon in their quest to increase student learning. Our meaning of "improvement ethic" will become clear in this chapter as reasons why teachers continue in their profession are explored.

North Carolina's Teacher Working Conditions Initiative (2010) survey results, titled "Analyses of Current Trends," and previous Teacher Working Conditions Survey data have demonstrated that school leadership is one of the strongest predictors of teacher retention and future employment plans. In 2010, when asked which aspect of teaching conditions most affects their willingness to keep teaching at their school, almost 3 out of 10 (28 percent) educators selected school leadership, nearly 2 times more than any other working condition area assessed.

Cochran-Smith (2006) in *Policy, Practice, and Politics in Teacher Education* describes the importance of school leaders developing and maintaining school cultures that sustain and support teachers' learning over the long haul as critical impetus for staying. The research points to the importance of a greater understanding by school leaders and the public alike that schools differ from private sector organizations in that teaching and learning cannot be reduced simply to efficiency and profitability. Cochran-Smith asserts that "Teaching and learning are matters of both head and heart, both reason and passion" (p. 104).

In a report on research studying the impact of teacher attrition on policy making, Exstrom (2009) notes that educators have consistently indicated they need the following:

- Supportive school leadership
- Engaged community and parents
- A safe environment
- Sufficient facilities
- Enough time to plan and collaborate

- High-quality professional development
- An atmosphere of trust and respect
- Effective school improvement teams
- Appropriate assignments and workload

When these needs are met, research shows that teachers stay and that students achieve at higher levels. And when these needs are not met, teachers leave more often and student scores are low.

We agree with Csikszentmihalyi (1990) and Molinaro and Drake (1998) that good teachers will stay when they believe in an "improvement ethic" and have a personal sense of efficacy. We add that the MBWA principal must provide the support mechanisms needed to create the work conditions conducive to teachers' adherence to the "improvement ethic" and development of a sense of efficacy.

THE IMPROVEMENT ETHIC

Journalist Andrew Reinbach (2010) asked the following question of a veteran teacher assigned to English as a second language (ESL) students in New York City: "Considering what teachers endure—why do you do it?" The teacher responded as follows:

> It can't be that we are workaholics who enjoy marking tests and homework, writing tests and planning lessons for hours every night. It can't be that we prefer spending our evenings, weekends and "vacation" days this way instead of paying attention to our spouses and children. Or that we bask in the disrespect shown to us, as highly educated and dedicated professionals, by the mayor, the chancellor and, especially, the press. So, why do we do it? The reasons came to visit me the other day. They were former students—two boys from Africa who are now in their second year of college—one of them studying microbiology and physiology. They hugged me and said that I

had really helped them, although at the time, they had not understood it. Now, older and more mature, they said that I had changed their lives . . . that visit is all the evaluation that I need, and all the evaluation that really counts. *That* is why teachers teach. (n.p.)

We all know that the improvement ethic can be and should be a lifelong goal regardless of whether we are talking about our craft, our trade, or our personal life. Getting better at what we do, producing better products, and helping young people learn more are our sources of energy. We also gravitate to the term because of the word *ethic*. This word addresses the principle of conduct governing an individual or a group. In our case as educators, when we embrace the improvement ethic, students learn, and this results in satisfaction and motivation for us. The target is improvement, a realistic and manageable goal. Improvement may come in fits and starts and is not continuous, but it is the focus that keeps district resources and personnel on target. That is what an ethic does—if we believe in an ethic, we try to live in accordance with it.

In a survey sample of teachers in Georgia (Inman & Marlow, 2004), the majority of teachers with 4 to 9 years of experience indicated that employment factors play a significant role in determining if they will continue teaching. It appears that teachers newer to the profession, with 0 to 3 years' experience, tend to be less sure of how their ideology compares with that of others and whether or not the working conditions are compatible with their expectations for their life's work. The more experienced teachers were better able to identify their own ideology, the ideology of others, and satisfactory working conditions that allow for a more collegial and professional atmosphere. Beginning teachers need colleagues around them with whom they can share ideas, make plans, and attempt to solve problems that might otherwise inhibit improvement. When teachers are supported in this way by the MBWA principal, they express fewer feelings of isolation and benefit by gaining knowledge from more-experienced teachers. This feeling of empowerment, gained from the support of colleagues and a positive work environment, assists the beginning teacher in gaining positive self-esteem and a sense of efficacy in providing instruction that leads to student improvement. On the other hand, teachers without this support are more likely to perceive themselves as isolated and be resigned to failure.

As a young superintendent, Larry Frase remembered hearing one of the district's administrators say that the district had an "improvement ethic." He explained that "Each of us believes that we can do better and we focus on improvement, from the superintendent on down." He captured what the district's leaders were doing in these few words. The building and central office administrators in the district were MBWA administrators. They were in the schools every day, watching and learning, and asking the following questions:

- What were the working and learning conditions?
- What could be done to make the teachers' work more effective?
- Was training needed?
- Was the distribution of students with discipline problems in classrooms equitable?
- Was the scheduling hindering teaching and learning?
- Were provisions of materials adequate?

When external influences were found to be problematic, changes were made. The MBWA administrators knew that the teachers needed high-quality working conditions that give them the chance of doing their best work.

We observe this ethic in many schools and school districts. As the Learning First Alliance (Togneri & Anderson, 2003) discovered, successful districts have the courage to acknowledge poor performance and the will to seek solutions. We found that one behavior common to all of the highly effective principals in our earlier studies was the ability to "face the brutal facts" and do something about them. This is a crucial first step. The school principals and other professionals in these districts strive to improve their work results. They are focused on improving learning for students and bettering the conditions for all employees within the district.

Unfortunately, we have also worked with districts that have essentially given up, either overtly or covertly. Some imply their students cannot learn, while others have resorted to purchasing the magic elixirs from the pedagogical pharmacy. Most of these quick fixes do not work, and they never have. In contrast, we describe in Chapters 5 and 6 curriculum practices that do result in greater student learning.

By focusing on the improvement ethic, we will learn how to stop the hemorrhaging of teacher talent. When their work conditions are so adverse that success is unlikely and a sense of efficacy is virtually impossible, teachers leave—and kids fail to learn.

How, then, does the MBWA principal set up schools so that teachers have better opportunities to experience success? When teachers receive effective professional development, support, and mentoring to develop their skills, it is highly likely they will succeed in helping their students learn. When teaching is successful, teachers are more satisfied, motivated, and efficacious. This is a success formula for our public schools.

Fostering the Improvement Ethic and Sense of Efficacy in Teachers

Consider the following four major factors for the MBWA principal in fostering the improvement ethic and sense of efficacy in teachers:

1. Support "flow" experiences.

2. Provide professional development.

3. Promote collaborative leadership.

4. Recognize successes.

Support "Flow" Experiences

So what is this thing called "flow," and why is it important? The short answer is that flow experiences represent optimal life experiences, that is, the best, most gratifying experiences we can have. It is a legitimate psychological concept with powerful implications for improving the quality of teaching workplaces and productivity (Csikszentmihalyi, 1990; Csikszentmihalyi & Csikszentmihalyi, 1988; Zhu, 2001).

Flow experiences are periods of deep, intense involvement in activities that challenge but do not overwhelm one's skills. This is a crucial aspect. We can attain flow when we are challenged, but the challenge should not be so far out of our reach that we cannot succeed. It must be beyond our current skill level, must require us to exert effort, and must require us to concentrate in order for us to succeed.

Do teachers experience flow? They have and do when conditions are right (Basom & Frase, 2004). Teachers have described flow experiences in a variety of contexts, as evidenced here (Caouette, 1995):

- "being able to get lost in my work with the kids because I'm so focused on them." (p. 73)
- "you realized you've got them, like they're with you—and I honor that experience and wonder. It's a feeling of wonder." (p. 74)
- "a sense of relaxing, fulfilled, self-fulfilling feeling." (p. 99)

Another study (P. Gray & Frase, 2003) revealed similar flow experiences described by teachers.

- "To watch them discuss, it felt like they were having so much fun—but they were getting so many good ideas at the same time. . . . I could have done that forever and not stopped because it was so involved." (p. 38)
- "Time stops, I'm not bored. I'm feeling very challenged. I know that I can make this work." (p. 39)

Most importantly, teachers noted that flow is experienced more often when they are actively engaged in a difficult enterprise that stretches their mental or physical abilities. Very practical actions MBWA principals can take to promote teacher flow experiences are provided in Table 4.1.

Table 4.1   MBWA Principal Actions for Building Environments Conducive to Teacher Flow Experiences

MBWA Principal Actions	Rationale
1. Visit classrooms often.	Principal classroom presence is positively correlated with frequency of teacher flow experiences (Frase 2001, 2003; Galloway & Frase, 2003). This practice allows school principals to gain an excellent understanding of the classrooms and teachers' work lives.
2. Minimize the use of the school bell, intercom, and presentations by outside agencies not directly aligned to the curriculum.	Teachers report that flow experiences were broken by such events since they disrupt teaching and concentration and, hence, flow (Caouette, 1995; P. Gray, 2003).
3. Provide adequate time for teachers to conduct lesson planning.	The research of Caouette (1995) and P. Gray (2003) revealed that teachers believed that sound preparation was a precedent to flow experiences.
4. Provide training on the design of a high-quality curriculum.	The curriculum defines what students are to learn. If the curriculum is not well-formed, it is likely that the desired learning is ill-defined and the curriculum is difficult for the teacher to use. When these poor conditions are present, it is less likely that teachers will experience success in helping students learn, let alone experience flow (English & Steffy, 2001).

(Continued)

Table 4.1 (Continued)

MBWA Principal Actions	Rationale
5. Find time for quality training on instruction.	Administrators need to make it a priority to know and understand the research on best instructional practices associated with increased student achievement and provide a plethora of opportunities for all teachers to learn and apply such instructional strategies (Marzano, 2003).
6. Assure that the conditions of the teachers' work environment are conducive to continual development and proud accomplishments.	Administrators need to reevaluate the teaching workload to assure that schools have embedded opportunities for collaboration and for ongoing learning in the daily work of the staff and faculty. Teachers should be afforded ongoing, content-rich professional development opportunities that link to the school's curriculum and assessment efforts (Darling-Hammond, 2003).
7. Provide well-designed mentoring and induction programs.	Studies have found that well-designed mentoring and teacher support programs raise retention rates for new teachers by improving their attitudes, feelings of efficacy, and instructional skills (Darling-Hammond, 2003; Inman & Marlow, 2004). Districts that supplement principal instructional leadership with teacher mentoring are more successful (Togneri & Anderson, 2003).
8. Provide teachers time to discuss, analyze, and reflect on their classroom successes and failures.	Arrange for teachers to observe each other's teaching. Stigler and Hiebert (1999) suggest that teachers organize themselves into teams based on common interests, systematically employ specific techniques for specific lessons, and observe each other's teaching. Veteran teachers could

MBWA Principal Actions	Rationale
	be paired with nonveteran teachers in a mentoring protocol such as peer coaching (Gottesman, 2000) for modeling and reflection, professional learning communities (DuFour, Eaker, & DuFour, 2005), and assessment teams (Boudett, City, & Murnane, 2007).

The ideas listed in Table 4.1 are focused and very doable. These are hallmarks of MBWA principals promoting the improvement ethic.

FOR REFLECTION

What are your thoughts about these ideas for promoting teacher flow experiences? What actions do you want to take in your school to build a flow environment?

Provide Professional Development Opportunities

Jack McCall (1997) declares that *"Students learn only from teachers who are themselves in the process of learning"* (p. 23). You, as the administrator in charge, support the improvement ethic and the development of a sense of efficacy in teachers by providing effective professional development. You can bring out the best in your teachers and provide an atmosphere of continuous learning. Unfortunately, teachers often describe their professional development with disgust, in the following terms:

A waste of time

Flavor of the month

Sit 'n' git

Unrelated to their classroom jobs

One-shot hot stuff

Superficial and faddish

Feel-good sessions

Make-and-takes

Bags-of-tricks

Consultant-driven presentations

The primary reason for their lackluster reactions to current professional development is that it does not relate to what they do in classrooms. Current and past professional development practices have failed. They have relied on unproven and non–research-based innovations.

The good news is that in spite of existing faddism and many teachers' negative statements, professional development can be highly valuable in further enhancing teachers' skills—the ones they need so desperately to succeed in classrooms. Professional development is effective when it is ongoing, long term, and related to the teacher's content area and classroom work (Garet, Porter, Desimone, Birman, & Kwang, 2001; National Staff Development Council [NSDC], 2001; Zepeda, 2008). In other words, professional development is welcome and effective when it is done right. Teachers appreciate it because they see it as a means of complementing their repertoire of skills. They want the skills they need to help students learn successfully. This success is the very thing that builds confidence in teachers—the *can-do* spirit that promotes the improvement ethic.

Assess yourself. The National Staff Development Council (2001) has developed Standards for Staff Development. In addition, the Colorado Statewide Systemic Initiative for Mathematics and Science (CONNECT) (1999) includes a guide for developing a professional development strategic plan. From both of these documents, we have developed some questions to ask yourself about the professional development program at your school. Assess your professional development program by circling yes or no for each question.

1	Do you or your district have a policy directing professional development efforts?	Y	N
2	Do you have a professional development mission in place?	Y	N
3	Does your professional development program promote "learning communities" (teams of teachers that meet on a regular basis for the purposes of learning, joint lesson planning, and problem solving)?	Y	N
4	Do you and your district leaders promote continuous instructional improvement that improves the learning of all students?	Y	N
5	Is your professional development program built using a long-range planning approach emphasizing long-range follow-up and reinforcement?	Y	N
6	Does your leadership foster an expectation for professional growth?	Y	N
7	Does your professional development program provide for three phases of the change process: initiation, implementation, and institutionalization in the school?	Y	N
8	Are your professional development efforts aligned with district goals?	Y	N
9	Does your professional development program focus on proven research-based approaches that assist students in meeting rigorous academic standards?	Y	N
10	When designing professional development for your teachers, do you focus on learning strategies appropriate to the intended goal?	Y	N

(Continued)

(Continued)

11	Does your professional development program provide educators with the knowledge and skills to collaborate?	Y	N
12	Does your professional development program prepare educators to understand and appreciate all students; create safe, orderly, and supportive learning environments; and hold high expectations for students' academic achievement?	Y	N
13	Are your professional development training techniques based on human learning and change?	Y	N
14	Does your professional development program deepen educators' content knowledge?	Y	N
15	Does your professional development program prepare teachers to use various types of classroom assessments appropriately?	Y	N
16	Does your professional development program provide educators with knowledge and skills to involve families and other stakeholders?	Y	N
17	Do you require an evaluation of professional development that is ongoing and includes multiple sources of information based on actual classroom behavior?	Y	N
18	Does your professional development program fit identified teacher needs while being linked to the school mission, the district mission, and the curriculum?	Y	N

FOR REFLECTION

How did you do? If you marked at least 14 questions as "Yes," your professional development program is on the way to becoming an effective program. For those you marked "No," improvement is always possible. What are some ways you can improve the professional development program at your school?

Recognize tenets of effective professional development. A study by the Western Regional Educational Laboratory (2000) examined the professional development programs at eight public schools that had made measurable gains in student achievement. The study found that the schools' professional development programs were characterized by collaborative structures, diverse and extensive professional learning opportunities, and an emphasis on accountability and student results. The Consortium of Chicago School Research (Smylie, Allensworth, Greenberg, Harris, & Luppescu, 2001) conducted a study of high-quality professional development programs—that is, those characterized by "sustained, coherent study; collaborative learning; time for classroom experimentation; and follow-up"—and found that these activities had a significant positive effect on teachers' instructional practices.

We count numerous other studies (DuFour & Eaker, 1998; English & Poston, 1999; Ferguson, 2006; Tienken & Stonaker, 2007; Zepeda, 2008) in which tenets of effective professional development are described. The NSDC standards and the CONNECT criteria discussed earlier were generated in part by the earlier of these studies and serve as criteria to follow in selecting professional development activities for your staff.

Much of this research negates the long-term effectiveness of stand-alone training. Too often, school leaders find themselves using a nonstudent planning day as an opportunity to bring in the expert on current topics for the day. Don't get caught in this trap. It is more likely going to be a waste of resources, most certainly won't be effective in the long term, and may result in teachers losing confidence in your leadership.

Promote Collaborative Leadership

Collaborative leadership in schools takes many forms and holds many labels, such as site-based management, collaborative decision-making teams, and professional learning communities. Our purpose here is not to describe the various forms of collaborative leadership. Instead, we look at the skills and strategies the MBWA principals use to promote collaborative leadership in any form.

Our MBWA principals reject the notion of top-down decision making and instead exercise skill in guiding their teachers to act together as professionals to deal with agreed-upon issues. Collaborative leadership assumes that the more we do as a group, the more we can accomplish. In effect, the principal is making use of the social capital of the relationships of a diverse group of people based on a common set of expectations, a set of shared values, and a sense of trust among those involved. As an added plus, faculty members grow in their knowledge and experience through collaborative leadership activities. This growth manifests itself in individual teachers' sense of efficacy in their own classroom work and in the allegiance they have for the school as a whole, thus providing more glue to keep the right people.

Molinaro and Drake (1998) propose that principals who wish to share leadership must replace "control over" with "support for" teachers and present them with opportunities to grow and develop (p. 6). To do this, you must be ready to engage in the actions listed below with your teachers.

- Avoid isolated decision making whenever possible. This is a critical mind-set change you must make first.
- Encourage teacher autonomy over instructional practices. Teachers collectively are the best resource for instructional best practices.

- Engage in reflective inquiry with teachers. An excellent resource for this discourse is found in *Advancing the Three-Minute Walk-Through: Mastering Reflective Practice* (Downey et al., 2010).
- Promote teacher responsibility for problem solving and follow-through. Once you have assured teachers that you have faith in their capacity for solving problems, they will expect themselves in return to be accountable and to hold each other accountable for following through on their collaborative decisions.
- Build the school schedules carefully in order to ensure that teachers have the necessary time to meet together. S. P. Gray and Streshly (2010) suggest possible times as follows:
  - Before or after school-scheduled staff meeting time
  - Scheduled district professional development nonstudent days
  - Yearlong shared prep periods (secondary schools)
  - Shared schedules for physical education, music, or art so teachers can meet together while students are being instructed by specialists (elementary schools)
  - Grade-level, department, or course-specific teacher nonstudent days using creative funding to hire substitutes
  - Shortened student days once a week for collaborative teamwork by increasing the length of the year (p. 96)

Collaborative leadership requires that you adopt a new mind-set for coping with some ambiguity, empowering others, and maintaining a momentum of continuous change. Throughout, you will balance your role of co-learner and collaborator in some matters with that of supervisor and school authority in others.

Recognize Successes

Studies have demonstrated how important it is to recognize teacher accomplishments (Blase & Kirby, 1992; Buckingham & Coffman, 1999; Peters, 1987). Gostick and

Elton (2009) assert that the best managers (our MBWA princi-pals) use recognition to engage the people they work with and retain them. In their book *The Carrot Principle: How the Best Managers Use Recognition to Engage Their People, Retain Talent, and Accelerate Performance,* Gostick and Elton offer a plethora of ways to recognize people for their efforts. We have included a few here as a sample:

- Revel in a new teacher's first day with the whole staff.
- Ask an experienced teacher to mentor a new teacher in the area of the experienced teacher's expertise, thus turning a responsibility into a reward.
- Say good morning to teachers every day, and call them by name.
- Gear up recognition during difficult times to communi-cate that you trust in a teacher's ability to turn things around.

Recognizing successes as a way to promote continual growth and keep the right people at your school is a simple skill that can go horribly wrong if implemented insensitively. An important rule for recognizing successes in schools is this: Recognize group successes in public and individual successes in private. Kohn (1999), in his book *Punished by Rewards,* dedi-cates one complete chapter to ways in which praising people can be detrimental. Critical to crediting others in schools is to avoid praise that sets up competition between teachers. Complimenting an individual teacher in front of his or her peers can cause unexpected dissention. After all, if a teacher is doing something right, does that mean the other teachers in the room are doing something wrong? Assuming you have promoted a culture of collaboration and shared responsibility and commitment at the school for increasing student achieve-ment, you should be recognizing the whole team for successful efforts, not just one individual on that team. Save individual congratulations for a private conversation.

Teachers thrive and are highly motivated in an environment where they are successful and where they believe they can affect the learning of their students. MBWA principals promote teachers' sense of efficacy that, in turn, helps create a school environment in which an improvement ethic can flourish and student learning will increase. In Chapter 5, we explore the importance of MBWA principals having a working knowledge of designing and identifying high-quality curriculum, instruction, and assessments.

5

Promoting Quality Curriculum Through MBWA

Nam et ipsa scientia potestas est. (Knowledge is power.)

—Sir Francis Bacon

T he MBWA principal as curriculum leader has moved to the forefront of school improvement with the dawn of the No Child Left Behind (NCLB) Act of 2001 and its emphasis on testing student achievement. Principals and district leaders are now more publicly accountable for the performance of their students on high-stakes tests. Increasing evidence points convincingly to a direct link between the curriculum leadership provided by the principal and the effectiveness of the school in raising student performance (Commission on No Child Left Behind, 2007; Glatthorn, 2009; Hall & Hord, 2006; Sanders & Simpson, 2005).

In Chapter 4, the importance of MBWA principals promoting a school environment in which the improvement ethic can thrive and student learning improve was highlighted. This chapter explores the importance of the MBWA principal developing a deep knowledge base with respect to the design and delivery of a high-quality curriculum.

We do not deny that our students' standardized test scores are not what we want them to be or what the NCLB law or the more recent Race to the Top (U.S. Department of Education, 2010) requires them to be. Many solutions have been proffered and many have been tried, but nearly all have failed to produce greater sustained learning. We believe knowledgeable curriculum leadership of the MBWA principal is key. First, the principal must know what is of the most value for students to learn.

Quality of Curriculum Content

Fraser, Williamson, and Tobin (1987) identified the quality of the curriculum as one of 10 factors influencing student achievement. Glatthorn (2009) agrees when he states, "The best teaching methods, when used to deliver poor content, result only in a great deal of mislearning" (p. 38). Ravitch (2010) supports this focus when she advocates that a well-conceived coherent and sequential curriculum is critical for meeting our expectations for what schools should accomplish for our children.

The ultimate goal of the MBWA leader is to maximize student learning by providing quality curriculum content. Given the pressure on schools for student performance on high-stakes tests, it is inevitable that we look to a question that has long been at the center of decisions made about curriculum.

Teaching to the Test: Ethical or Unethical?

As states have adopted various types of high-stakes tests and the scores on these instruments are made public, the impact of testing has become the driving force identifying what is of most value to teach or learn. The curriculum has become *whatever the test is assessing*. Thus, "teaching to the test" becomes inevitable. Why? Because it is the test results that have come to define "successful teaching" and "successful schools" (English, 2010, p. 22).

FOR REFLECTION

Is teaching to the test ethical? Why or why not?

Curriculum research establishes that students who have been taught the skills and knowledge required on a test do better on it than those students who have not been taught these skills (English, 1992, 2010; English & Steffy, 2001). We've learned after working with hundreds of teachers and administrators that typically a question follows asking whether or not teaching the test is cheating. This question misses the point. We most certainly do not advocate teaching the exact test items. That, of course, is inappropriate. Teaching *to* the test, that is, teaching students the content and knowledge needed to perform well, *is* fair. It is the only way some students have to learn what the test demands of them. Many students from lower socioeconomic backgrounds do not come to school with the cultural capital presented on the test, so preparing them for the test is an educator's moral obligation.

This is crucial in closing the achievement gap. The rationale for teaching to the test is clear—it is the only way to help prepare students for the tests. How many of us have ever prepared for the Miller Analogy Test, the GRE, the SAT, or any one of numerous other exams? Did you note the high degree of alignment between the preparation manuals and the exam? These manuals, designed to acquaint students with the contents of these tests, are available and are intended for use. They teach to the test. What about the typical driver's test or a real estate license test? Classes and manuals are available for both, and the tests include only those items covered in these manuals, without exception. The bottom line is that failure to teach the test content translates to unfair measurement—and haplessly the student is labeled with the results (English, 2010; English & Steffy, 2001)!

Designing an Aligned Curriculum

Standard setting by the states has its problems. Individuals who are often far removed from local schools set the standards. What should the MBWA principal do about state standards? We agree with Glatthorn (2009), who believes, "State standards should be treated as the floor for curriculum, not the ceiling" (p. 9). Under the active leadership of the MBWA principal, the school customizes its own curriculum that builds on the state and district's broader curriculum. The school curriculum takes into consideration special needs of their students while preparing them for high-stakes tests and their future as successful citizens. Curriculum development is a challenge for the MBWA principal, and the tasks involved in succeeding are not quick and easy—but they can be achieved. These tasks are explored in this chapter.

It is important to remember that curriculum development is not the sole responsibility of the MBWA principal. It is a collaborative team process. The more teachers are involved, the more buy-in is generated for implementing the curriculum in their classrooms. However, an MBWA principal must have the knowledge base to facilitate such a task. We look more fully at collaborative structures later on in this chapter when we discuss ways to monitor the effectiveness of the curriculum. We begin our discussion of curriculum development by first clarifying certain key terms.

Basic Definitions

- **Written curriculum:** The book, curriculum guide, or other materials that define what it is that students are to master
- **Taught curriculum:** That which the teacher teaches—content, attitudes, beliefs, values, etc. It could be anything, including the written curriculum (the guide).
- **Tested curriculum:** The content (information, skills, attitudes, etc.) that the test assesses
- **Aligned curriculum:** The overall key to ensuring high student achievement is by aligning the written, taught, and tested curriculum as portrayed in Figure 5.1.

Figure 5.1 Alignment of the Written, Taught, and Tested Curriculum

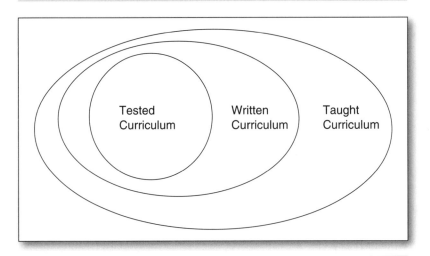

Source: Adapted from English & Steffy (2001, p. 88).

- **Topological curriculum alignment:** A one-to-one match between the test item and the objectives in the written curriculum for

  o content (the topic, concept, process, skill, knowledge, and attitude to be learned);
  o context (the conditions under which the student must demonstrate mastery of the content); and
  o cognitive type (the type of thought process required to demonstrate mastery). Bloom's (1956) taxonomy, including knowledge, comprehension, application, analysis, synthesis, and evaluation, is useful here and presented in Table 5.1.

Table 5.1   Condensed Version of Bloom's Taxonomy

KNOWLEDGE—Includes those behaviors and test situations that emphasize the remembering, either by recognition or recall, of ideas, material, or phenomena.

- Range from the specific and relatively concrete types of behaviors to the more complex and abstract ones—including the interrelations and patterns in which information can be organized and structured
- Remembering is the major psychological process involved here.

COMPREHENSION—When confronted with a communication, students are expected to know what is being communicated and to be able to market some use of the material or ideas contained in it.

- Three types: translation, interpretation, and extrapolation.
- Emphasis is on the grasp of the meaning and intent of the material.

APPLICATION—Applies comprehension in a situation new to the student without prompting, requires transferring of knowledge and comprehension to a real situation.

- Emphasis is on the remembering and bringing to bear upon given material the appropriate generalizations or principles.

ANALYSIS—Break down the material into its constituent parts, make explicit the relationships among the elements, and then recognition [*sic*] of the organizational principles, the arrangement, and structure, which holds together the communication as a whole.

- Emphasis is on the breakdown of the material into its constituent parts and detection of the relationship of the parts and of the way they are organized.
- Not to be confused with comprehending the meaning of something abstract (Comprehension)

SYNTHESIS—Putting together elements and parts so as to form a whole, to a pattern or structure not clearly there before.

- Focus on creative ability of the student but within limits of a framework
- Must draw upon elements from many sources and put these together in a structure or pattern not clearly there before
- Should yield a product

EVALUATION—Making of judgments about the value, for some purpose, of ideas, works, solutions, methods, material, and so on.

- Involves use of criteria as well as standards for appraising the extent to which particulars are accurate, effective, economical, or satisfying
- May be quantitative or qualitative
- Are not opinions but judgments based on criteria

Source: Bloom (1956, appendix). Adapted from condensed version in Downey et al. (2010, pp. 38, 39), *Advancing the Three-Minute Walk-Through: Mastering Reflective Practice,* Thousand Oaks, CA: Corwin. Reprinted by permission of Carolyn Downey.

- **Deep curriculum alignment:** Topological alignment plus (1) a broad yet reasonable range of content application and (2) real-life contexts that expand alternative ways of assessing the contents and (3) provide a variety of cognitive types for student mastery.

- **Frontloading:** Developing a written curriculum first, and then selecting or developing the appropriate measuring tool to assess it.
- **Backloading:** Analyzing the knowledge and skills required on the test, and then including these in the written curriculum.

The question now becomes, how does the MBWA principal facilitate the creation of a curriculum that reflects the state standards and high-stakes tests, while meeting the special needs of the students at the school and preparing them for the world at large?

Backloading the Curriculum From the Test

When the written curriculum is backloaded from the test so that 100 percent of the test is covered in the written curriculum, and when the teacher teaches 100 percent of the written curriculum, students learn. Moreover, they prepare themselves for the test. There are no surprises, and test scores go up. A note of caution here: Backloading the curriculum from the test is a measure to improve test scores by helping all students learn what is being tested, but it is not the whole curriculum. It is not intended for determining what the breadth and depth of a curriculum should be in the first place.

The process of developing the curriculum from the test is especially difficult when the high-stakes test itself is not available for analysis. Textbook publishers attempt to help us in this regard by telling us that their text is aligned with all state frameworks (tests) and all subject matter areas tested. Many times, unfortunately, this has proved to be more a sales pitch than a reality. Early alignment studies showed a lack of alignment between textbooks and standardized tests (Floden, Porter, Schmidt, Freeman, & Schwille, 1981; Freeman et al., 1980; Goodman, Shannon, Freeman, & Murphy, 1988). More recent studies (Kulm, Roseman, & Treistman, 1999; Price-Baugh, 1997) unearthed similar results. This continuing lack of alignment between what is tested and the adopted textbooks leads to unfair surprises for the students and results in lower scores.

Topological alignment. Downey et al. (2003) describe the following steps used by many school districts to overcome the problem of poor alignment, steps that if used, result in a one-to-one match between the written curriculum and the high-stakes test.

1. Review each item on the test, or on a similar test. Alternate tests or test items are available in many states. In places where these are not available, use sample test items published on the State Department of Education website, or purchase such tests from other states. Studies have shown that most tests used across the United States are highly similar. As a double check, match the items against the frameworks used in your state.

2. Deconstruct each test item by identifying what is being taught (the content) and how it is being tested (the context). The context of the test item is the conditions under which the student must demonstrate mastery of it, such as the format of the items—multiple choice or word problem. In addition, determine what type of cognition is required.

3. Determine the grade level at which each item is first tested in your state. Remember that these grade levels vary from state to state. Place the test items at the proper grade level for your state.

4. Determine the frequency of test items on your state test for each objective. This frequency varies from state to state, and your taught curriculum and practice tests should reflect these percentages. Vary the time spent teaching to each objective based on these frequencies.

5. Place the objectives in content standards—use the state or district content standard/framework areas as a tool.

6. Develop a correlation matrix displaying the tested objectives in relation to the state or national standards or frameworks. We suggest that you keep the matrix on file for legal purposes based on our own experience with state mandates.

A sample of a topologically aligned (one-to-one match in content, context, and cognitive type) and backloaded objective is presented in Figure 5.2 and Table 5.2. The item presented in Figure 5.2 is a fifth-grade mathematics practice test question. This test item uses a gridded response question in which students must arrive at a numeric answer independently, and then write the answer and bubble in the circle.

The deconstruction of the test item for topological alignment to the curriculum is shown in Table 5.2.

Table 5.2   Deconstruction of Fifth-Grade Test Item for Topological Alignment

Content:

- Specify the number in a repeated number pattern that requires a skip in the pattern using the simple operations of addition and/or multiplication.

Context:

- Given a word problem that is split by a visual depiction of the word problem
- Given a visual depiction that is only part of the problem
- Vocabulary specific to learning that includes ordinal and cardinal numbers, and words such as *row*, *continued*, *pattern*
- Student writes answer and then bubbles answer into a number grid

Cognitive Type:

- Knowledge (Bloom's Taxonomy)

Source (for Table 5.2 and Figure 5.2): Downey et al. (2003, p. 18–19), *Leaving No Child Behind: 50 Ways to Close the Achievement Gap*, Johnston, IA: Curriculum Management Systems. Reprinted by permission from Carolyn Downey.

Figure 5.2   Fifth-Grade Test Item

1. The gymnastics class stood in rows to have their team picture taken. The photographer told 2 people to stand in the first row, 4 people to stand in second row, and 6 people to stand in the third row.

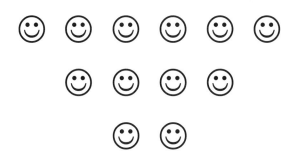

The photographer continued the pattern. How many people did he tell to stand in the sixth row?

Test Questions			
1	2	3	4
⓪	⓪	⓪	⓪
①	①	①	①
②	②	②	②
③	③	③	③
④	④	④	④
⑤	⑤	⑤	⑤
⑥	⑥	⑥	⑥
⑦	⑦	⑦	⑦
⑧	⑧	⑧	⑧
⑨	⑨	⑨	⑨

Deep alignment. Although topological alignment as just described will be a major improvement for the large majority of districts, it will lead to limited test score improvement—and those improvements are generally short-lived. Several studies conclude that deep alignment, focusing in depth and in multiple contexts on a smaller number of skills and concepts, will produce major sustained test score improvement (English & Steffy, 2001; Erickson, 2007; Marzano, 2007). Schools and districts should write curriculum that goes beyond the state test in order to assure that students have adequate and rich learning. This is called "deep alignment." Deep alignment requires that the content of the objectives be broadened to a reasonable range of learning, that the variety of ways of assessing mastery be expanded, and that students be moved to higher levels of cognition. Multiple contexts must be developed—that is, use the tested context; the textbook context, which is usually of the "write the answer" variety; and a real-world context. Multiple contexts bring purpose and reality to learning and increase the probability that students will transfer this learning to multiple situations.

Table 5.3 includes an example of how you as principal and your teachers would take the topically aligned objective from the fifth-grade test item shown earlier and write it in a deeply aligned way. Italics indicate the changes that move the objective from topical alignment to deep alignment. Note also the additional contexts.

Table 5.3   Objective Deeply Aligned to the Fifth-Grade Test Item

Content:
- Specify the number, *letter,* or *visual symbol* in a repeated number, *letter, or visual symbol* pattern that requires a *next in line* and a skip in the pattern using the simple operations of addition or multiplication, *subtraction, or division.*

Context 1: (gridded response)

- Given a word problem that is split by a visual depiction of the word problem
- Given a visual depiction that is only part of the problem
- Vocabulary, which includes ordinal and cardinal numbers, words such as *gymnastics, photographer, row, continued, pattern*
- Student writes answer and then bubbles answer into a number grid

Cognitive Type:

- Knowledge

Context 2: (multiple-choice test)

- Given a word problem that is split by a visual depiction of the word problem
- Give a visual depiction that is only part of the problem
- Vocabulary, which includes ordinal and cardinal numbers, and words such as *gymnastics, photographer, row, continued, pattern*
- Student selects answer from four possible answers with distracters, most frequent errors, and a "none of the above" answer
- Student bubbles correct answer on Scantron-type separate answer sheets

Cognitive Type:

- Knowledge

Context 3: (multiple-choice test)

- Given symbolic pattern
- Student selects answer from four possible answers with distracters, most frequent errors, and a "none of the above" answer
- Student bubbles correct answer on Scantron-type separate answer sheet

(Continued)

Table 5.3 (Continued)

Cognitive Type:

- Knowledge

Context 4: (typical textbook approach)

- Given symbolic pattern, student writes in answer and explains the answer

Cognitive Type:

- Comprehension

Context 5: (real-world pattern simulation, requiring student to show reasoning, per writing objective)

- Given a word problem depicting a real-world situation
- Given a direction to determine a pattern
- Student writes the pattern and a descriptive paragraph explaining the reasoning behind the correct answer
- Paragraph must meet fifth-grade writing rubric

Cognitive Type:

- Application

Source: Downey et al. (2003, pp. 20–21), *Leaving No Child Behind: 50 Ways to Close the Achievement Gap,* Johnston, IA: Curriculum Management Systems. Reprinted by permission of Carolyn Downey.

Deep alignment is based on Thorndike's (1951) concept of *transfer*—that is, when students are taught concepts and information in a certain context, they will more likely be successful performing the task in identical/similar situations or contexts. Therefore, the best way to ensure that students will have high transferability of their learning is to teach it to them in many contexts. This is very important, since students will be challenged with many situations in different contexts. In regard to curriculum, this means the curriculum must not only mirror the test, but also include many contexts going beyond the test. Deep alignment does this; it maximizes the curriculum design and gives teachers the material they need to help their students perform well. Students will demonstrate that they have learned and, more important, are able to use their learning in life. Using a real-life context example is the best way to ensure that students can successfully use their knowledge in real-life situations.

FOR REFLECTION

How is the process of collaborating to align the curriculum a form of professional development for teachers?

Providing a deeply aligned curriculum is an important way the MBWA principal ensures successful teaching and student learning. As stated in earlier chapters, teachers leave because of their lack of success in helping their students learn—in many cases as determined by low scores on the high-stakes test. Working closely with teachers to develop deeply aligned curriculum is the MBWA principal's way of giving teachers the tools they need to get the job done! When students achieve, teachers are motivated, morale is high, and the community recognizes the school's excellent work. It's a win-win-win proposition.

ENSURING HIGH-QUALITY INSTRUCTION

MBWA principals are driven to share high-quality instruction tactics with their teachers. High-quality teaching comes through research-based best practices, and we can provide the training needed so teachers can acquire high-quality instructional skills, as well as knowledge about when to use them. As stated earlier in this book, teachers are the most important element in the formal education of their students, and they need and deserve attention in the form of professional development programs and supervision. These can be their lifelines. Darling-Hammond (2000) illustrates the importance of this to teachers when she states,

> Policy investments in the quality of teachers may be related to improvement in student performance [and] measures of teacher preparation and certification are by far the strongest correlates of student achievement in reading and mathematics, both before and after controlling for student poverty and language status. (pp. 1–2)

The MBWA principal works with the teachers as a team to implement high-quality instructional practices. So what are these practices?

Having a strong working knowledge of research-based instructional practices is crucial to the MBWA principal's effectiveness. Marzano (2003) borrowed findings from previous research (Brophy, 1996; Cotton, 1995; Creemers, 1994) to identify three teacher-level factors that have high impact on student learning: instructional strategies, classroom management, and curriculum design.

High-Impact Factor 1—Instructional Strategies

Numerous studies on instructional strategies exist, and we found it helpful to sort them into three distinct study groups:

1. The "I think" variety;

2. Level 1 research-backed studies; and

3. Level 2 research-backed studies.

The "I Think" Variety of Studies

The first study group consists of the generic "I think" type. These studies typically appear in teacher and administrator trade journals and are expressions of their author's ideas about the effectiveness of certain instructional strategies. Frequently, these articles expound upon the worth and value of a program with which the author is familiar and do not deal with research results.

Level 1 Research-Backed Studies

This second study group highlights instructional strategies backed by one or more research studies that indicate their effectiveness. One group of these researchers found that the following teacher behaviors are positively related to higher student learning:

- Teacher clarity
- Teacher enthusiasm
- Student task-oriented behavior
- Variability of lesson approaches
- Student opportunity to learn criterion material (Bennett, 1986; Creemers, 1994; Hattie, 1992)

The conclusion of this research study group is further articulated by other researchers, namely, that a teacher's ability to use varying instructional strategies with different student groups and individual students takes on great importance, since no one instructional strategy is unvaryingly successful (W. Doyle, 1985; McBer, 2000; Walberg & Waxman, 1983). The argument for use of multiple instructional strategies has been made for many years. The researchers also indicated that student perceptions of teacher effectiveness are frequently right on target. In one study, students were asked to identify characteristics of the "best" and "worst" teachers. The students responded that the number one characteristic of "good" teachers is their good sense of humor, and the number one characteristic of the "worst" teachers was that they were dull and boring (National Association of Secondary School Principals [NASSP], 1997). This matches our experience with interviewing junior high students to get their opinion regarding the characteristics of good and not-so-good teachers. They resoundingly reported that good teachers were the ones who explained the material well and engagingly.

Level 2 Research-Backed Studies

This third type of research is different from the second in that it ratchets up the level of research sophistication. These studies include *effect size*, a key and most valuable statistical term. For example, in addition to saying that one strategy is significantly more effective than another, conclusions about effect size tell us exactly how much more the students learn. The Marzano, Pickering, and Pollock (2001/2004) seminal work falls into this category. They analyzed the extant research on instructional strategies and summarized the findings into the following nine categories of strategies that lead to increased student achievement:

1. Identifying similarities and differences
2. Summarizing and note taking
3. Reinforcing effort and providing recognition
4. Homework and practice
5. Nonlinguistic representations
6. Cooperative learning
7. Setting objectives and providing feedback
8. Generating and testing hypotheses
9. Questions, cues, and advanced organizers

These categories, along with examples of related teacher behaviors for each, are provided by Marzano (2003) in his book *What Works in Schools: Translating Research Into Action*.

High-Impact Factor 2—Classroom Management

Classroom management means maintaining a classroom environment where effective instruction can occur, where students attend to the lesson, and where learning actually does happen. Classroom management is a major problem in many classrooms across the United States, particularly in low socioeconomic status (SES) schools, and it has been identified as the variable having the most impact on student achievement (Wang, Haertel, & Walberg, 1993). This makes sense. Without good classroom management, teachers cannot teach effectively. Students must participate in a reasonable manner. Teachers who perform poorly frequently attribute their problems to their lack of classroom management and to inadequate preparation (J. E. Miller, McKenna, & McKenna, 1998). So, as we can see, classroom management skills are crucial to both teacher and student success. That is why it is imperative that MBWA principals be very knowledgeable and skillful in conveying techniques that help teachers establish and maintain effective classroom management.

Firm, well-communicated schoolwide rules and procedures established collaboratively by teachers and administrators provide a beginning in the endeavor to attain good classroom management (see Chapter 8). Well-defined rules and procedures that establish expectations for specific behaviors are present and utilized in all effectively managed classrooms. But those of us with experience in preK–12 classrooms or even graduate classrooms know that the best-laid plans, in this case classroom management rules and procedures, are not always followed. Students do break rules, and teachers must monitor behavior and react appropriately.

The following list is a summary of key research findings on the most effective strategies for establishing and maintaining good classroom management and student discipline.

- Minimize discipline time and accentuate instructional time.
- Realize that time spent disciplining students adversely affects student achievement outcomes.
- Realize that the least effective strategy is failure to deal with discipline and rule breaking.
- Realize that the most effective strategy is using a combination of punishment and positive reinforcement.

- Interpret and respond to inappropriate behaviors promptly.
- Maintain clear rules and procedures and establish credibility with students through fair and consistent implementation of discipline.
- Scan the room frequently, particularly when working with a small group or with an individual (Berliner, 1986; Brophy, 1996).
- Reinforce and reiterate the expectations for positive behavior.

Successful teachers monitor their own attitudes about specific students by mentally reviewing their students before class, noting those with whom they anticipate having problems, forming a mental picture of these students exhibiting appropriate behavior, and then keeping positive expectations when interacting with these students (Good, 1982; Rosenshine, 1983).

In one study of cases where rules are broken, the use of a variety of interventions resulted in a reduction of disruptive classroom behavior among 78 percent of the treated subjects (Stage & Quiroz, 1997). The strategy yielding the largest effect size was use of a combination of punishment and reinforcement, the second-largest effect size was reinforcement, and the third was punishment. The least-effective strategy was using no immediate consequence. These findings are also supported by the work of A. Miller, Ferguson, and Simpson (1998).

High-Impact Factor 3— Classroom Curriculum Design

As discussed earlier in this chapter, classroom curriculum design is a most important factor affecting student learning. The reason has become quite clear. Ensuring high-quality instruction in these days of high-stakes testing requires us to prepare students to perform well on these tests. This means that districts, administrators, and teachers must deconstruct the test items to determine the skills required to attain mastery of the item and the context in which competence is to be demonstrated. All of this then becomes the curriculum. Without doing this first, no amount of inspired or instructionally sound teaching of content and context of the test is going to help students perform well on high-stakes tests. The teaching must first be focused on the skills required by the test.

MONITORING THE CURRICULUM

Once the deeply aligned curriculum is developed and implemented, the MBWA principal is responsible for monitoring its effectiveness. This is accomplished in a variety of ways, including faculty, grade-level, departmental, and vertical team meeting discussions; analysis of assessment data; lesson study; and, of course, classroom observations. In Chapter 6, we explore in detail various protocols MBWA principals utilize for classroom observations. In practice, there are a variety of ways schools can organize to effectively support ongoing conversations about the effectiveness of curriculum implementation. Deciding which approach is most appropriate for your school will require you as school leader to think creatively about how you can organize your school's time, people, and other resources. Table 5.4 lists 4 of the many research-based collaborative models for monitoring the curriculum.

Table 5.4   Collaborative Models for Monitoring the Curriculum

Collaborative Model	Description	Source
Professional Learning Communities	Teachers work in teams, engaging in an ongoing cycle of questions that promote deep team learning. This process, in turn, leads to higher levels of student achievement.	What Is a "Professional Learning Community"? (DuFour, 2004)

(Continued)

Table 5.4 (Continued)

Collaborative Model	Description	Source
Data Teams	Small grade-level or department teams examine individual student work generated from common formative assessments; collaborative, structured, meetings are scheduled that focus on the effectiveness of teaching and learning.	*Data Wise: A Step-by-Step Guide to Using Assessment Results to Improve Teaching and Learning* (Boudett, City, & Murnane, 2007)
Lesson Study	Japanese teachers engage in a professional development process to systematically examine their practice, with the goal of becoming more effective. This examination centers on teachers working collaboratively on a small number of study lessons. Working on these study lessons involves planning, teaching, observing, and critiquing the lessons.	*Lesson Study: A Japanese Approach to Improving Mathematics Teaching and Learning* (Fernandez & Yoshida, 2004)
Curriculum Design Cycle	Curriculum design consists of (1) establishing design standards; (2) protocols and schedules for self-assessment, review, and field testing; and (3) opportunities for revision.	*Understanding by Design* (Wiggins & McTighe, 2005)

CAVEATS ON RESEARCH

Now that we have a more solid research base supporting MBWA, we absolutely need to use it. Improved student learning and enhanced public perception of education is at stake. However, you as the school's leader should be cautious of your expectations of research and what it means. A research study may show that students experiencing Treatment A scored 0.5 standard deviation points higher than students experiencing Treatment B and that the level of significance is .01. Does that mean that using Treatment A will always have those effects? The answer is no. Statistics simply report probabilities, and the probabilities are diluted when we consider the contextual differences in the experiment and in the application setting. A better way to interpret the research is to think that there is a higher probability that students will learn more if we use Treatment A rather than B, if the contexts are as similar as possible. It is important to remember that research results are never guaranteed. For a full discussion of how to use and interpret research, see *Making Sense of Research* by McEwan and McEwan (2003).

The research described in this chapter should be used to influence supervision and instruction, and further research will add strength. In this sense, it is worth considering the quote by 19th-century educator and researcher Mark Pattison (as cited in Firth & Pajak, 1998): "In research the horizon recedes as we advance . . . and research is always incomplete" (p. xiii). We recommend that you as school administrator forge ahead with what research we currently have. Use these findings in your professional development programs, and discuss them at faculty and team meetings. Make research findings and the teachers' experiences with implementing them the fabric of your school and the key topic of all meetings and supervision activities. After all, high-quality instruction delivers the curriculum to the students. The knowledge that the principal has of the written, taught, and tested curriculum is put to work in Chapter 6, "Getting Into Classrooms."

6

Getting Into Classrooms

The great end of life is not knowledge but action.

—Thomas Henry Huxley

T he MBWA principal must have an in-depth understanding of the well-developed written, taught, and tested curriculum. However, equally important are the MBWA strategies for putting these tools to work. Short and frequent classroom observations by the principal constitute an important strategy for acquiring firsthand information about what is taking place in classrooms, and having thoughtful, research-based conversations with teachers about curriculum. The MBWA principal sees and acts upon informal observations of classrooms as an integral part of the school's culture. The many classroom visit protocols vary in name, purpose, and implementation steps; however, they all have in common brief, yet focused observations in classrooms that provide data for conversations about teaching and learning. It is important to emphasize the supportive nature of these visits. They are not meant to be formal evaluation of teachers (Pitler & Goodwin, 2008). The occasionally sensitive problems of separating the summative evaluation from the formative observations and conversations are discussed in detail in Chapters 9 and 10. This chapter delves into the following topics concerning informal classroom observations:

- Research supporting classroom observations
- Purposes for conducting informal classroom observations
- Some general rules of "etiquette" for principals to follow when informally visiting classrooms
- Information gathered when making informal classroom observations
- Uses for the information gathered
- A sampling of informal classroom observation protocols

Take a moment now to reflect on the following questions.

FOR REFLECTION

- How does classroom observation fit into your beliefs about the role of supervision, and how do you carry out this essential task?

- What is the lens that you as the school administrator use when you walk into classrooms?
- How do you remember what you have observed?
- How do you use the information you gather from observing in a classroom?
- What would motivate you to walk around on a more regular basis?

RESEARCH SUPPORTING FREQUENT PRINCIPAL CLASSROOM OBSERVATIONS

Sather (2009) affirms that "The walk-through [classroom observation] can influence real change in schools by getting administrators close to the classroom" (p. 132). Thus, these administrators build their stature and capacity as instructional leaders. Informal principal classroom observations are robustly linked to important benefits as confirmed by numerous studies. These benefits and the related research studies for the MBWA principal are presented in Table 6.1.

Table 6.1   Benefits of Principal Classroom Observations and Supporting Research

Benefits of Classroom Observations	Supporting Research
Improved teacher motivation and work satisfaction	Chester & Beaudin, 1996; Frase, 2001; Freedman & Lafleur, 2003; Glickman, 2002; P. Gray, 2003; P. Gray & Frase, 2003; Varrati & Smith, 2008
Increased trust between principals and teachers	Glickman, Gordon, & Ross-Gordon, 2005; P. Gray, 2003; S. P. Gray & Streshly, 2008; Tschannen-Moran, 2004
Improved teacher attitudes toward professional development	Annunziata, 1997; Frase, 2001, 2002, 2003; Keruskin, 2005; Rossi, 2007; Stiggins & Duke, 1988

(Continued)

Table 6.1 (Continued)

Benefits of Classroom Observations	Supporting Research
Increased understanding of teachers' work context	Freedman & Lafleur, 2003; Fullan & Hargreaves, 1991; Glickman, 2002; P. Gray, 2003; Sather, 2009; Supovitz & Weathers, 2004
Improved classroom instruction	P. Gray, 2003; Kachur, Stout, & Edwards, 2010; Marzano, Pickering, & Pollock, 2001/2004; Teddlie, Kirby, & Springfield, 1989; Varrati & Smith, 2008
Improved teacher perception of principal effectiveness	Andrews, & Soder, 1987; P. Gray & Frase, 2003; Heck, Larsen, & Marcoulides, 1990; Sager, 1992; Wimpelberg, Teddlie, & Stringfield, 1989
More positive relationship between principals and students	Blase, 1987; P. Gray, 2003
Higher student achievement through an increase in teacher reflection on curricular and instructional issues	Andrews & Soder, 1987; P. Gray, 2003; Hallinger & Heck, 1997; Heck, 1991, 1992; Keruskin, 2005; Leithwood & Mascall, 2008; Louis & Miles, 1991; Robinson, 2007; Stronge, Richard, & Catano, 2008

During research conducted in Shawnee Mission School District, Kansas, we noted comments made by principals and teachers when asked what they liked about informal principal classroom observations or principal walk-throughs. Table 6.2 includes a sample of those comments (P. Gray, 2003).

CONDUCTING INFORMAL CLASSROOM OBSERVATIONS

The MBWA principal does not simply wander around, in and out of classrooms, or what Marshall (2009) terms "Managing by rushing around" or making "drive-by visits" (p. 43). We prefer instead, as Kachur, Stout, and Edwards (2010) describe it, "Wandering with a purpose" (p. 27).

Table 6.2   Principal and Teacher Comments About the Benefits of Informal Principal Classroom Observations or Walk-Throughs

Benefit	Comment
Teacher motivation and work satisfaction	From Principals: • "Teachers know we value the work they do when we come into the classroom. They take pride in what they are doing at that moment." • "When I visit teachers' classrooms often, the teachers know that I respect their professionalism and trust them to do good work." From Teachers: • "It is a little bit of a motivating factor and it's also a nice message to me to know that my building principal is interested in what is going on in the classroom." • "It's motivating. It's kind of nice to be recognized for it." • "I always tell [the principal] she strokes my ego." • "My principal is good about noticing things [when in the classroom]. He tells me things like 'I can tell you exactly what your objective is.' That is always encouraging." • "Comments from my principal are good. They make my whole day." • When I know the principal will be visiting my classroom often, it inspires me to do my very best all the time."
Increased trust between principals and teachers	From Principals: • "Teachers have an easier time doing what I ask of them when I visit their classroom and see what they are actually doing." • "It's about building a relationship and getting to know the teachers so that they feel comfortable with me and trust me."

(Continued)

Table 6.2 (Continued)

Benefit	Comment
	• "I think you have to build relationships and I don't think people know me enough to trust the relationship unless I'm out there [in classrooms]. I mean they don't know who I am."
	From Teachers:
	• "That [trust from teachers] comes from his credibility as a person who has one foot in the classroom."
	• "It is a lot easier to take suggestions from someone who has been observing and not just on a formal basis."
	• "I am very comfortable with it [principal classroom visits] now that it has happened a lot. I feel like the principal and I have a great working relationship. He doesn't intimidate me when he walks into the room. I just know he is not coming in just to get on me about anything. It is never like that."
Higher student achievement through an increase in teacher reflection on curricular and instructional issues	From Principals:
	• "They [teachers] are more focused on curriculum."
	• "They are writing their agenda on the board with more specificity . . . a connection to the curriculum, and it is not just a curriculum number either."
	• "The teacher knows that I'm there making sure he/she is making the right decisions about teaching the curriculum."
	From Teachers:
	• "It's helpful to get suggestions [from the principal] as to how exactly to prioritize when we are trying to integrate reading and writing into the math curriculum."
	• "When the principal comes into my classroom, it is to be sure that I am following district curriculum. I know that my students do better because of that."

Benefit	Comment
Increased principal understanding of teachers' work context	From Principals: • "It [knowledge of teacher work context] gives me a chance to talk about the things I'm seeing, when I talk to the faculty." • "I think [knowledge about the teacher work context] has value in just bringing in a spectrum of communication about education." • "Well, you look at what the teacher is teaching and what the kids are doing. You see what is out and around, on kids' desks, teachers' desks, and in the halls. You try to get a picture of what is happening." • "[We look for] the level of instruction. What kind of learning is going on? Is it just a rudimentary type of knowledge or higher level?" From Teachers: • "[Suggestions] are a lot easier to take from someone who is going around and observing [in classrooms.]" • "A principal's knowledge of teachers' work may give teachers more permission to say, 'What did you think?' or 'Did you notice anything?' It gives teachers an opportunity to say, 'Did you have any feedback for me?'"
Improved teacher perception of principal effectiveness	From Principals: • "I think they [teachers] perceive me to be more effective because I'm out in their world." • "If they believe I know what I'm talking about, which gives me validity, it allows me a chance to successfully support them." From Teachers: • "I enjoy principal visits because I think that way they know what is going on. I think it's for them to see the big picture and kids interacting and learning the objectives that we teach. I really don't see how they [principals] know that unless they're there."

Table 6.2 (Continued)

Benefit	Comment
	• "The principal of this school knows what is going on in the classrooms." • "Principals do this [visit classrooms] so they can maybe have a better understanding of what teachers do." • "You know, I think it [informal classroom visits] is a better way to see us as real teachers because otherwise they just see this great lesson that we plan on the day we are being formally observed." • "I think it helps principals by just seeing what makes us tick."
More positive relationship between principals and students	From Principals: • "I do classroom visits so they [teachers and students] know who I am and that I am interested." • "I tell the kids that my job is three things: to make sure they are learning and to make sure they are safe. The third one is that I want them to have fun while they are learning and being safe in school. I think that the best way to make sure that these three things are happening is by being hands-on and in and out of the classrooms." • "I think the kids will see that their administrators are not just disciplinarians, that they are actually here to lead the school somehow to success." From Teachers: • "I think principal classroom visits let me and the kids know that we are working together." • "The students are aware of the principal. They probably sharpen up a bit when the principal visits." • "The principal asks the students what they are doing, what they are learning, and makes comments to them about their work." • "I think principals visit classrooms just because it serves as a second accountability for kids."

Purposes for Conducting Informal Observations

The MBWA principal could design a special classroom observation protocol that meets the special purposes of a particular school or targeted population, or select one of many approaches that are being advocated throughout the educational profession.

Which type is most suitable? To decide on the approach, you as school administrator must first decide the purpose of your supervision. Educators view the purposes of supervision in different ways. Historically, the intent of supervision was to improve teaching. According to Frase (2005), there is little evidence that we have been successful in this purpose. This is a result of several factors, not the least of which is a belief among some principals that supervision is the means by which employees are forced to work. A more productive supervisory approach is based on the belief that people want to do a good job, want to work, and have an internal motivation to grow and learn (Drucker, 1974). We contend that the type of informal classroom observations that will be most effective in improving teaching and learning is that which reflects a supervisory purpose congruent with McGregor's Theory Y approach (see Chapter 2).

Motivational practices based on extrinsic rewards and relying on inspectional approaches to see if the work is being carried out are proving to be unproductive in effecting long-lasting change in teacher behavior. Yet many administrators continue to use such processes. Checklists documenting easily observable and often trivial aspects of a teacher's performance are developed, with ratings, rankings, and degrees of proficiency built right in, and their implementation is being pursued with single-minded intensity. The accountability movement brought about by the adoption of state and national standards has resulted in too many administrators falling back on supervisory processes that seldom work. The influx of these checklists on the market gives rise to the concern we have about the misuse of informal classroom observations as an "inspectional" practice of the Theory X variety.

A humanistic and intrinsically motivational approach is congruent with Theory Y, and one that helps people reflect on their practice and grow professionally. In a conversation with Carolyn Downey in 1991, W. Edwards Deming stated, "Stop rating and ranking people, stop the competition within the organization, stop rewarding people and put joy back into the workplace" (cited in Downey, Steffy, Poston, & English, 2010, p. 4). It was a powerful message for school leaders who supervise others: Put joy into supervision, joy into the culture of learning, and joy into the profession of serving children.

Steffy (1989) believes that most districts' formal procedures for evaluating teachers will be ineffective in maintaining and supporting the growth process. We do believe in the value of the teacher appraisal process, but it must emphasize quality appraisal processes that focus on growth (Downey & Frase, 2003) and that can be used to engage teachers in intrinsically motivating reflective questioning.

The MBWA principal must abandon the traditional approach to supervision as no longer a viable means for effecting lasting change in the classroom. In a 2004 conversation with Downey (as cited in Downey et al., 2010), current Deputy Superintendent for the San Antonio Independent School District, Betty Burks, shared her belief that informal classroom observations are about "expecting rather than inspecting and respecting rather than directing" (p. 6). Blase and Blase (1998) report that teachers like the type of supervisor who has most helped them develop professionally as a coach and a person who is "value added" to their lives. They have little respect for the person who is a "fix-it, tell-it" personality, even though such a person might mean well.

The MBWA principal's perspective is that supervision is a human development enterprise. It creates the conditions that increase teachers' zest for continuous growth. They will then be in the preferred position of making decisions about their professional growth and making changes on their own out of an intrinsic desire to do so. The role of the MBWA principal is to facilitate the reflective inquiry that encourages introspection and individual decision making. We believe the curriculum and assessment accountability movement has palpable merit; however, this does not mean that we must revert to inspecting people.

How can the MBWA principal help teachers successfully teach the standards and objectives and appropriately use the assessment tools? The informal classroom observation is a great vehicle for achieving this balance. With these observations, one can informally gather relevant data on the decisions teachers are making regarding what to teach. The goal is to help each teacher be committed to teaching the standards effectively at the right level of difficulty for students. The informal classroom visit yields the type of information the MBWA principal needs to assist the teacher in reflecting on personal practices and in making decisions about how to best improve the delivery of the curriculum. This type of decision making is most effective, and is best accomplished through reflective inquiry and providing needs-based professional development for new knowledge. This means coaching and mentoring approaches are needed to assist the teacher in being responsible for decisions for professional growth. When principals try to force teachers to teach the standards, they may move teachers away from a commitment to these learnings. Forced compliance often brings on resentful or even belligerent behavior. It is difficult for people to carry out work they do not believe in, or in which they are not invested.

The research we conducted and reported in *From Good Schools to Great Schools: What Their Principals Do Well* (S. P. Gray & Streshly, 2008) supports the importance of the MBWA principal getting and grooming the right teachers—teachers who have decided on their own to value the standards and understand the inherent benefits in using powerful strategies to teach to those standards. Those types of teachers self-direct their behavior, and because what they value and believe is congruent with the vision of the principal, they are more likely to act accordingly.

Informal classroom observations and the follow-up activities that ensue are important inducements assisting teachers to examine their values and beliefs regarding their teaching and the needs of their students. The aim is to use tactics that reinforce a teacher's capacity for greater reflection and resourcefulness in making improvements in classroom teaching and learning. To do that, school leaders should first understand their own core beliefs about working with others (Glickman, 2002). Supervision should not be viewed as an end in itself, but as a *means* to an end, and should facilitate the growth and development of the teacher (Steffy, 1989). Of course, there are times when we find a teacher not performing at a satisfactory level, and a decision is made that the individual will require an intensive assistance approach for marginal teachers. What we must not do is create tools and approaches for the marginal employee and then use them for all employees. Strategies for dealing with marginal teachers and incompetent teachers are described in detail in Chapters 9 and 10.

Information Gathered

Informal classroom observations allow the MBWA principal to collect valuable and pertinent information not readily available from formalized observation structures/processes. Some of the very successful principals we studied regularly gather with three or four teachers after school and walk into classrooms, just looking at the various artifacts and other materials in the rooms. They talk about the curricular objectives being addressed and the instructional approaches being used. It is a great time for teachers to learn from one another and for the principal to become more informed about a teacher's intentions.

A sampling of the types of information gleaned from frequent, informal classroom observations by the MBWA principal are highlighted in Table 6.3.

Table 6.3   Information Gathered During Informal Principal
Classroom Observations

- Receive an overall picture of teaching and learning practices in classrooms
- Obtain data on the standards being taught in the classrooms
- Note different types of curricular and instructional decisions being made by individual teachers
- Sample different areas of subject matter to obtain trend data over time
- Note groupings of students and any differentiation of learning
- Ease teachers' apprehension of formal evaluation processes by increasing their comfort level (the "trust factor") for classroom visits and observations
- Consider possible areas for reflective discussions with teachers (individual or groups)
- Identify possible areas for professional development activities
- Ascertain the progress teachers are making in implementing new practices after participating in professional development efforts
- Gain credibility as an "instructional leader" by demonstrating a focus on teaching and learning
- Identify possible areas of marginality (see Chapter 9) that need to be addressed quickly
- Note equality or equity issues
- Note safety, health, and facilities issues in classrooms and on the school campus
- Be informed if parents call with a concern
- Have students see you demonstrating instructional leadership and an interest in their learning

The term *monitoring* (the curriculum) was not listed above as one of the many benefits of informal classroom observations, although it certainly is. However, many people approach the implementation of monitoring from a negative, "catch what's wrong" perspective, while many teachers confuse monitoring with inspection. When we use the word *monitoring*, we use a term meant to be "nurturing, supportive, mentoring, and coaching in nature" (Downey et al., 2003, p. 156). Monitoring the curriculum has become an expectation for the MBWA principal, and visiting classrooms is one way to more accurately monitor the delivery of the curriculum. Such monitoring is critical to the role of supervision, and allows for frequent data collection about the most essential components of education: teaching and learning. However, how you as principal of the school use these data is important.

Using the Information Gathered

Massive data gathering is of little use if the MBWA principal doesn't use the data gathered to improve teaching and learning. Table 6.4 includes potential uses for data gathered by the principal in classrooms.

Table 6.4   Uses for Data Collected During Informal Classroom Observations

- Reflective conversations with individual teachers
- Trend data analysis in collaboration with groups of teachers
- Planning lessons
- Planning interventions
- Planning formative testing
- Decisions about materials selection
- Decisions about differentiating instruction
- Planning for professional development
- Observing issues of concern to follow up with formal evaluation

Observation Rules of "Etiquette"

The following rules of "etiquette" for principal classroom observations are important for a variety of reasons that will be obvious as you head out.

Signal That the Visit Is Informal

When you as principal informally walk into classrooms, it is important to make it clear to the teacher that you are not there to formally evaluate him or her. Our suggestion is to communicate to the teachers beforehand some signal that they will recognize, to convey that the visit is informal and not evaluative. The signal could be something as simple as telling teachers that when you enter the classroom with a clipboard in hand, the observation is a formal evaluation, and when you enter the classroom without the clipboard, the visit is a data-gathering episode and not evaluative. Or, you could use something like a "thumbs-up" or an alert (oral or written) prior to the visit. Most collective bargaining contracts require notice of formal observation.

Enter Without Disruption

Teaching and learning need to be ongoing and continual, and you must not be seen as a disruption to those processes or an evaluator of the teacher. Teachers report that they like principals in their classrooms, but not if they are disruptive (Blase & Blase, 1998). You need to be careful that you do not distract students. If you are a former teacher, you may find it hard to remain an observer and refrain from engaging with students. Students may even attempt to engage you on their own. Although there are times when you would engage students, those times need to be for a purpose. It should also be noted that sometimes we enter a classroom at an inconvenient moment and need to depart immediately. For example, if students are taking a big test or a timed activity, our visit might be an unwelcome distraction. Or perhaps the teacher is having one of those "family conversations" where the room is very quiet, the tone is serious, and all eyes are on the teacher. Our presence during something so personal and important can only be a distraction, so we should leave immediately. Teachers also, in being courteous, stop their teaching to greet you and share what is happening. To keep disruptions to a minimum, it is important to inform them prior to your visit that you simply want to observe them teaching and gather information for all the reasons we mentioned above. They should continue what they were doing.

Keep Confidential the Individual
Classroom Data Collected

Exposing individual classroom data to others is a good way to destroy any trust the MBWA principal has built. The information gathered over time through informal classroom observations for one identified classroom is data meant for reflective conversations with an individual teacher. If collecting information from many classrooms over time, the data may be shared in a group setting *if* classroom data cannot be attached to an individual teacher. The principal of a small school runs that risk when the data are disaggregated by grade level or specific course and there is only one teacher assigned to the grade level or course.

INFORMAL CLASSROOM OBSERVATION PROTOCOLS

The sampling of protocols in Table 6.5 is all based on brief, frequent, and focused observations in classrooms that provide food for reflection about teaching and learning. Our own experience with classroom observations protocols has led us to appreciate the need for highlighting those that have been found to be more productive at the different school levels of elementary, middle, and high school. Each of these protocols is considered from the following lenses: (1) purposes, (2) data gathered, (3) tools used for data gathering, and (4) appropriateness to your individual school level and culture. The protocols we have selected for inclusion here represent a sampling of approaches being used in schools.

Table 6.5 Informal Classroom Observation Protocols

Protocol	Source	Purposes	Data Gathered	Tools Used	Personnel	School Level
Downey Walk-Through With Reflective Inquiry	Palo Verde Associates, La Jolla, CA	To provide short, informal observations that may result in reflective conversations	Primarily curricular and instructional decisions made by the teacher	Informal note taking for observer use only	Principal, coaches, mentors, teachers	K–12
Walk'bout	Association of California School Administrators (ACSA), Burlingame, CA	To provide information about schoolwide, department, or grade-level implementation of specific educational practices	Information about the classroom setting, instructional modes and practices, and the match between classroom activities and the California Content Standards	Data can be collected on any computer or hand-held device that is connected to the Internet	Principals, department heads, teachers	K–12

(Continued)

Table 6.5 (Continued)

Protocol	Source	Purposes	Data Gathered	Tools Used	Personnel	School Level
The Learning Walk Routine	Institute for Learning, University of Pittsburgh, PA	To inform decisions about professional development	Focus on the institute's Nine Principles of Learning; content-specific and generated from professional development	Open-ended form that lends itself to notes; form is for observer only	Administrators or teacher-leaders	K–12
McRel Power Walkthrough	Mid-continent Research for Education and Learning, Denver, CO	To observe, evaluate, and record extent to which teachers are using 1. *Classroom Instruction That Works* strategies; 2. Technology; 3. Levels of Bloom's Taxonomy (1956); also, evaluate and record evidence of student learning	The nine strategies described in *Classroom Instruction That Works*; teacher and student use of technology	Recorded on hand-held device loaded with McRel's web-based software	School and district administrators, curriculum directors, teachers	K–12

Protocol	Source	Purposes	Data Gathered	Tools Used	Personnel	School Level
Teachscape CWT	Teachscape, San Francisco, CA	To improve instructional practices that lead to increased student learning	Research-based questioning and other instructional practices; student engagement; differentiation	Recorded on hand-held device loaded with Teachscape software	Instructional Leaders— principals, assistant principals, department heads, coaches	K–12
High School Walkthrough	Northern High School (Calvert County Public Schools, Prince Frederick, MD)	To collect patterns of data on instructional activities learned through professional development	Dependent on the staff development teachers experienced	Record five different pieces of information as evidence of the staff development initiative	Principal, assistant principals	6–12
The Bristol Central HS Walkthrough	Bristol Central High School (Bristol School District, Bristol, CT)	To collect data on instructional effectiveness, identify professional development needs, encourage reflective dialogue	Objectives of lesson; learning environment; level of engagement; instructional decisions; student work	Recorded on team-developed data-gathering forms	Principal, assistant principal, department chairs, district curriculum coordinators, teachers	6–12

Note: A comprehensive study of many more informal classroom observations protocols may be found in *Classroom Walkthroughs to Improve Teaching and Learning*, by Kachur, Stout, and Edwards (2010).

The Downey Walk-Through
With Reflective Inquiry

We include a more comprehensive description of the *Downey Walk-Through With Reflective Inquiry* (Downey, Steffy, English, Frase, & Poston, 2004; Downey et al., 2010) here because we believe it to be possibly the most effective short and frequent classroom observation protocol (referred to as a "walk-through" in this protocol) MBWA principals use to promote teacher professional growth and reflective conversation. Carolyn Downey is a colleague of ours at San Diego State University; a nationally recognized speaker and trainer; and a senior board member of Curriculum Management Systems, Inc. (CMSi), an organization known for curriculum management audits and school leadership training. The protocol she has developed over the many years of her experience in schools features two major components: the five-step observation structure and the reflective conversation.

The Five-Step Observation Structure

The walk-through component, as described in Table 6.6, is a 1- to 3-minute walk-through observation in classrooms using a nonjudgmental lens.

Table 6.6   Five-Step Observation Structure of the Downey Walk-Through

Step 1	**Orientation to the Work:** Are students doing what the teacher wants them to do? Are they attending?	
Step 2	**Curricular Decisions:** What standards and objectives is the teacher teaching to, and how do they match system curricular standards/expectations?	
	Part I: Taught Objectives	What is the content of the taught objectives? What is the context of the taught objectives? What is the cognition type being used in the taught objectives?

Part II: Intended Objectives	What is the congruence between the actual taught objectives and the teacher's intended (stated or written) objectives?	
Part III: Calibrated Objectives	What is the alignment between the content of the taught objectives and the system curricular standards/expectations?	
Step 3	**Instructional Decisions:** What instructional teaching practices is the teacher choosing to use in the teaching of the standards and objectives?	
	Part I: Generic Practices	What instructional practices is the teacher using that research has indicated are powerful when teaching in most instructional situations?
	Part II: School or District Focused Practices	What instructional practices is the teacher using on which there is a school or district focus?
	Part III: Subject- Specific Practices	What instructional practices is the teacher using that research has indicated are powerful when teaching a particular subject area?
Step 4	**If Time, "Walk the Walls":** What previous curricular and instructional decisions can be noted by examining easily accessed materials—student products on the wall, teacher-made charts, student portfolios, future worksheets, past quiz papers, and so on?	
Step 5	**Safety and Health:** Are there any safety, facility, or health situations noted to which attention needs to be paid?	

Source: Downey et al. (2010, pp. 28–29), *Advancing the Three-Minute Walk-Through: Mastering Reflective Practice,* Thousand Oaks, CA: Corwin. Reprinted by permission from Carolyn Downey.

During the observation, teacher decisions are observed but are not evaluated as good or bad, present or not present, complete or incomplete, accurate or inaccurate—or any of the ways one can judge a teacher's performance. There is no checklist. The observer takes a few notes that may be the impetus for a reflective conversation with the teacher.

The Reflective Conversation

The heart of the Downey Walk-Through is actually not the structured classroom observation described above but the reflective follow-up dialogue. "The overriding goal is to provide an environment that helps each person become a self-reflective, self-analytical, self-directed person who is always learning and improving one's practice" (Downey et al., 2010, p. 1). With the Downey protocol, after several frequent diagnostic observations, a principal might choose to have a reflective conversation with the teacher that is of a growth-producing nature. This second part involves the use of the reflective question as part of an ongoing, collegial conversation between principal and teacher. The reflective question is generated by the data gathered in the informal walk-through structured observation and is based on five positive presuppositions that teachers

- plan lessons around the curriculum;
- think about how they will relay information to students;
- make choices based on some criteria to decide strategies for relaying information; and
- make these choices based on factors that will promote the high likelihood of each student learning the objectives.

A sample of questions around teacher decisions that promote a conversation between the teacher and the principal follow.

Reflective question about a curriculum decision: "As you plan your lessons around the district's curriculum, and if you are desirous of integrating objectives from other disciplines into your lessons some of the time, what factors do you consider in deciding which curricular objectives to use across various disciplines in order to provide efficiency in student learning of objectives?" (Downey et al., 2004, p. 65)

Reflective question about an instructional decision: "In planning your lessons around the district curriculum, and in thinking about activities you might use, what thoughts go on in your mind about which activities to select to impact student achievement?"(Downey et al., 2004, p. 65)

(Note: This is an important time to put into play your thorough knowledge and understanding of curricular and instructional practices.) When applied with many teachers, the school culture is altered one teacher at a time, eventually resulting in a community of learners.

Downey (2004) has also created a structure for observing classrooms across the school called the *SchoolView: Gathering Diagnostic Trend Data on Curricular and Instructional Classroom Practices.* This tool, which has a computer tablet or PDA (personal desk assistant) enhancement, does have a list of teaching practices on which to make observations. However, the data are not kept by the teacher; rather, the data are aggregated into reports to show the information, and new data are collected every so often as a repeated-measures tool. Such data collection is only to be used in a diagnostic way to help the principal and other instructional leaders identify possible staff development areas or observe the effects staff development is having on faculty. It is also used to identify possible interventions and their effects, as measured through classroom practices.

The Walk'bout

Many school leaders today are making efficient and effective use of technology in the form of hand-held devices in conducting informal classroom observations. Most of these products contain a teacher evaluation component. However, one product continues to follow the premise followed in this book that the MBWA principal's purpose for informal classroom observations is to encourage conversation around teaching and learning—not to formally evaluate the teacher. The Walk'bout protocol (Association of California School Administrators, 2010) was originally developed by one of California's top educational leaders, George Manthey, Assistant Executive Director for Educational Services for the Association of California School Administrators (ACSA), and is accessed through a web browser. Synchronization with any web-enabled personal digital assistant, such as a Palm or iPad, or a smartphone such as a Blackberry or iPhone, is immediate.

This technology-driven protocol is worthy of more comment here, especially given the nationwide standards initiative, No Child Left Behind (NCLB), and now "A Blueprint for Reform: The Reauthorization of the Elementary and Secondary Education Act." The California Content Standards are embedded in the Walk'bout, so standards that may match the classroom activity being observed are automatically suggested for selection by the observer. This protocol allows the observer who conducts frequent short classroom observations to efficiently gather and synthesize data from those observations. It is designed to provide data about whether or not a school, grade level, or department is meeting goals set by stakeholders related to the implementation of best instructional practices around the state content standards. The data from the Walk'bout are organized into three distinct areas: basic classroom information, basic information about the activity being observed, and use of effective teaching practices to teach the content standards. This last area may be modified to reflect individual district priorities for effective practices.

Most technologies available for collecting classroom data assist principals in conducting formal teacher evaluations. The Walk'bout is not designed to be a substitute for the formal evaluation/appraisal process. Any sort of individual teacher rating or appraisal has been purposefully left out of the Walk'bout—the MBWA observer simply indicates when a strategy is being used or not. The reports show the percentage of time a given strategy was marked by the observer. In this way, the Walk'bout is superior to most other technologies available for classroom observations, since we doubt if evaluating an individual or even a school with walk-through data ever leads to growth—which is the real purpose of supervision.

FOR REFLECTION

- Consider this reflective question: As you walk into classrooms, and are thinking about the many ways you could gather data and the structure you could use in your observations, what criteria do you use to decide on your walk-through lens at any given time to be of value to the teacher and his or her practice?
- Compare the observation framework you use now with the Downey Walk-Through With Reflective Inquiry or the Walk'bout. What are the similarities and what are the differences? Do you think there might be some changes you would like to make in your lens, based on your reading of this chapter?

When confronted with the research related to frequent classroom visitations, many principals simply throw up their hands and exclaim, "I haven't got the time to spend several hours a day in classrooms." The next chapter addresses this dilemma.

7

Finding Time for MBWA

SUPERVISION

DISCIPLINE

PUBLIC RELATIONS

PLANT MANAGEMENT

COUNSELOR

We spend too much of our time worrying about the mosquitoes and not enough time concerning ourselves about the health of the pond.

—Anonymous

Management by Wandering Around takes time! When recently we asked principals how they schedule their time during the day, some responded with excuses for why they couldn't be the MBWA administrators they knew they needed to be. A sampling of such responses includes the following:

- "I get 200 e-mails a day. It takes me 2 hours to deal with them."
- "The paperwork that comes with the job is a Goliath."
- "There isn't enough time in the day to take care of the phone calls, irate parents, discipline issues, and paperwork, much less get into classrooms."
- "I spend most of the school day putting out fires. That leaves me with the hours after school and into the evening hours taking care of all the bureaucratic work that comes with this job."
- "How does the district office expect me to be an instructional leader when they are constantly pulling me off campus for meetings?"

head teacher

Principals deal with literally hundreds of brief tasks each day, sometimes 50 to 60 separate interactions with others or assorted other activities in one hour (Peterson, 2001). This level of activity is amazing and so fragmented that there seems to be little opportunity to reflect on problems or improve performance. Principals are required to be educational visionaries; instructional and curriculum leaders; assessment experts; disciplinarians; community builders; public relations and communications experts; budget analysts; facility managers; special programs administrators; as well as guardians of various legal, contractual, and policy mandates and initiatives. In addition, principals are expected to serve the often conflicting needs and interests of many stakeholders, including students, parents, teachers, district office officials, unions, and state and federal agencies.

In spite of this outrageous activity level, effective administrators find the time to be out on campus, in classrooms, on playgrounds, and in the hallways practicing MBWA. One such principal was highlighted in an article in the *San Diego Union Tribune* (Moran, 2009) for improving student learning significantly in two different schools over relatively short periods of time. Matthew Tessier has been credited with first leading Loma Verde Elementary School in San Diego County out of federal sanctions with 2 consecutive years of dramatically improved test scores. Then, he moved a second school, Harborside Elementary, off the federal watch list to become the most improved school among San Diego County's 700 public schools—all within 2 years. The *Union Tribune* article stated that Tessier estimates he spends 80 percent of his time in classrooms. We wanted to find out how true that statement was and, if so, how he is able to do that. So, we arranged to interview him at his school. When we met him in his office and asked him that question, the first thing he said to us was, "Well, I don't do anything here [in the principal's office]." He then qualified that statement by describing where and when on the campus he conducts the office work that comes with the job of principal while having teacher conversations, building trust, and getting teacher commitment. He follows a specific routine when he enters classrooms with his laptop in hand. He looks at student work displayed on the classroom walls and compares that with test data he has on his laptop. He has conversations with students about that work. He observes what the teacher is doing and makes notes on a memo pad about his findings. When there is a pause, transition moment, or silent reading session in the classroom activities, he deals with the administrative minutiae of answering e-mails on his laptop. As he exits the classroom, he leaves the notes he has taken on the teacher's desk. Harborside teachers verify Tessier's explanation of how he spends 80 percent of his time in classrooms.

This chapter examines how MBWA principals find the time, like Matthew Tessier, to be the instructional leaders they need to be. First, we explore the research that looks at exactly how principals spend their school day. Next, we offer activities to assist readers in (1) analyzing how they spend their time, (2) prioritizing their time, and (3) planning activities to meet those priorities. We clarify some time management myths and provide strategies for effective time management. The chapter concludes with some specific tactics for reducing or even eliminating four potential and troublesome time wasters: telephone calls, drop-in visitors, mail/e-mail, and meetings.

FOR REFLECTION

- How do you, as principal of your school, schedule your daily routine?
- How much time, if any, do you allocate to visiting classrooms?
- What sorts of job demands seem to take up the most valuable MBWA time?

THE RESEARCH ON
HOW PRINCIPALS SPEND THEIR TIME

The research has clearly and convincingly concluded that strong leadership is a key characteristic of effective schools. Leaders in effective schools are highly visible through frequent classroom visiting, touring the campus, and participating in the instructional program. These leaders are out and about in the school and classrooms, keeping the school on target and helping in all phases of the school—all characteristics of the MBWA principal. The question is, if these administrators are spending 2 to 4 hours a day practicing MBWA, what are the other administrators doing with the same 2 to 4 hours? Let's take a look.

Table 7.1 lists the various principal job dimensions and the time spent on each by average and strong principals as reported by the Association for Supervision and Curriculum Development (Brandt, 1987).

Table 7.1   Principal Job Dimensions and Time Spent on Each

Job Dimensions of the School Principal	How the Average Principal Spends Time	How a Strong Leader Spends Time
A. Educational programmatic improvement	27%	41%
Community relations	7%	7%
B. Student-related services and activities	28%	18%
C. Building management operations and district relations	39%	34%

In 1987, the "average" principal spent 27 percent of the day on program improvement in comparison to the 41 percent spent by the "strong" principal. This discrepancy is reflected in the amount of time spent on managing buildings and student-related services. The average principal spent 67 percent of the day on these activities, while the strong leader devoted only 52 percent of his or her time. Job dimensions A, B, and C in Table 7.1, in particular, call for principals to be out of the office and with people—in other words, close to the classroom.

Early studies by Howell (1981), Peterson (1977–1978), Morris (1981), Martin and Willower (1981), Kmetz and Willower (1982), and Stronge (1988) and described in Table 7.2 reveal large variations in time allocated by principals.

Table 7.2   Principal Time Allocations

Location of Principal	Percentage of Time
In the office area	40%–80%
In hallways and on the grounds	10%–23%
Off campus	11%
In classrooms	2.5%–10%

More recent research (Camburn, Spillane, & Sebastian, 2010; Gilson, 2008; P. Gray, 2003; Hallinger, 2005; McEwan, 2003; PriceWaterhouseCoopers, 2007; Reeves, 2006) finds that the discrepancy between time spent on managerial tasks and time spent out and about on campus and in classrooms continues in many schools. Principals continue to be locked into office activities, report writing, meetings, commuting between meetings, and communicating with various individuals by phone and e-mail. Reeves declares bluntly, "The demands of leadership almost invariably exceed the capacity of a single person to meet the needs at hand" (p. 32).

One of the most noticeable findings of research conducted by McPeake (2007) is the consistent increase from the 1960s to 2007 in the total amount of time that principals spend per week doing their job. The literature review conducted by McPeake indicates that the mean time dedicated to the job was 49.31 hours in the 1960s and had risen to 61.1 hours in the early 2000s. McPeake finds the mean time worked by principals in 2007 to be 60.3 hours per week. The percentage of increase in time spent by principals performing various tasks for a 3-year period is displayed in Table 7.3.

Table 7.3   Principals' Time-on-Task Increase, 2004–2007

Task	Percentage of Time-on-Task Increase
School management	57.5%
Personnel	64.8%
Program development	64%
Student activities	38.4%
Student behavior	30.6%
Planning	60.8%
Community relations	42.5%
District office	38.8%
Professional development	52.9%

Source: McPeake (2007).

Fifty percent of the principals interviewed in McPeake's study pointed to the mandates of No Child Left Behind as a cause for the increase in time on task.

According to several recent Public Agenda surveys of principals (Johnson, 2008), 75 percent report that they spend more time working with such things as curriculum, teaching techniques, mentoring, and professional development than they did in the past. Even so, most principals surveyed would like more hours to devote to this aspect of their work. Just 1 in 10 principals is satisfied with the time spent on this area; 70 percent of principals say they would like to do a lot more. In fact, fighting for time for MBWA activities appears to be one of the main frustrations of being a principal today; nearly three quarters of principals surveyed say that daily emergencies rob them of time that could be better spent on instructional issues.

The significance of the problems identified here is amplified by the fact that the principal's accessibility, being out and about on campus and in classrooms, is strongly correlated and related to numerous highly desirable results as discussed in Chapter 6. These desirable results are lost when the principal is locked into office activities.

How MBWA Administrators Find the Time

In Southern California more than a half-century ago, in a suburb of San Diego, Helix High School distinguished itself as an outstanding educational institution. By all measures of student achievement, the school excelled. Much of the credit went to a highly respected principal, Ben Hart, whose leadership has since become legendary. So it was not surprising that new principals would seek his counsel and quiz him about the secrets to his successes. Ben would remind these aspiring young administrators that the primary mission of the principal is instructional leadership. This meant the principal is involved with program planning in every department. It also meant that the principal visits every classroom regularly to keep track of instruction and promote ongoing conversation about learning.

Usually at this point, a new principal would ask how visiting all classrooms regularly was possible at a school like Helix with more than 100 teachers. "The secret," Ben would explain, "is what I call 'Many Peeks.'" He then described a practice similar in structure and intent to our present-day "walkthroughs." The classroom visits were only 2 or 3 minutes long—just enough time for the principal to understand what the teacher was teaching and how.

Still, the process required Ben to organize his days so that time was set aside for his "Many Peeks." This, according to Ben, was not a problem. He explained that parents, community members, and even board members and district office personnel understood that supervising instruction was what a principal was supposed to do. It was normal for these people to arrange their own schedules to respect Ben's uninterrupted classroom visitations.

Today, there are administrators who plan their day to include classroom observations, teacher supervision, and even teaching and who continue to spend the majority of the day checking out what is going on, serving as the school spokesperson, disseminating information to staff members, and handling disturbances. Matthew Tessier is one, and we were able to find others in the course of our investigations of highly successful principals (S. P. Gray & Streshly, 2008). However, research has long told us that most principals fail to spend more time in the classroom and less time in the office, even though they say they desire to do so and are given discretion to do exactly that (Hager & Scarr, 1983).

Mere dissatisfaction with the status quo is unlikely to lead to change. As we have worked with principals, we've become convinced that making a change in the way we do things, for instance, managing our business and our time, requires an understanding of how a well-run school operates, a devoted desire to change, and a plan for doing it—plus a means of monitoring the plan.

Finding time for MBWA is a matter of values and attitude, and it is not dependent on intellect. If you accept the idea that you can control your day and the demands on your time, you are halfway there. The other half is found on the pages that follow. They contain ideas and suggestions that are not magic. They require effort, but they are not difficult. Embrace them, and you'll have the time to be out on campus and in the classrooms.

When you finish this chapter, you will have accomplished the following:

- Rated the importance/priority of nine "life roles"
- Set aside time to accomplish the essential school leadership activities
- Specified the number of hours per week spent on each
- Determined any mismatches in the time spent in each role
- Developed goals and specific action plans to help you gain more balance in your life so you spend more time on those life roles you prefer
- Explored strategies for dealing with time wasters

Analyzing the Big Picture

Let's get started. First, take a look at the big picture—all your time, not just the workday. It is commonly thought that there are nine life roles:

1. Personal-Spiritual

2. Family

3. Spouse

4. Social

5. Community

6. Professional

7. Cultural

8. Recreational

9. Physical Exercise

Each deserves attention and time. The exact amount of time is up to you, but the general view is that a well-rounded person participates in all nine areas. Soon, we will ask you to rate the priority of each of the nine life roles. But first, note that rating any of these nine roles as lowest priority does not mean it is not important. It simply means that you want to give the others more time. Each of these nine life roles should receive time each week. What we generally find is that some school principals end up spending very little or no time for exercise, recreation, spouse, or family, and instead give all their time to the professional role. Think back to what you read in Chapters 3 and 4 about what motivates people and the improvement ethic. Avoiding any one of these areas is damaging mentally and physically, leads to lesser satisfaction, and ultimately can lead to burnout and unhappiness. Following are six steps you as the school leader can use to prioritize life roles and develop a plan for the most effective use of your time.

Step One: Rate Your Life Role

Rate each life role. What is the relative priority of each to you? The nine life roles are presented in Column 1 in Table 7.4. Rate the importance of each using a 1–5 scale, with 1 being *lowest priority* and 5 being *highest priority,* in the second column labeled *Priority Rating.* Avoid rating more than three life roles as having the highest priority. If you rate too many as high, you will not be able to complete the exercise meaningfully. Or, it may mean that you simply lump everything in the high-priority pile and therefore cannot do an adequate job with any one of the roles. Remember, we cannot do them all and do them all well. We must pick our priorities and act accordingly. Now, take a shot at rating each role.

Step Two: Log the Hours

In Column 3, *Time Devoted,* log the number of hours you spend each week in each role. This is an estimate, but be as accurate as possible. Take time to think about it.

Table 7.4   Life Role Analysis

Roles	Priority Rating (1–5 High)	Time Devoted (Hours)	Discrepancy (Hours)
Personal-spiritual			
Family			
Spouse			
Social			
Community			
Professional			
Cultural			
Recreational			
Physical exercise			

Step Three: Compare Your Priorities

Now, compare your priorities and the number of hours spent on each. Do your time allocations match your priorities? If you rated "Family" as your number one priority, did you also give it a larger amount of time than the other categories? If physical exercise is important to you, and it should be, are you devoting time to it? Remember that all of us should exercise for at least 30 minutes, 5 days a week. Compare the priority rating assigned to each role and the relative number of hours spent on each. Write the discrepancies in Column 4, labeled *Discrepancy*. This takes consideration. If you find that you are only spending 3 hours a week with your family, but you consider your family a high priority, write +6, +8, +10, or another number in Column 4 indicating that you want to spend this many more hours with them. Do this for each of the nine life roles.

Step Four: Study a Sample Analysis of Time Spent

A sample analysis of life roles is provided in Table 7.5.

Table 7.5 Rating My Life Roles for Importance and Priorities

Roles	Priority Rating (1–5 High)	Time Devoted (Hours per Week)	Discrepancy (Hours per Week)
Personal-spiritual	4	2	+2
Family	5	3	+7
Spouse	4	2 (also included in family)	+5
Social	3	3	+0
Community	1	1	+0
Professional	4	60	−15
Cultural	2	2	+0
Recreational	3	4 (also included in family)	+4
Physical exercise	4	2	+4

Note that the sum total of column 4 is +7. So what is going on here? First, too much time is being spent at work at the expense of family, spouse, recreation, and exercise—all very important life areas. Overall, 15 hours need to be taken from work and 7 hours have to come from other activities such as watching TV. We will find a way to do this later in the chapter. This is where it becomes difficult. We all have 24 hours. We must make some hard decisions about how we use our time.

Step Five: Consider a Sample Plan for Spending Time

A sample plan for reducing discrepancies regarding time spent with family, spouse, and doing exercise is provided in Table 7.6. In Step 6, you will develop goals and activities designed to reduce discrepancies in the way you use your own time.

Table 7.6   Sample Plan for Reducing Discrepancies

Life Role:	Family
Discrepancy:	I value my family very highly, but I spend only 3 hours per week with them.
Goal 1.0:	Spend 7 hours more per week (10 hours total) with my immediate family.
Activities:	Take the family to the local university basketball game on Friday evening. Visit my folks on Wednesday evening. Eat with my children and spouse at least 4 nights a week. Monitor my children's homework, and work with them on it.
Life Role:	Exercise
Discrepancy:	I engage in no aerobic exercise and should engage in 5 thirty-minute sessions per week.
Goal 2.0:	Spend 3 half-hour sessions per week working out at the club, and do speed walking for half an hour, 3 times a week.
Activities:	Call for appointment with club trainer for Saturday morning. Schedule my workout times on my calendar and the trainer's calendar.

(Continued)

Table 7.6 (Continued)

	Set my smartphone's alarm to remind me of the time.
	Follow my schedule religiously!!
	Schedule my half-hour speed-walking sessions. Ask my wife for a reminder and to join me.
Life Role:	Spouse
Discrepancy:	I seldom spend quality time with my spouse talking, dining, attending cultural events, or engaging in physical exercise.
Goal 3.0:	Spend at least 5 hours of quality time per week with my spouse.
Activities:	Engage in three speed-walking sessions with my spouse each week. These are great times alone, and we can talk about the day, the children, and our lives.
	After the children retire for the evening, spend half an hour on at least 4 nights talking with my wife about our day, our children's day, priorities for the following day, and planning our activities.

Step Six: Develop Your Own Plan

Now, give it a try. In Table 7.7, write the life roles you want to work on (room is provided for two life roles). First pick one life role and write it down. Then write the discrepancy, the goal, and the activities.

Table 7.7   Planning My Life Role Activities

Life Role:	
Discrepancy:	
Goal 1.0:	

Activities:	
Life Role:	
Discrepancy:	
Goal 2.0:	
Activities:	

Do not feel guilty if your activities call for more time for something other than work. Work is not all of our lives, and our lives should not be all work! St. Thomas Aquinas said that work and the quality of our lives are linked, but he did not say life was only work! So take plenty of time for the other roles. Take time to smell the roses! Medical and psychological evidence clearly shows that exercise increases enthusiasm, health, and work effectiveness among many other benefits. Effective leaders take time to reflect and relax. They work hard *and* play hard.

TIME MANAGEMENT MYTHS

Managing and controlling your time well will help you free up time at work for MBWA. A good way to start is by clarifying what time management is not. Six common time-management myths follow.

Myth 1: More Time Spent is Better

The more time spent at work, the more will get done; more is better. This is a myth. Eventually, mental or physical fatigue will consume you. When either occurs, productivity goes down, and your time is essentially wasted. A task that ordinarily takes 15 minutes takes 45, and the quality is poor. Frequently, you must revise and correct it the next day. This is neither efficient nor effective, and it leads to frustration.

Point: The relationship between time and productivity is curvilinear—initially, as time goes up, productivity goes up, but after a point, productivity goes down as time goes up! Don't perseverate at a task when it starts to hurt!

In fact, it's inefficient and ineffective and a perfect example of diminishing returns.

Myth 2: An Open Door Policy Is Always Good

Operate on an open door policy. It's smart to greet everyone who comes into the office. Being open and visible is good policy and crucial to good PR. Another myth! Aristotle's Golden Mean applies here: *everything in moderation.* Seeing, greeting, and chatting with everyone who comes through the office doors is not moderation. People like seeing the administrative head, but if they see you on every occasion, they may start to wonder if you do anything other than operate the "glad hand." Plus, it is a great time waster. You certainly must greet people, but you have other responsibilities, too. Attend to them, and do not feel bad that not everyone walking through the school's doors will see you. Regular visits to classrooms will make you visible where it counts most.

Point: Take time to greet people, but take time for other duties, too. Start by organizing your time, and plan to close the door for specific periods to get your paperwork done, make calls, and make plans for MBWA. Many things that you may do now can be scheduled before or after school operating hours, thus giving time for MBWA. Instead of wasting time idly chatting with others, use this time for pointed conversations and for doing other work. Note: This does not mean that you should add hours to your workday.

Myth 3: You Must Do It All Yourself

Your job is very important; you had better do it all by yourself. Nonsense! The top executives of America's most successful corporations don't do it all themselves. The best leaders hire capable people and delegate tasks to them. More than delegating tasks, they also delegate responsibility and give the necessary autonomy to get the job done. Teachers who are ready for the challenge can benefit from this job enrichment (see Chapter 4). New responsibility and autonomy will give them new life and greater enthusiasm for their job. Blase (1987) reported that delegation of authority was not only associated with effective performance, but also resulted in increasing teachers' self-esteem and sense of professionalism, morale, and efficiency. School administrators are not the only capable people. Chances are that a number of very capable parents and teachers would respond most favorably to the opportunity to "head up" many of the functions that go on in our schools. Assess their abilities, plan with them, and give them the reins. It is called "team building."

> **Point:** You are responsible for the organization, but you cannot do it all. So do not try—delegate.

Myth 4: There is Not Enough Time to Do It All

You just do not have the time for it (an important task) with all the expectations placed on you. Yet another common myth. Who is in control? Who is running the ship? The personality variable known as "locus of control" (Rotter, 1966, 1971) offers insight here. At one end of the locus-of-control continuum is the internal personality, and at the other is the external personality. The internal personalities believe they can control their lives, while the external personalities believe their lives are controlled by external factors such as fate, spirits, powers, and significant others. Those who believe that they have an impact on their own destiny (internals) are more likely to act that way. They are more likely to stop smoking, start exercising, and wear their seat belts. Externals, on the other hand, do not engage in these measures. They take a passive stance of *que sera, sera*—whatever will be, will be: If I get lung cancer, if I'm thrown against the dash of the car in a fender bender, or if I get flabby and my heart is overtaxed, that's just the way it is. This is the defeatist's attitude. The fact is that you can be in much greater control of your life, and you should be. If necessary, take control by letting people know you can't do everything and that they may have to do something themselves if they want it done; that includes your boss. Learn to say no.

Learn to argue for district meetings to be scheduled after the normal student day. In our experience, the district administrators will work to make this possible. Much of the district's business can be conducted without pulling the site administrators away from the schools while regular classes are in session. While we recognize that some site administrators prefer meetings during the school day, we believe that schedules should be established to support the MBWA administrators' classroom visitation priorities.

> **Point:** You are responsible for your organization, so take control and run it; start with your time.

Myth 5: You Should Read It All

You must read your mail and e-mail—all of it. Not so—if much of your mail never reached you, you would be no worse off and would never miss it. Like the postal mail and e-mail we receive at home, much of the mail to administrators is sales literature and other forms of spam. Leave it alone or "deep six" it—trash it. If you needed it, you would already have known about it. Reading the stuff just creates "wants." After developing a want, you may want to buy it. Something purchased primarily as a result of an enticing sales brochure or sound-and-motion animated e-mail attachment is often destined only to gather dust on the shelf, never to be used. Time spent reviewing the e-mail and postal mail, placing the order, and leafing through literature after it arrives costs the organization big money in personnel time and costs you from 20 minutes to 2 hours of your own precious time each day. (More about handling mail and e-mail later.)

> **Point:** Do not let the mail control you—you control it!

Myth 6: Ignore Problems, and They Will Go Away

Some problems will just go away if you pay no attention to them. Besides, you really don't have time now to deal with it. There are two points about this myth. The first is a matter of semantics.

Sometimes we perceive things as problems when they really aren't. These will go away, and we shouldn't devote time to them. Second, if a problem really does exist, acting like an ostrich won't help. The problems must be dealt with; otherwise, they fester and spread throughout the organization. If you thought the problem would take too much time when it first presented itself, it will quadruple later!

> **Point:** The ostrich's problems do not go away when it sticks its head in the sand, and neither will yours. Spend a half hour now and save 2 hours down the road!

FINDING TIME AT WORK FOR MBWA

Those are some of the myths. Now, get started on your plan for more effective use of time so that you can accommodate MBWA. Everyone has the same amount of time each day, 24 hours, and each of us wastes some of our allotment. Some of us waste more than others.

Time Wasters

Time wasters have been studied for many years, and some very useful lists have been developed. R. A. Mackenzie (1972/1997) identified the top 20 time wasters:

1. Management by crisis
2. Telephone interruptions
3. Inadequate planning
4. Attempting too much
5. Drop-in visitors
6. Ineffective delegation
7. Personal disorganization
8. Lack of self-discipline

9. Inability to say no

10. Procrastination

11. Meetings

12. Paperwork

13. Leaving tasks unfinished

14. Inadequate staff

15. Socializing

16. Confused responsibility or authority

17. Poor communication

18. Inadequate controls and progress reports

19. Incomplete information

20. Travel (p. 61)

A. Mackenzie and Nickerson (2009) have now added various technology time wasters to the list. Since with e-mail it seems everyone has open access to us, spam control is of the utmost importance! Gaining policy agreement on this with administrators and teachers in the district is crucial. Principals report that they receive 100 to 150 e-mails a day, and time spent dealing with them can take 2 hours of their day. This is ludicrous. E-mail makes it easy for people to request reports and other information from you—help the organization get a grip on it! E-mail is frequently not worth reading, let alone taking action on. This is a huge time waster. Learn how to vet the incoming mail, just as you vet the postal mail. Develop screening processes. Facilitate the formation of a school and district policy regarding use of e-mail.

Time wasters are essentially of two types: internal and external. Drop-in visitors, telephone calls, e-mail messages, meetings called by others, and addressing the needs of others are examples of external time wasters. Internal time wasters come from us, the people in charge, and frequently appear in the form of procrastination, handling the same paper multiple times instead of once, not planning the day or week, not saying "no" when we really should, trying to do everything ourselves, and not discriminating between tasks in terms of importance and value. Here is where Pareto's (cited in Conway, 1992) dreaded 80:20 law—the law of the vital few—confounds our efforts: Eighty percent of the results come from 20 percent of our decisions. The key is to focus on those 20 percent that yield big results. When we devote 80 percent of our energy to time wasters, we are not being productive, and we are not accomplishing the "big" results from MBWA. If we do not focus on them, they won't get done—at least not to the level of quality required.

Planning for More Effective Use of Time

Time wasters are the enemy and must be eliminated, or at least significantly reduced. We get that. Before we can declare war on them we must better know what and who "the enemy" is. First, let's affirm the fact that the product of schooling is learning. This is a crucial understanding, and it should provide the needed focus for using our time.

Technique 1: Embrace Value-Added Work

Conway (1992) conceptualized Pareto's law for us and offers a means of overcoming the problem. He clusters work activities into three categories: value added, waste of time, and necessary.

"Value added" work includes activities such as

- conducting investigations regarding effective instruction;
- observing and supporting classroom learning;
- being in classrooms;
- offering teachers reflective questions; and
- focusing dialogue on learning.

"Waste of time" work includes activities that do not directly contribute to learning because they involve work that could have been avoided had it been done properly the first time, such as

- correcting or redoing any mistakes of your own or of others;
- dealing with teacher, parent, or student complaints;
- conducting a meeting without appropriate personnel present; and
- wasting time during meetings.

"Necessary" work includes tasks that keep the school running but have no direct impact on learning, such as

- signing purchase orders,
- writing reports, and
- approving supply orders.

The problem with tasks like these is obvious—too much wasted time, which does not result in positive impact on learning. Eliminating or greatly reducing these activities will allow devotion of much more time to the value-added work of MBWA and ensure that the focus is on learning. The key here is that doing more value-added work is directly proportional to the amount students will learn.

Conway (1992) used an interesting technique for informing us about how we spend our time. Principals and industrial managers wear a beeper set to vibrate or emit a sound three to four times per hour. At those times, the person tallies the current activity on a sheet of printed activities organized into the three key categories: value added, wasted time, or necessary. The activity is recorded in its appropriate category. This recording must take place immediately following the signal and must be very honest. Anything else will nullify the integrity of the process, and the goal of finding more time for MBWA as well as the focus on learning will be lost.

Four to 8 weeks of conducting this activity usually yield approximately 800 data points. These will present a very clear pattern of how you spend your time. Time-wasting patterns emerge, and the "culprits" are identified that take your time away from MBWA and focusing on learning. Principals we have worked with find that a process such as this helps them convert 20 to 40 percent of their time from wasted-time activities to value-added activities. Even a minimum gain has tremendous implications for learning.

Technique 2: Separate the Wheat From the Chaff

The second technique has proved very successful also and is designed to help you separate the wheat from the chaff—to give you the data needed to analyze how you spend your workday time. Later, you will use these data to identify activities that are less important than others. As a result, you will be able to focus on the more important activities and build them into your workday plans to ensure that you invest the proper amount of time and energy in them. A description of the technique with directions and rationale for using the form is presented in Table 7.8.

A series of 15-minute time segments is listed on the vertical axis. Fifteen-minute segments may seem excessively small, but early research supports their usage. For example, Sproul's (1976) study of managers revealed that the average length of an activity was only 9 minutes. Morris, Crowson, Nicherson, and Keefe (1984) found that face-to-face contacts range from 5 minutes and 20 seconds to 2 minutes and 30 seconds per contact. The frequency of contacts is further exacerbated by interruptions, which occur at a rate of 1.7 per task (Kmetz & Willower, 1982). Peterson (1977–1978) suggests that a principal may be involved in as many as 60 activities in an hour—an average of 1 per minute. If anything, 15-minute increments are too large. Should you find that the 15-minute segments do not work for you, record your data more frequently. Every 15, 10, or 5 minutes (whichever you choose), check the appropriate column to indicate the activity or activities for that period.

(Text continues on p. 145.)

Table 7.8 The Principal Activity Record, or What I Did Today

Activity:	A Telephone	B Mail/E-mail	C Meetings—Parents	D Meetings—District Office	E Meetings—School Staff	F Reports	G Lunch	H Civic Duty	I Drop-in Visitor	J Discipline—Student	K Classroom Observation	L Directing Office Staff	M Curriculum/Instruction	N Planning the Day/Week	O Dealing With Emergency	P Resting	Q	R	S	T	U	V	W	X I or E	Y P or U	Z 1 to 5
7:15																										
7:30																										
7:45																										
8:00																										
8:15																										
8:30																										
8:45																										
9:00																										
9:15																										
9:30																										

	Telephone	Mail/E-mail	Meetings—Parents	Meetings—District Office	Meetings—School Staff	Reports	Lunch	Civic Duty	Drop-in Visitor	Discipline—Student	Classroom Observation	Directing Office Staff	Curriculum/Instruction	Planning the Day/Week	Dealing With Emergency	Resting								I or E	P or U	1 to 5
9:45																										
10:00																										
10:15																										
10:30																										
10:45																										
11:00																										
11:15																										
11:30																										
11:45																										
12:00																										

(Continued)

Table 7.8 (Continued)

	Telephone	Mail/E-mail	Meetings—Parents	Meetings—District Office	Meetings—School Staff	Reports	Lunch	Civic Duty	Drop-in Visitor	Discipline—Student	Classroom Observation	Directing Office Staff	Curriculum/Instruction	Planning the Day/Week	Dealing With Emergency	Resting								I or E	P or U	1 to 5
12:15																										
12:30																										
12:45																										
1:00																										
1:15																										
1:30																										
1:45																										
2:00																										
2:15																										
2:30																										
2:45																										

	Telephone	Mail/E-mail	Meetings—Parents	Meetings—District Office	Meetings—School Staff	Reports	Lunch	Civic Duty	Drop-in Visitor	Discipline—Student	Classroom Observation	Directing Office Staff	Curriculum/Instruction	Planning the Day/Week	Dealing With Emergency	Resting								I or E	P or U	1 to 5
3:00																										
3:15																										
3:30																										
3:45																										
4:00																										
4:15																										
4:30																										
4:45																										
5:00																										
5:15																										

(Continued)

Table 7.8 (Continued)

	Telephone	Mail/E-mail	Meetings—Parents	Meetings—District Office	Meetings—School Staff	Reports	Lunch	Civic Duty	Drop-in Visitor	Discipline—Student	Classroom Observation	Directing Office Staff	Curriculum/Instruction	Planning the Day/Week	Dealing With Emergency	Resting								I or E	P or U	1 to 5
5:30																										
5:45																										
6:00																										
6:15																										
6:30																										
6:45																										
7:00																										
8:00																										
9:00																										
10:00																										
Totals/%																										

A series of typical school principal activities is listed on the horizontal axis. This is not intended to be a comprehensive list. So that you might modify the form to best fit your particular activities, four columns have been left untitled—T, U, V, and W. Note that Column M is "classroom observations." For your purposes here, observations in this column are defined as lasting more than 4 minutes—these are typically formal classroom visits. In the space for Column S, write "brief classroom visit." The definition for this column is being in a classroom for 30 seconds to 4 minutes.

Log your activities. Once you have completed the revision of the form (see Table 7.8), place it on a clipboard or something that will allow you to write easily. After each 15-minute time segment, check the primary activity you were involved in. Place only one tally mark for each 15-minute block. Most of the time, you will experience more than one activity; however, one tally mark keeps the task manageable and will be fully adequate for this analysis.

Completing this record takes time and commitment. It will distract you and seem to be in the way at times. It may be viewed as an inconvenience or even a waste of time. Consider it an important investment in that there are many crucial benefits to managing our time according to priorities. Completing the record is simply the best way to gather evidence so you can document your time and energies being devoted to the more important duties.

An "I" (for internal) or "E" (for external) should be placed in Column X to record whether the activity was initiated by you or someone else: Use "I" for self-initiated and "E" for other-initiated. Next, place a "P" (for planned) or "U" (for unplanned) in Column Y for each activity. Last, rate each activity in terms of its importance, and write the rating in Column Z. Use a 5-point scale, with 5 being highly important and 1 being unimportant. Keep the log for 2 consecutive days. Record the totals for each column at the bottom.

Remember, consider this analysis an investment! For instance, Blase (1987) found that teachers in schools where principals managed their time effectively experienced decreases in feelings of frustration and increases in productive faculty meeting interactions. In addition, both students and teachers experienced decreases in time wasted. Think of the great dividends of MBWA described earlier in this book. There is no doubt that time management will pay big dividends by allowing you more time for MBWA. It takes time to save time, and the initial investment you make now will pay benefits well into the future.

Analyze the data. Now that you have recorded your week's activities and have the totals, analyze the data. Start with the following questions:

- What percentage of your activities were planned? The acceptable range is 60 to 80 percent. If your percentage is not between 60 percent and 80 percent, go to the next question.
- How important do you perceive the unplanned activities to be? Which activities account for most of your unplanned activity? If the relative importance rating is less than 4, circle these in red and record them in Column A of Table 7.9. These activities are likely to be telephone calls, meetings, and drop-in visits. A little further on, we will make plans for cutting back on these.

Table 7.9   Activity Analysis, or Separating the Wheat From the Chaff

"A" *Unimportant, Unplanned* *Activities*	"B" *Unimportant, Not Initiated* *by Me*
1.	
2.	
3.	
4.	

"A" Unimportant, Unplanned Activities	"B" Unimportant, Not Initiated by Me
5.	
6.	
7.	
8.	
9.	
10.	
11.	
12.	
13.	
14.	
15.	
16.	
17.	
18.	
19.	
20.	

- Examine the activities entered into Table 7.9 and ask, "What percentage of my activities were initiated by someone other than me?" The ideal is 20 percent for someone else and 80 percent for you. Note which activities others are initiating, and circle them. Is someone or something else initiating more than 20 percent of your activities? If so, go to the next question.
- How important do you perceive these activities to be? Record those unplanned activities with an importance rating of less than 4 in Column B. The biggest time wasters are likely to be uninvited telephone calls, drop-in visits, and paperwork from the state or district office.

Do some unplanned activities with importance ratings of less than 4 appear in both columns? Your answer is likely to be yes! There they are, the triple-threat team, unplanned by you, uninitiated by you, and unimportant to you—stealing your time! Go ahead. Be outraged! They have taken your time from MBWA or reading that book you've been hoping to get to. Remember the nine life roles discussed a few pages ago? You may have just found the time for balancing them out and creating a healthier lifestyle *and* practicing MBWA.

Strategies for Dealing With Time Wasters

The following are some time management strategies for reducing or even eliminating the "big four" time wasters: telephone calls, drop-in visitors, mail/e-mail, and meetings.

Too Much Time on the Telephone

There are two possible problems here: too many phone calls and too much time per call. Who initiated the calls? If they are being initiated by someone other than you, structure the time you will devote each day to returning calls—maybe a half hour before lunch and a half hour in the afternoon. Just before lunch is a good time because people tend to be brief when lunch is waiting. This will give you time to engage in "outside the office" activities like MBWA and evaluating staff.

True emergency calls are another story—take them. Also, remember that definitions of "emergency" differ for parents, principals, board members, and superintendents. Train your secretary to discriminate and give only the true emergencies to you.

The cardinal rule about phone calls is to return all calls. The parents will love it when they receive a call from you, even if it is later in the afternoon. They will think of you as a very considerate person for taking the time to do so. Also, their problem may have shrunk just a little bit by then and be easier to resolve.

Make a list of calls that you must make, and prioritize them. Start with the most important, and use a timer. Set the timer at 3 minutes to keep you on schedule. When the time is up, say, "Joan, I have a bunch of calls to return, so I better move on." Being put on hold is a time waster. Don't let it happen. If for some reason you feel it is necessary, have work organized on your desk so you can be productive while waiting. A conference phone works wonders here; it frees your hands to do other things. Chitchatting on the phone is also a big time waster. Be mindful of drifting into too much casual talk; stick to the point. Be sure to set your timer. If the person you are talking with seems intent on rambling, use one of the following techniques to bring the conversation to an end, being certain that what you say is truly the case:

- "Gloria, it is clear that this issue is important to you as it is to me as well. Let's make an appointment to continue this conversation when we both have more time."
- "Let's plan to get together regarding this idea, but I must go now."
- "John, it's been great talking with you but I must hang up so I can prepare for the superintendent's meeting."

Sometimes you can treat the problem preventively. When a call is initiated by someone who has a reputation for rambling on and on, start off with saying, "I have 2 minutes unscheduled and then I must run." If you initiate the call, begin the call the same way. If this doesn't work, your administrative assistants can help here. Have them primed to interrupt when the conversation hits the 2-minute mark.

Too Many Drop-in Visitors

Fact 1: Schools and school districts are service agencies and must serve the people of the community and affiliated organizations.

Fact 2: You do not always have to serve at the drop of a hat and at others' convenience. Following are some ideas for controlling (reducing) the number of drop-in visitors:

- Position the secretary's desk so that he or she can screen visitors, answer questions that do not require your attention, route visitors to other qualified officials, take messages, or schedule appointments for you. Before implementing this strategy, be certain that the secretary understands this role and has the required skills. If you believe training is needed, check with your central office's staff development department, state administrators association, or local community college for training programs. These strategies can backfire if you have an unqualified secretary, so be sure the secretary possesses all the skills needed to do the job. She or he is the first line of PR and can make you look like a hero or an insensitive dolt.

- Position your desk so it is not visible from the outer office. Eye contact will invite passersby into your office. If they do not see you, they will be much less likely to drop in, unless they are particularly aggressive. That's where your secretary earns his or her money.

- Your office should promote comfortable and efficient meetings with your visitors without being *too* comfortable. Chairs should be straight, a bit hard, and definitely not plush. This will help keep the visitation to a reasonable length. Sometimes it is difficult for visitors to end the conversation. You can terminate the conversation with "closers" such as, "My next appointment is in 2 minutes, but it's been great talking with you," or "I'm sorry I don't have more time, but I hope to see you again." Movement toward the door will help deliver the message.

Chairs are for planned guests. Unless you feel it very important, drop-in visitors should not be offered a chair.

Remain standing. If you sit down, they will, too. Give them 2 minutes, walk them to the door, thank them, and say good-bye.

A large percentage of drop-in visitors are salespeople, and they can be aggressive. Unless highly trained, the receptionist or secretary will succumb, pity them, and bring them in to see you. These visits often take a half hour at least and can take up to an hour or more. The unknowing receptionist will say, "But he was very nice and seemed to have a great spelling series, so I thought you would want to see him." Wrong! You didn't and you don't want to see him. Not now, not ever! Unless you call *him*. Help your secretary or receptionist understand that you are not being unkind; you are simply doing your job. Share with her or him the fact that the Educational Sales Representatives Association of Maryland, the District of Columbia, and Delaware listed 156 representatives in their 1979–1980 directory (Shipman, 1983) and that by now there's likely to be another 100 plus out there looking for ways to occupy principals' time. A half-hour drop-in visit from only 50 percent of them will take 65 or more hours. You can't and shouldn't afford them that much time. Tell your receptionist that you are not available on a drop-in basis to salespeople. You do not see them at all unless you ask them to come in. If you need something, you'll know it; *then* you'll call a salesperson. Remember, few principals have been fired because salespeople thought they were unkind, and few are ever promoted because they score in the top 5% on the salesperson's "how I feel about the principal" inventory.

Inevitably, you will have an unscheduled visit from an angry or distraught parent, teacher, or community member. The critical issue here is to be certain that the visitor knows you are listening and that you care about him or her. Taking notes can help convey that. Use all your communication skills to ascertain quickly whether the issue is something that needs immediate action such as a condition threatening the safety of students or an employee. If the issue can be delayed by scheduling a meeting for a later time, do that with a comment such as

I can see that you are very upset about this, and I understand your concerns. I am scheduled to be visiting classrooms right now. So please have my administrative
assistant schedule a time later today or tomorrow when
we can meet to resolve the issue.

Delaying the conversation does several things: (a) It provides
you the opportunity to be the one in control of the conversation, (b) it allows time to do some data collecting about the
issue, and (c) it gives the visitor time to settle her or his emotions enough to carry on a more rational conversation with
you. Of course, there will be the rare time when a drop-in visitor demands your full and undivided attention on the spot.

Stay in control; time is a finite resource. Don't give 5 minutes away any faster than you would a hundred-dollar bill.
Some bosses have ways of dropping in. They feel comfortable
dropping in to your office, dropping in through the phone or
e-mail, and dropping you into their meetings. They tend to
have lots of ideas, and all of them take your time. We most
assuredly advocate developing a good rapport with bosses,
but are they taking too much of your time with activities that
significantly detract from your ability to keep your school at
the level the district expects? If so, you have a problem and the
monkey is on your back. Honesty is the best policy, and it is up
to you to initiate the conversation. Here are the steps to follow
in helping bosses get a grip on the effects of their demands, so
you can better do your job as an MBWA school leader:

1. List the unplanned jobs your boss gave to you this past
   week.

2. Estimate the amount of time you devoted to these
   demands.

3. List the tasks you were prepared to do this week.

4. List those tasks from Table 7.7 that you did not get done
   or did not get done to the same level of excellence you
   and the district expect.

5. Put yourself in the boss's shoes. Are the demands really excessive? Can you juggle things to make it all happen?

6. If you conclude that the demands are truly excessive and that spending time on them will hurt the school, schedule a meeting with the boss. Highlight those tasks you planned to do that were displaced by your boss's "unplanned" interruptions. Share with your boss the problem you are having. Be open but not accusatory!

7. Share Items 1 through 4 and ask if these reflect your boss's expectations. Add others if appropriate.

8. Get in agreement with the boss on the expectations and the reality of the problem. Offer your thanks and be sure to keep your boss updated on your activities.

This process takes a lot of tact. You will never be totally comfortable with the prospect of presenting such information to the boss—so don't expect it to be comfortable. If you do not know the boss well, it may be wise to confer with a trusted colleague about the problem and the meeting beforehand. But don't wait; do it! It is very important that all supervisors know the problems their team members are having.

The Mail/E-mail Trap

As we stated in Myth 5, if you never saw 60 percent of your mail and e-mail, you would not have missed anything you couldn't live without. In-baskets, out-baskets, and other paraphernalia such as file folders (e-mail has those folders, too!) can be helpful in controlling mail, but not necessarily for everyone. Some people use desk tray organizers well: Ideally, the trays should serve as organizers for incoming and outgoing mail and for those items that you want to let sit for a few days to prove their worth—that is, if you are unsure about their importance, initially give it a couple days. If they then look important, take action as needed. The trays should be convenient to you and your secretary. The bottom tray is for incoming mail. Have the secretary deliver it to you in three groups: junk mail, correspondence, and immediate action. It will take you less than a minute to assess the value of the junk mail and funnel it to the round file. Ask the secretary to draft a nice "take me off your mailing list" form letter and send it to those who send you junk mail. Don't worry about missing something. When was the last time you were introduced to a great idea via the brochures and catalogues that constitute junk mail? Your response is likely to be *never*. Depend, instead, on other people and a few tried-and-true publications to give you the hot ideas.

You should act on your mail and e-mail correspondence immediately; otherwise, it simply builds. If the message requires a response, pound out your response. If you need information before you can respond, attach a note and give it to the secretary. He or she may even be able to prepare the response. If someone else can act on the item, send it to that person and note the action required. Spend 15 minutes a day for 3 or 4 days training your secretary in the fine art of handling mail and e-mail. Your secretary is a valuable asset and frequently can act as an administrative assistant. Let this person use and expand her or his talents to save you time.

If you are in a quandary as to whether you should respond, ask yourself what will happen if you do not. Put the item in question in a hold tray, or ask someone else to give it back to you in 1 week. Most of these items will be forgotten. Learn to throw them away. Don't clutter your files with this stuff. If you find yourself ordering additional file cabinets each year, you are saving too much. There are no awards for the principal, assistant superintendent, or superintendent "who has the highest volume of paper" in files. Make it one of your objectives to cut way back on the paper load. Keep your eye on the ball. Concentrate on your primary mission.

This is the technology age. We all have computers in our offices, and they are the very best means of communicating, other than face-to-face. In this age, e-mail messages have largely taken the place of formal memos. Seeing your work on a screen, knowing that if you make a mistake it can be easily corrected, and being able to move your sentences and rearrange your thoughts in a moment help reduce the need for further revision prior to sending your message. This is a time saver and tends to produce higher-quality communiqués.

New software products are always entering the scene, and it is now possible to dictate to your computer. You can tell it what changes to make! This is terrific for those who lack keyboard skills, but we still like typing our own e-mail messages and memos and find that we are more involved in the task.

The most current hand-held technology available today is an efficient tool for the MBWA principal, particularly when driving (with your device on speaker, of course) or in the field where your computer or administrative secretary isn't. Many of the very successful principals we recently interviewed reported reading and responding to e-mails and text messages with their iPhone or Blackberry as they walked the halls and visited classrooms, thus virtually eliminating the need to carry that laptop while on campus and cutting down on the time needed for reading and responding to e-mails later on in the day or evening. One principal said that not only does she text thoughts and ideas to herself when she is out on campus, but she has conversations via e-mail or text messaging with her teachers as well. The faculty of one high school we visited has developed a "for teachers only" online chat room for informal discussions about curriculum and instructional practices.

MEETINGS: WASTING TIME
VERSUS MAKING PROGRESS

Meetings take time. Doyle and Straus (1976/1993) report that managers sit through more than 9,000 hours of meetings in a lifetime—that's more than a full year's time. As your professional success goes up, so does your time spent in meetings. Middle managers, such as principals, spend 35 percent of

their time in meetings. Superintendents spend at least 50 percent of their time in meetings. That means a very significant
part, 35 to 50 percent, of your organizational life will be spent
in meetings. With that kind of time commitment for higher-
paid personnel, Doyle and Straus extrapolate that as much as
15 percent of the organization's budget may be spent on
meetings.

Meetings also distract from value-added time (time spent
that directly contributes to student learning), a concept discussed earlier. A group of educational leaders found that only
12 percent of their governance council meeting time was value
added—only 5 of the 30 hours spent in these meetings per
year was value added—and the rest was wasted. Our reviews
of over 100 faculty meeting and administrative meeting agendas revealed that only 10 percent of the time spent was productive and resulted in a value-added effect. In the Microsoft
Office Personal Productivity Challenge (Microsoft Corporation,
2005) survey of 38,000 people worldwide, 70 percent felt that
meetings are unproductive. Others have found that some secondary school faculty meetings are zero percent value added
(Freeston & Costa, 1998). This is a travesty considering the
many important tasks that need to be accomplished and the
limitations of time.

When we hear of another meeting, we groan! When teachers hear of another meeting, they groan. So why are we having
all these meetings? Can we (and the organization) do without
them? The answer is yes, sometimes. Schools are people organizations, and people must meet in groups in order to accomplish some tasks. Some meetings are considered so important
that legislators mandate them; for example, school boards,
boards of directors, boards of supervisors, and many other
bodies are required to meet a certain amount of times a year.
Meetings are the most efficient and effective way to debate
ideas and solve problems. Organizational problems sometimes need group participation or input before an effective
solution can be developed. Participation of the group equals
involvement, involvement leads to ownership, ownership
leads to cooperation, and cooperation leads to successful

problem resolution. Ultimately, educational programs improve and result in greater student learning.

The key is to have meetings when they are needed and not to have them when they are not needed. A few rules will help you weed out the unnecessary meetings. Meetings should not be held when

- a memo (paper or e-mail) or telephone call would accomplish the mission as effectively. The importance or urgency of the message can be coded to ensure that emergency information is read and acted on.
- adequate preparation has not taken place.
- the subject is confidential and should not be shared with all members of a group.
- the subject simply does not warrant the time of those attending.
- the meeting involves a controversial, hot topic, and people need time to calm down before they can work together in a collegial manner.
- the topic is simply about something that is routine.

The first rule in the list above is the most frequently broken. If the task is to "disseminate" information about schedules and routines, a memo will work just as well and will save both you and the teachers time. We have all been in this type of meeting and just as we resented it, so do the teachers. They have better things to do with their time. For many years, we've had our university students bring their school meeting agendas to class where we analyze them. Over half are simply information-dissemination meetings. If you are a superintendent, consider analyzing those monthly or weekly meetings you call. Unless you provide great entertainment and food, your principals would probably prefer spending their time at their schools taking care of business. These meetings may be the external force wasting a good bit of their time. Principals, middle managers, and coordinators, if you have such a meeting on your calendar (team meetings, coordinator meetings, superintendent meetings), take action by not going. But be sure to cover bases; that is, if the meeting is optional, call and ask forgiveness, but do not attend. Sending another person is an option. Do not misunderstand: We are not recommending insubordination; if it is required, go! If the meetings are required, and they keep you from accomplishing important tasks, talk to your boss as discussed earlier in this chapter. A poll of thousands of people (Douglass & Douglass, 1992) revealed the indicators and causes of unproductive and time-wasting meetings that hold true in current school settings:

- No purpose
- No agenda
- Not sticking to the agenda
- Starting late
- Too long; no time limits
- Not relevant to their work
- Ineffective meeting leader
- Poor participation
- A few people dominate the meeting
- Participants not prepared
- No decision or conclusions
- No follow-up
- Redundant, rambling discussion
- Actions already determined before the meeting
- Hidden agenda introduced
- Side issues discussed
- Key people missing
- Too many people at the meeting
- Wrong people present
- Short notice or lead time
- Not knowing what is expected
- Too many interruptions (p. 124)

Meeting Types

Basically, there are three types of meetings, and each type has a different purpose.

Information Meetings

These meetings are for sharing information. Examples are the final briefing before a big event at the school, a progress report, or discussions of a new policy. All of these are highly likely to elicit questions, and these should be discussed. If the information is not likely to elicit questions, send it to the members in the school mail. If necessary, go over a few of the highlights at the next "necessary" meeting.

Action Meetings

When there is a need to discuss a problem, clear the air, or build esprit de corps, then a well-planned meeting is a must. Decision making is another very legitimate reason for having a meeting. In these meetings, all participants share responsibility for

- bringing and defining the problem.
- establishing priorities for the agenda.
- offering and discussing solutions.
- determining steps for implementing solutions.
- establishing evaluation and follow-up procedures.

Information and Action Meetings Combined

Purposes of information and action meetings are combined here. For instance, in the case of a committee working on a discipline problem, it may be necessary for committee members to report the findings of their investigations (information) so that the next steps can be formulated and subsequently implemented (action).

PLANNING A PRODUCTIVE MEETING

Leading productive and successful meetings is a challenge, one that is seldom met. Hawkins (1997) offers four key ideas for making meetings highly effective:

1. **Focus**—Is the meeting needed? The fact that "we always have this meeting" doesn't cut it.

2. **Facilitation**—For problem-solving meetings and debates, it is a good idea to have an outside facilitator present. This takes the principal or the leader off the hot seat of solving disputes or monitoring and limiting talk time for those who go on and on. Plus, a trained facilitator can work with the group toward identifying solutions and gaining consensus.

3. **Fellowship**—Participants in effective meetings are able to share openly and relate to each other effectively. This results in feelings of success and develops the "we can do it" spirit. Always keep in mind that schools are people organizations, and having high-quality discussion time is crucial.

4. **Feedback**—Participants should always be aware of how the meeting is faring, that is, is the meeting accomplishing its goals? Intermittent assessments following the meeting are important. Conway (1992) encourages leaders to offer members ample opportunities to give feedback on content issues in a constructive way. Using phrases such as the following is most helpful:

   • "What works . . ." or "What I like about . . ."
   • "I wish we could find a way to . . ." or "How can we . . . ?"

Sources in the literature for planning productive meetings are plentiful (Delehant, 2007; Doyle & Straus, 1976/1993; Jennings, 2007; Lencioni, 2004; Mundry, Britton, Raizin, & Loucks-Horsley, 2000). Principals meet with parents (special interest groups), PTA groups, districtwide teacher or administrator groups, teacher committees from within the school, custodians, aides, bus drivers, student councils, and special event committees. We, too, have met with these groups and have found our meetings to be more productive when meeting protocols are planned and implemented. It takes a bit more planning time, but the meetings are shorter, there are fewer of them, and you accomplish more.

Guidelines and forms follow for planning and implementing productive meetings regarding what to do (1) before the meeting begins, (2) at the beginning of the meeting, (3) during the meeting, and (4) at the end of the meeting.

Identify a meeting coming up at your school, and make it your project to complete the forms provided on the following pages.

Before the Meeting

Before the meeting, you need to build an agenda, communicate expectations, and arrange the room.

Build an Agenda

Table 7.10 is a meeting planner that requires identification of the five Ws (who, when, where, what, and why), the type of meeting, and the name of the leader. Ever had trouble determining the intent of a meeting? We have, and we have even conducted a few of them without a clear intent. Use of this planning strategy will help you avoid this problem. Let's start.

Table 7.10   Meeting Planner

Who	
Group/Meeting Name:	
Participants:	
Where	
Location:	

(Continued)

Table 7.10 (Continued)

When	
Date:	
Time:	
What (agenda for the meeting)	
1.	
2.	
3.	
4.	
5.	
Purpose (desired outcome):	
Meeting Type:	
Meeting Leader:	

What's the name of the group, and who will attend? When and where will the group meet? Provide this information on Table 7.10. Now for the hard part: What is the purpose of the meeting? Be specific. If you can't specify the purpose, the meeting need not be held. If you're stuck, think about what you want from the meeting, the desired outcomes: a decision, a list of ideas, a process, and so on. If you simply want to present information, the meeting may not be needed. But if you think there will be questions about the information, your purpose may be to ensure that the group fully understands the information and its implications. In this case, the meeting is needed. If you are facing a rash of discipline problems, the purpose may be to derive a solution to those problems. In this case, too, the meeting is needed. What is the purpose (desired outcome) of your meeting? Record it on Table 7.10.

Now that the purpose, time, place, and other needed details are decided, it's time to tackle the meat of the agenda. The agenda provides the leader with a road map to success. It lets participants know in advance what will be covered at the meeting and how they can participate. It serves as a guide for the meeting, and it serves as the basis for evaluating the success of the meeting.

The well-planned agenda includes a statement of the topics to be dealt with, the process to be used in dealing with each topic and the desired product/decision (if any), who will present each topic, and the time allocated to each topic. Each of these must be completed for each topic to ensure the success of the meeting.

A detailed agenda works wonders. Establishing the agenda and analyzing the agenda items serve several functions and benefit the leader in that they

- determine whether the meeting is needed;
- serve as a map for accomplishing the results;
- ensure that appropriate participants attend;
- identify needed preparation;
- keep the meeting on track; and
- provide a tool for evaluating success of meeting.

At the same time, the benefits for the participants are that the agenda

- identifies the topic(s) to be addressed at the meeting and what participants should study before the meeting;
- indicates what to prepare/bring; and
- communicates what is expected by way of participation.

A sample agenda is presented in Table 7.11.

Participants are responsible for studying the agenda and discussions from previous meetings, preparing new information needed for the meeting, and formulating ideas for use in the meeting. The leader should share these expectations with the participants in a memo or letter accompanying the agenda.

Table 7.11   Sample Meeting Agenda

What: Council Agenda

When: November 13, 2012—3:30 PM

Topic:	What:	Who:	Time:
Mathematics CRT test scores	Review of scores Test score analysis— compare item analysis to the taught curriculum	Mary and John (fifth-grade teachers)	1 hour
Marginal teacher evaluation schedule	Discussion and consensus	Harry (Personnel Director)	30 minutes
New student rights policy	Presentation, questions and answers, discussion	MaryAnn (Assoc. Supt.)	30 minutes
Lock-down procedures	Analysis and discussion of lock-down problem at Clapton High	Jake (Assistant Supt.)	20 minutes
Administrators out of office	Explanation and discussion of rules	John Henry (Principal)	10 minutes

Communicate Expectations

Expectations for participants during the meeting must also be communicated. Depending on the purpose of the meeting, participants are expected to play an active role in clarifying purposes, providing information, offering solutions, evaluating solutions, observing ground rules, clarifying each other's opinions, calling for a decision, encouraging hesitant participants, asking questions to seek information, making suggestions for keeping the group on track, and protecting the rights of those with minority opinions.

Be sure the agenda is complete and sent out in advance. Participants should receive it at least 2 days prior to the meeting and should be notified of the date, time, and place at least 1 week in advance.

Arrange the Room

Room arrangements sound rather custodial in nature, but they are key to the success of your meeting. Consider the purpose of your meeting, and choose an appropriate room arrangement (see Figures 7.1 and 7.2 for examples). If the purpose is to provide information and conduct some discussion, Plan A will work. If it involves problem solving, lots of discussion and give and take, then Plan B is appropriate. The advantage of Plan B is that it allows participants to see each other. This is a very important consideration in problem-solving meetings. In order to downplay your position as the "boss" during these meetings, don't hold them in your office and don't sit at the head of the table. Be a participant! Everyone knows the principal is the boss. The desired effect is for all to participate so that the best possible solution is attained. Trying to maintain the image of "the boss" may restrict the emergence of that sought-after solution. "Group Memory" in Figures 7.1 and 7.2 is the record of the meeting and is most readily kept on an easel, a whiteboard, or an interactive board such as a SMART Board or document camera. Keeping the record is the recorder's job. Information to be recorded varies with the purpose—decisions, lists of ideas, processes, questions, and special information related to the purpose for the meeting.

Come to the meeting place early to be sure things are just right. Is the chair and table arrangement correct? Are the group memory materials in place? Is the temperature comfortable? Are paper, pencils, and name tags in place? And last, are refreshments appropriate? Everything set? Let's begin the meeting.

Figure 7.1   Plan A—Meeting Room Arrangement for
Information and Discussion

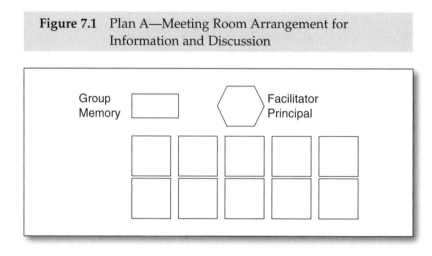

Figure 7.2   Plan B—Meeting Room Arrangement for Problem
Solving

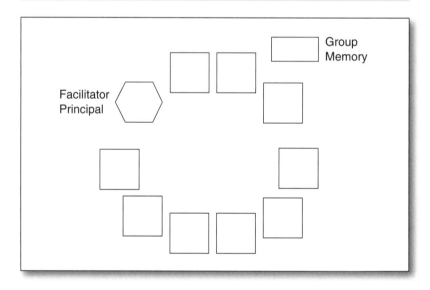

Beginning the Meeting

What you do during the first few minutes may determine the effectiveness and efficiency of the meeting. Starting on time, selecting a recorder, and establishing ground rules for discussion are key.

Start on Time

Starting on time may not be popular, but you should do it. The latecomers will either learn to arrive on time, or they will drop out. The group may want to establish fines for latecomers. This may help to get people there on time and provide funds for refreshments or the next party. If a significant number of participants are late, the meeting time for the next meeting should be changed. Put it on the next agenda for discussion.

The beginning of the meeting should always be devoted to introductions, where appropriate, and to review and gain agreement on the agenda and its desired outcomes. Are there any comments on the topics, on the purpose, and on its stated outcome? Are the time limits appropriate? Should other topics be included? If there is agreement among the group to change something, do so. If an additional item will take more time than is available, put it on the next agenda. This procedure may sound like a big time waster, but in the long run it is a time *saver.* You really can't have a total team effort until you do, and when you do, the force of the team will be much stronger and will help eliminate dissension down the road.

Select a Recorder

A recorder will be needed, and this person should not be the leader or facilitator, whose time and attention must be free for leading or facilitating. Prerequisites for a good recorder include legible handwriting or fast keyboarding and the ability to listen to the conversation of the meeting. You may want to call for a volunteer or use the job as a means to get the non-participator to participate. Determining what should be recorded is also the responsibility of the group, but guidance may be needed. The leader must know what types of things should be recorded before the meeting. The rest of the group may offer other helpful ideas.

If the recorder is not sure the ideas of the group have been accurately recorded, he or she should call for clarification. This will ensure accuracy of the group memory (record) and facilitate future progress. The memory should be brief. Lengthy minutes cause overload and are difficult to deal with from a historical perspective.

Establish Ground Rules to Guide the Meeting

Establishing ground rules for discussion is another crucial factor. They need not be fancy, and they must be to the point. Some old standbys that really help keep a meeting on track are the following ground rules:

1. Treat each other with respect. We're in this together, and we are not the enemy.

2. All opinions are welcome and needed. Be honest. If you disagree, it's okay. Say so.

3. Look and listen as an ally, as a teammate. Don't look and listen for fault.

4. Participate, but don't dominate.

5. Adhere to the time limits.

6. Wait your turn. One person talks at a time.

These six rules work wonders, and each is discussed in more detail below.

Ground Rule 1. Respect is the key. We have observed absolutely ridiculous behavior on the part of some people during meetings. They are belittling, insulting, ornery, and otherwise just not nice. The inclination is to take them out back and paddle them, but sometimes they are too big, and paddling is not an appropriate behavior in a people organization like school, anyway. So, do your best to emphasize adherence to the ground rules, because they work. The bullies may mutter, but the rules give strength to the oppressed to quiet the bullies. Let the ground rules work for you. The participants will use them to get the job done. Give it a try.

Disrupters may be people with hidden agendas, that is, those whose issues do not appear on the formal agenda. Ask them what their issue or their point is. If they will address it forthrightly, it should go on another agenda, if the group agrees. Regardless, the issue must be addressed, or the person will never be a contributing member of your team.

Ground Rule 2. All opinions are welcome and help the timid types participate. Also, knowing that no one will yell at them or make fun of them (Ground Rule 1) may be the encouragement some people need to speak their mind.

Ground Rule 3. Be allies. That sets a tone of cooperation. It may take time to establish a spirit of cooperation if there are a lot of skeletons in the closet and a hidden agenda is stuck in someone's craw. Some "group building" and "group processing" may be required, but not much will be accomplished until these skeletons and hidden agendas are dealt with.

Ground Rule 4. Everyone participating enhances productivity by encouraging those who typically sit there like a bump on a log grading papers or not paying attention. This may take some one-to-one counseling outside the meeting if the person is particularly shy or rude. Frankly, reticence is a pretty unusual find in a faculty and is more likely to be found in a PTA where the participants are not accustomed to speaking in groups. Make all members feel relaxed, wanted, and comfortable. The arrangement of the room and chairs, a relaxed yet purposeful presentation of topics, and your demeanor will go a long way in helping "bring out" the participants. First and foremost, let them know their participation is valued.

Ground Rule 5. Adherence to time limits keeps the meeting on track. This one also helps limit the proverbial marathon talker. A simple reminder that "we have only 5 minutes remaining for this topic" will keep them on target.

Ground Rule 6. Waiting your turn takes care of committee members who typically monopolize the conversation. We have all experienced this type of behavior. They have something to say about everything, and they don't give others an opportunity to speak. Let the ground rules do the work: Remind them of the rules, which were agreed upon before the meeting. If that doesn't work, the other members of the group should exercise their option of speaking up to control the person breaking this rule.

During the Meeting

Stick to the agenda, and follow the ground rules. If someone brings up a topic she or he won't drop and it's blocking progress of the meeting, put it in the "bin" or the "parking lot." That simply means that the recorder notes it in the group memory to be dealt with at another time. It also communicates that the group must continue with the agenda. The recorder should record this on another easel or notebook page for safekeeping. This is the place for revealing the hidden agenda. Get the issues out in the open so people know what's bothering this person and the person knows the group is listening. Make it clear that the group will deal with the problem at another time. Of course, this should be the group's decision. If the group does not want to deal with it or feels it is not appropriate for the group, take it up at another time privately with the person in question. It is mandatory that intervening topics not cripple the progress of the group's agenda.

At the End of the Meeting

Before you bring the meeting to a close, you need to complete two very important tasks: review and evaluate.

Review Actions Taken

Review the group memory for actions taken and directions established by the group. Remember the "who, what, when, and where" format. If assignments were given, make sure the persons responsible know exactly what is expected of them and when it is due. This will help ingrain the decisions in the minds of the participants. Set the time and place of the next meeting. It is much easier and much less time-consuming to do this now than after the group has disbanded.

Evaluate the Meeting

A thorough evaluation lets you, and the group, acknowledge what was good about the meeting and what should be changed next time. Take this task seriously; making meetings more effective and efficient is a key to your continued success. Critiquing meetings for 5 to 10 minutes at the end serves as a reminder of the criteria that contribute to conducting and enjoying good meetings. Give people an opportunity to voice their opinions about the meeting and to use the information constructively to make their meetings more effective. The questions that can be asked are numerous. A few are provided below from which you can select:

- Was the agenda followed?
- Did the facilitator remain neutral and effectively facilitate the group?
- Did the recorder appear to keep an accurate group memory?
- Was the pre-meeting planning adequate?
- Were the purposes of the meeting accomplished?
- Was there a free flow of ideas and participation?
- Was the seating arrangement appropriate?
- Were there too many items on the agenda?
- Was a win–win solution reached as opposed to a unilateral decision?
- Were all participants prepared?
- Was the decision made or outcome already accomplished before the meeting? (Was the meeting a rubber stamp?)

Administrators spend from 30 to 70 percent of the workday in meetings of one kind or another. Running better meetings results in greater effectiveness overall—we get more done more effectively; we look good to the boss or board; and most important, students will learn more.

FOR REFLECTION

Given the potentially overwhelming list of responsibilities you as school principal may face on a daily basis, how will you go about organizing your time to focus on MBWA?

This chapter has examined how MBWA principals find the time to be the instructional leader they need to be. Tools for analyzing, prioritizing, and planning your time have been provided. Once these tools and strategies have been implemented, you will have the much-needed time for MBWA. Chapter 8 explores the role of the principal in establishing superior levels of student discipline and maintaining a safe and orderly campus through Management by Wandering Around.

8

Promoting Good Student Discipline and a Safe Campus

There is no more fundamental obligation of a government than to protect those who cannot protect themselves: namely, our children.

—James McGreevey, former governor of New Jersey

I n addition to supporting the educational mission of the school, Management by Wandering Around promotes a safe and secure learning environment. The MBWA principal's habit of being out and around—during lunch hour and class breaks as well as times when classes are in session—has a powerful impact on student deportment as well as threats from off campus. In addition to spotting problems before they happen, the MBWA principal has an important opportunity to interact with students in informal settings. These small events add warmth and humanity to school institutions that for some students can be cold and foreboding.

PLAN A TEAM APPROACH TO SCHOOLWIDE STUDENT DISCIPLINE

When it comes to student discipline, the MBWA principal's "wandering" must be accompanied by the support and cooperation of the faculty, the co-administrators, the parents, and the community. This requires skillful planning and coordination by the principal; however, the effort is essential. Student discipline and the resultant campus climate are part of the MBWA principal's core mission. Few aspects of a school are more basic to the conduct of education than good school discipline. As one experienced professional noted, "It isn't the most important thing we do; but until order is established, nothing else will be accomplished." Because school administrators are ultimately responsible for the conduct of effective school operations, planning for good school discipline starts with them. Ultimately, however, it involves every member of the school community: the teachers, the custodians, the secretaries, the aides, the administrators, the students, and the parents.

KNOW THE BOARD'S POLICIES AND REGULATIONS

The MBWA principal's planning for good school discipline requires knowing and understanding the board's policies relating to student behavior. These documents, along with their administrative regulations, empower the administrators and teachers to deal with the multiplicity of behavior problems faced in modern American schools. Typically, these policies delegate to the staff the responsibility for maintaining good student discipline. They usually prescribe processes for formal disciplinary action, such as the grounds for suspension and expulsion; the limits on detention and other punishments; requirements for notifying parents; and other board requirements for addressing student behavioral problems of special local importance. We advise that the administrator also have a working familiarity with the state's laws and regulations governing schools and students. A special effort by the MBWA principal to stay abreast of the constantly changing legal framework is smart. This is especially important if the district-level administration fails to keep the district's policies and regulations up-to-date.

CREATE A STUDENT DISCIPLINE PLAN

The following are key processes for designing a workable student discipline plan for implementation by the MBWA principal.

1. Develop a code of student behavior. The first step is to identify the possible problem areas and draft a code of student behavior for discussion by faculty, students, police, community advisory groups, and the school district's attorney. Reducing school rules to concise written statements is an important part of the U.S. Supreme Court's requirement that students be afforded due process. It is also particularly relevant to the supervisory duties of the "wandering" school administrator.

2. Involve the staff and community. The next step is to gather advice and input from as many sectors of the community as possible for use by the staff in adopting the final code of student behavior. The result should be a written set of student rules, regulations, consequences, and processes fully supported by the staff responsible for enforcing them. The resulting code should be reviewed and discussed regularly by the staff, and the whole process should be repeated every 4 or 5 years. Moreover, adjustments to the code can be made by the wandering administrator as problems emerge.

3. Publish the code. The next step is to publish the code and circulate the written rules and regulations. Then, establish a process for orienting the students. This has been done successfully in a number of ways. At the high school and middle school levels, the most formal method is to publish a student handbook containing not only the school rules, but also other useful information about the school, such as school calendars, various schedules, and school services. Typically, these handbooks are distributed to students at the beginning of the year by the teachers. Some staffs go a step further by testing the students to help ensure a high level of understanding of the behavior code.

The content of the handbooks varies widely from school to school. Typical topics covered in a student handbook are presented in Figure 8.1. You should modify your list of topics to focus on the important issues in your school.

Figure 8.1   Hills High School Student Handbook Table of Contents

STUDENT HANDBOOK
TABLE OF CONTENTS

(Continued)

178 The New School Management by Wandering Around

Figure 8.1 (Continued)

4. Communicate with the parents and the public. Last, the MBWA principal should communicate the disciplinary code to the parents and the wider community. Including school discipline as a part of parent orientation programs and bulletins is a good beginning. One successful principal in a suburban high school found that mailing a summary version of the school's disciplinary code to all residents in the school's attendance area reaped big dividends in school support. The residents were accustomed to stories of disruptive behavior in the nation's schools and assumed that the local high school was part of it. They were surprised and gratified to learn that the local school demanded orderly behavior from its students.

The written code of behavior also should be distributed to all members of the staff, both certified and noncertified.

A faculty handbook is probably the most convenient location for information of this sort. Included with the rules should be guidelines for faculty response to various problematic student behaviors. Again, the key is good orientation. Periodic whole-faculty discussions and other means of communication about the purposes and processes of the disciplinary plan are essential.

The importance of full staff cooperation in establishing good school discipline can't be overemphasized. An alert staff can prevent major problems developing from minor disciplinary infractions. As one successful MBWA principal put it, "Many students learn good school behavioral habits simply because they don't have opportunities to misbehave."

FOR REFLECTION

- Consider the most pressing student discipline problems on your campus.
- What approaches would you propose, and what processes would you establish to address the problems?
- Where would you begin, and how would you proceed?

MAKE THE CAMPUS SAFE

The MBWA administrator has a fundamental duty to protect students. Over the years, courts have recognized this duty by granting school officials broad latitude to act quickly and decisively in protecting or defending the children in their charge. Although individual students are generally afforded the constitutional guarantees of all citizens, the courts recognize the necessity to abridge these rights when the safety and well-being of the student body is at stake. Principals understand that students do not leave their constitutional rights at the schoolhouse gate; at the same time, school officials are not held to the same standards as law enforcement officers. They have far more authority to maintain order on campus than the police force has to keep order in a city. In general, they don't have to prove "probable cause," just a "reason to suspect."

Supervise Adequately

When it comes to student safety and safe campuses, at the top of every school principal's list is supervision. Over the years, the legal duty to supervise and protect students has become a well-established principle. Consequently, lawsuits against schools failing to provide adequate supervision have resulted in hefty monetary awards. This means the school leader must take extraordinary steps to avoid negligence.

Avoid Negligence

To school principals, negligence usually means they have not taken reasonable precautions to prevent injury to students or other citizens attending the school, using the school facilities, or engaging in school-related activities. For a negligence claim to be sustained, the courts require four conditions to exist:

- First, there must be a legal duty to protect others from unreasonable risks of injury.
- Second, there must be a breach of that duty.
- Third, the breach must cause an *injury.*
- Fourth, damages must be suffered as a result.

Generally speaking, the courts will ask three questions to evaluate the judgment of the school officials who are responsible for assigning supervision. These questions serve to guide the MBWA principal in efforts to provide adequate supervision and avoid being negligent:

1. **Were any staff members assigned to supervise the area?** Here, the MBWA principal has an edge. School officials are obliged to control and supervise all areas of the campus where students might congregate. Even if a

danger is unforeseeable, the school will probably be held responsible for accidents that could have been avoided if supervision had been present. However, the MBWA principals are more likely to spot potential trouble as they wander with a purpose.

2. **Was the number of assigned supervisors sufficient?** Assigning a single supervisor to a large campus area with many visual obstructions will not protect a school district from a charge of negligence—especially if the supervisor was not immediately present when the injury occurred. To help ensure adequate supervision, the MBWA principal must take into consideration the physical features of the facility to be supervised as well as the number of students.

3. **Were the assigned staff members adequately supervising?** Staff members assigned to supervision must remain vigilant to stop potentially dangerous situations from developing. If the teachers on duty are congregated on one end of the playground chatting, the supervision is inadequate no matter how many staff members are assigned. School districts may even be held liable for accidents that happen off campus if they occurred because the school failed to provide supervision that could have prevented the students from leaving campus (Harutunian, 1980).

We advise that the MBWA principals add staff training to their yearly supervision planning and then follow up by observing implementation and making appropriate adjustments. At a minimum, the faculty and other supervisory staff should be schooled in the following four principles.

Principle 1: The obligation to report to the assigned supervision area on time. MBWA principals cannot be certain their plans for adequate supervision are being carried out unless the supervisors take their responsibilities seriously.

Principle 2: The necessity to stay alert and keep a watchful eye on the assigned area. The supervisors must constantly look for potentially dangerous activities, objects, equipment, and other threats to the safety of the students.

Principle 3: The duty to act in the event of a dangerous situation. Supervisors must act quickly to break up fights and prevent students from walking off campus. The supervisors do not have the luxury of ignoring a dangerous situation—even if it is personally uncomfortable.

Principle 4: A clear understanding of the authority of a faculty member assigned to supervision. In many cases, a designated school supervisor carrying out the duty to protect students has more power and authority than the police. As the circumstances warrant, supervisors should not hesitate to call on law enforcement. Police officers enjoy the greater freedom they have when working jointly with school officials.

ESTABLISH LINES OF COMMUNICATION WITH THE POLICE

Police and other law enforcement officials have the absolute right to enter a public school campus, at any time, to question or arrest students or school personnel. Usually, the police officers find it advantageous to work cooperatively with school officials. Accordingly, they normally contact the administration and conform to school procedures. It is important, however, that administrators recognize that cooperation with law enforcement is mandatory. School personnel do not have a right to be present with a student who is being questioned by the police, although the officers often allow this.

Police officers have the right to take students into custody without the permission of school officials. When this happens, however, common sense (and, in many cases, state law) requires the school administrator to inform the parents immediately. Typically, school districts have procedures for dealing with law enforcement officers on campus. We advise that all members of the administrative staff, including clerical staff, be acquainted with these procedures. In the absence of district procedures, the site administrator should develop site procedures, taking care to be certain they are consistent with the state's laws.

Making a campus safe, like child rearing, takes a whole community. It is everyone's responsibility. The MBWA principal is the central bearer of this responsibility, and it begins with the principal being on the campus and being connected with everything that is happening. This is the essence of Management by Wandering Around.

9

Dealing With Unmet Expectations

Marginal and Incompetent Teachers

*A clever arrangement of bad eggs
will never make a good omelet.*

—C. S. Lewis

T hus far in this book, discussions about faculty have been very positive and focused on what administrators can do to help capable teachers do their best work. Most teachers enter the profession to help youth learn, and it is the administrator's job to offer them tools and resources to help them succeed. We addressed this in Chapter 4 by presenting strategies for fostering the improvement ethic and sense of efficacy in teachers. In Chapter 5, we explored the intricacies of MBWA principals having knowledge and understanding of researched-based curriculum development and instructional strategies. In Chapter 6, we presented classroom walk-through protocols. All of these are intended to help top-quality teachers stay on the cutting edge and to offer other teachers resources and assistance to help them get there. Offering these tools to teachers is a noble venture and the right thing to do. Unfortunately, there is the flip side of the coin. Teaching is a very difficult job, and it requires a healthy quantity of artful abilities and scientific skills. The reality is simply this: *Not all people can become competent teachers.* The job is simply too difficult. To think that every person who enrolls in a teacher training program can or will become a capable teacher is simply naïve.

One of the most important responsibilities a principal has is to ensure that proficient teachers are present in every classroom. Every child deserves a well-qualified teacher. To deny a child this right is blatant administrative malpractice. Unfortunately, this sort of malpractice is rampant in our schools. Experts estimate that anywhere from 5 to 20 percent of the teachers in the nation are marginal or incompetent. Do these percentages seem small? The reality is that even though they may be small, they have devastating effects. Five percent of the teachers in the United States translates to about 145,000 subpar classrooms—or enough to place an incompetent teacher in every classroom in our 14 smallest states. If these teachers have 20 students in their classrooms, then the education and future of a full 2,900,000 students are jeopardized each year—a significant number by any standard.

What is a marginal or incompetent teacher? Lawrance, Vachon, Leake, and Leake (2001) define the marginal or incompetent teacher as lacking "the skill to ensure an efficient, orderly classroom and a safe learning environment for students" (p. 1). We agree. We also recognize that there is a distinction between marginal and incompetent. The *marginal* teacher has the ability to improve with remediation and assistance; the *incompetent* teacher is unable or unwilling to improve. However, we believe schools exist to produce high-quality learning, and both marginal and incompetent teachers lack the skill to actually inspire this learning. For this reason, we judge both marginal and incompetent teachers as *unsatisfactory* unless they respond quickly with visible and measureable improvement in classroom performance. The mission of our schools can only be accomplished with fully competent teachers in every classroom.

This point is easily lost because schools are humane and caring institutions. We educators try to help people, and we want to promote learning. Ridding a school of its inept teachers can be an emotional and demanding chore. Add to that the roadblocks presented by negotiated contracts, state tenure laws, and various court cases, and dismissal of a marginal or incompetent teacher becomes an onerous task—to say the least.

Often, we hear our fellow administrators lament that the most difficult problem in school administration today is dealing with the dismissal of incompetent teachers. As a top-flight attorney said after a 4-year teacher dismissal struggle, "Dismissing an incompetent teacher makes the O. J. [Simpson] case look like a cakewalk" (see Lewin, 1997, p. 1). To escape the political heat, some administrations move poor teachers from school to school, a practice dubbed "the dance of the lemons" or the "turkey trot," and the students they come in contact with lose.

Unfortunately, the situation is not improving (see Archer, 1998; Haycock, 1998; Schalock, Schalock, & Myton, 1998; Van Horn, 1999). Our experience in visiting thousands of classrooms over the past five decades leads us to believe that the 5 to 15 percent estimate of marginal or incompetent teachers is accurate but can be higher or lower depending on the school. It is likely that there is at least one marginal or incompetent teacher in every school.

THE DAY OF RECKONING

What happens next if unsatisfactory teachers do not respond to the principal's efforts to help them succeed? What do we do when we have determined that a teacher's competency level is unsatisfactory? As the supervising administrator, you must, at this point, shift gears and focus on the paper trail. Your warm, nurturing relationship must give way to the task of meticulous and comprehensive legal documentation. This requires that you, the administrator, change your mind-set. Your formative approaches to evaluations and observations of the teacher's performance must become summative and judgmental. Now, feedback to the teacher precisely documents performance deficiencies and demands specific action. Classroom visits are documented and signed by the observer and the teacher, with a notation that a copy will be placed in the teacher's file.

You can expect the relationship between you and the teacher to become strained at this point, but continuing to follow the proper procedures is absolutely essential in order to advance your case. Don't expect other teachers on the staff to support your action initially. They won't. However, our experience tells us that when the action is justified, the faculty will eventually approve—after the dust has settled. The key is to maintain your professional poise, keeping in mind your professional and ethical duty to put a competent teacher in every classroom of your school. This chapter examines the interaction between the supervising administrator and the marginal or incompetent teacher.

To begin, we advise mastering the following skills and information:

- Analyzing teacher performance
- Dealing with a marginal teacher—a four-phase process
- Avoiding or dealing effectively with grievances

MBWA principals benefit from the normal practice of being in every classroom many times each week conducting walk-throughs (see Chapter 6). They are able to observe clues regarding the educational environment. This helps them determine what they can do to clear the educational roadways of obstacles that may prevent teachers from teaching students. It also helps the principal accurately determine who on the faculty is not measuring up.

ANALYZING TEACHER PERFORMANCE

Strong supervision and evaluation programs identify top-notch teachers, capable teachers, and marginal teachers. The following model for conceptualizing employee performance is an adaptation of an employee performance analysis model used widely in the private sector. According to Businessballs.com (2011), the model has uncertain origins being claimed by more than five individuals or organizations. Figure 9.1 is based on an interpretation by George Odiorne (1983), who popularized "management by objectives." The two dimensions used are *performance* and *potential* of the individual.

The *workhorse* is the teacher whose performance is high but whose potential is moderate. This teacher comes to work every day and gives 100 percent and keeps the school going. Approximately 40 to 45 percent of all teachers fall into this category.

The *stars* are an inspiration to the whole staff. These teachers do it all and very well. They make administrators look good; parents love them and students love them. They do a *great* job for the students and the school. This is a relatively small group, though, approximately 5 to 10 percent of all teachers.

Figure 9.1   Teacher Performance Analysis Model

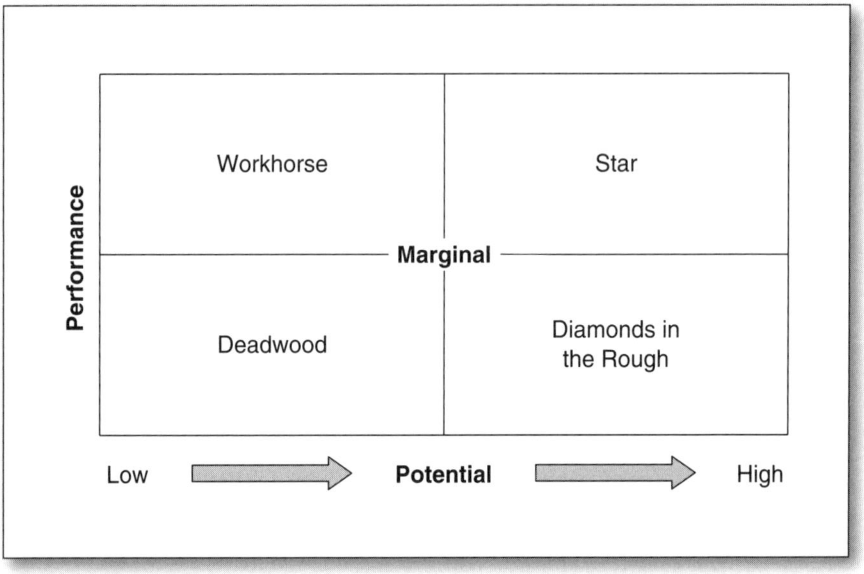

Source: Taken from www.businessballs.com/people_performance_potential_model
.htm. Origin unknown.

The *deadwood* is just that. Teachers in this category possess the same potential as the workhorses but are unable or unwilling to perform. They do not respond to help, advice, or encouragement. They stay in teaching for their own reasons and tend to drag others down to their level. Deadwood accounts for approximately 5 to 10 percent of teachers.

The *diamonds in the rough* have high potential but are short on performance. New teachers are in this category. Polishing with professional development will hopefully put them into the star or workhorse categories; 20 to 25 percent of teachers fall into this classification.

The *marginal* teacher is consistently low in performance, and has low-to-moderate potential; as we discussed previously, 5 to 15 percent of teachers are in this category.

No profession wants or condones the presence of deadwood or marginal employees. The question becomes what to do with them. The first action step is to extend a helping hand through professional development, counseling, or whatever other measure is appropriate. The school district should help its teachers for at least two reasons. The first reason is one of economy. The district should follow through with its original investment of hiring and training them. The second reflects a moral obligation. The teachers come to the district in good faith to do a good job, and the district has an obligation to help them succeed. Helping teachers improve reflects a basic value of a civilized and compassionate society, and that's what professional development is all about—helping teachers acquire the skills they need to succeed (see Chapter 4).

As you read this chapter, picture a teacher whom you believe *may* be marginal. Apply the information presented in each section to the teacher in question. For instance, in the following section, attempt to categorize the teacher's proficiency shortcomings. In the section on specifying deficiencies, write out the deficiency, being as factual and objective as you can. Remember, if it seems too tough or "not worth it," consider the consequences: the dulling of millions of student minds by mediocrity.

Teacher incompetence takes many forms, and many types of incompetence are interrelated. Observing an incompetent teacher and specifying the deficiencies take skill. It all can be quite confusing. But help is available. There are five categories of incompetence that help organize and make understandable the many forms of deficiencies: technical, bureaucratic, ethical, productive, and personal (see Bridges, 1990). Examples of each type of incompetency are provided to further define and illustrate the meaning of each category. Each example has been successfully used in court cases.

(1) Technical. The teacher is deficient in one or more of the following:

- Ability to maintain discipline
- Teaching methods (ability to impart knowledge and produce learning effectively)
- Knowledge of subject matter

- Explanation of concepts
- Evaluation of pupil performance
- Classroom instruction and instructional organization.
- Development and maintenance of lesson plans
- Respect from parents and students

(2) Bureaucratic. The teacher does not comply with school rules and regulations or directives of supervisors regarding the following:

- Following suggestions for improving performance, following the district curriculum
- Allowing supervisors in the classroom for purposes of observing performance
- Performing normal administrative duties or complying with the reasonable demands of the administration

(3) Ethical. The teacher does not conform to standards of conduct applicable to the teaching profession. Examples include the following:

- Physical or psychological abuse of students
- Negative attitudes toward students
- Indifference toward performance of teaching duties
- Immoral or unprofessional conduct
- Criminal acts
- Conviction of a felony or any crime involving moral turpitude

(4) Productive. Teacher fails to obtain certain desirable results in the classroom in the following areas:

- Academic progress of students
- Students' interests in school
- Respect of students for teacher
- Classroom climate

(5) Personal failure. Teacher lacks certain attributes deemed instrumental in teaching, resulting in one or more of the following:

- Poor judgment
- Emotional instability or other mental disability
- Lack of self-control
- Insufficient physical strength to withstand the rigors of teaching
- Alcoholism or other drug abuse

The large majority of competency problems in schools have to do with lack of teaching ability or classroom management skills. These generally involve teachers who simply bungle the job of teaching and hinder student learning. We have all seen incompetence in action. It is most frequently manifested in failure to maintain classroom control, or in excessive reliance on rote learning or drab techniques such as copying material and seeking answers to end-of-chapter questions.

Technical and productive incompetency are obviously related. That is, lack of ability to teach will logically result in productive failure—low student achievement. This chapter addresses technical incompetencies because they are by far the most prevalent in our schools and are the categories directly related to teaching skills.

Management of marginal and incompetent teachers, both tenured and probationary, generally is carefully prescribed by law, board policies, and the negotiated agreement. Efforts to provide resources to teachers to improve their teaching performance are required; records must be kept, and deadlines must be met. First and foremost, administrators have a legal and moral obligation to provide resource assistance to teachers who demonstrate teaching deficiencies. Doing this job right takes time, fortitude, and energy. Being organized and diligent in following a plan and all applicable rules makes the job easier and increases your chances of attaining a successful outcome. It is crucial that all relevant board policies; the teacher contract; and state laws regarding teacher observation, documentation, and due process be fully understood and followed. Remember, success is defined as having a competent teacher in the classroom.

Dealing with the marginal or incompetent teacher is a four-phase process. The remainder of this chapter grapples with the processes you as the supervising administrator must tackle. Chapter 10 outlines more precisely the competencies a district might expect from its teachers, and Resource C at the end of this book provides an outline of summative evaluation procedures.

The law requires quite different due process procedures for tenured teachers than for probationary teachers. Basically, tenured teachers have greater "property interest" in their job and therefore more stringent due process procedures than do probationary teachers. "Nonrenewal" of probationary teachers' contracts is subject to significantly fewer and less stringent legally prescribed due process requirements.

DEALING WITH UNSATISFACTORY TEACHERS: A FOUR-PHASE PROCESS

A comprehensive process for dealing with an unsatisfactory teacher, from the time problems are first detected through dismissal, is provided and discussed in the following sections and in Figure 9.2. Note that only Phase 1 and sometimes Phase 2 are required for probationary teachers, while all four phases are required for tenured teachers.

Phase 1: Initial Diagnosis

From initial diagnosis of possible inadequacies through successful remediation or termination, the administrator's primary responsibility is to offer resource assistance, follow all due process requirements, and compile documentation. The fact that some people lack the ability to teach must also

Figure 9.2   A Four-Phase Process for Dealing With the
Unsatisfactory Teacher

PHASE 1 INITIAL DIAGNOSIS	→	PHASE 2 THE FIRST FORMAL PLAN FOR IMPROVEMENT	→	PHASE 3 OFFICIAL CORRECTIVE ACTION	→	PHASE 4 THE TERMINATION PROCESS
1.1 Legal and ethical considerations		2.1 Seek legal advice.		3.1 Issue notice to implement improvement plan.		4.1 Notify teacher of board's intention to terminate services.
1.2 Specify deficiencies.		2.2 Teacher develops written performance improvement plan with admin. assistance.		3.2 Develop and implement second improvement plan.		4.2. Prepare for hearing.
1.3 Assist teacher in remedying deficiencies.		2.3 Appoint mentor teacher.		3.3 Evaluate progress.		4.3 Hold hearing.
1.4 Evaluate progress.		2.4 Review and validate plan.				4.4 Action of board or hearing body
		2.5 Initiate performance improvement plan.				4.5 Prepare for possible appeal.
		2.6 Monitor progress and evaluate for improvement.				

Source: Redfern (1983, p. 17–21), "Dismissing Unsatisfactory Teachers: A Four Phase Process," *ERS Spectrum,* 1(2). Reprinted by permission from Education Research Service.

be kept in mind from the beginning. This means that the teacher might not make adequate improvement to meet the profession's standards of acceptable performance. We hope that every teacher will, but holding yourself responsible for everyone's improvement is an impossible task. Remember, your job as supervising administrator is to provide resources and opportunities for improvement. It is the teacher's job to improve. This will help you keep your responsibility in perspective. Your ultimate goal is to ensure that all teachers in your school are competent. Some are already competent; some will improve; and some, who do not improve, will be dismissed. Procedures for offering resource assistance and for termination are very serious and strictly governed by law or "due process" rules that must be followed carefully. Failure to follow one step in due process usually means all bets are off—you lose. We discuss due process in more detail in Chapter 10.

The first question to answer after a performance problem has been detected is, what causes the deficiency? Is the teacher's poor performance a managerial or an organizational shortcoming? Are teaching supplies inadequate in quantity or in quality? Are too many duties assigned?

The second question is whether the problem is a personal weakness of the teacher and, if so, whether the deficiency is due to lack of skill or effort. The former is a matter of training; the latter is a matter of attitude. These demand very different types of remediation. The following questions will help determine whether the problem is a skill or effort deficiency:

- Could the teacher do what is expected if motivated to do so?
- Has the teacher ever shown in the past that he or she is able to do what is expected?

If the answers to these questions are yes, the deficiency reflects a lack of motivation or effort. If the answer to either or both questions is no, the deficiency is likely due to a lack of skill.

Statements of deficiency, regardless of their nature, must be objective and clearly written (see the section on Phase 2 and the section in Chapter 10 on documentation). Soft-soaping the problem will hinder the teacher's progress and will hurt your efforts in Phases 2, 3, and 4.

Maintaining written records of all contacts with the teacher and all attempts to assist in improvement is crucial. It is easy to slough off this chore. It takes time, and it is a pain. However, it is a crucial ingredient in the formula for success if the case proceeds to the hearing stage. Detailed, copious records are required.

Efforts to correct deficiencies must be well aligned with the statements of deficiencies. Professional development at this time may consist of clinical supervision, collegial mentoring by a highly skilled teacher in the school, having the teacher observe the mentor, or attending conferences. The teacher in question should receive close attention during this step. This is not a witch hunt; instructional improvement is the goal. Keep complete records of your attempts to offer resource assistance. Anecdotal notes from MBWA activities will serve you well throughout the case; however, memoranda to be used as evidence for a dismissal case must be placed in the teacher's personnel file. Moreover, the teacher must be informed of the documents and given an opportunity to respond. Should the teacher not demonstrate the required improvements and the case go to a hearing, the administrator *will* be called upon to show evidence of support given to the teacher.

This is a time for maintaining close contact with the teacher by making frequent supervisory visits to the classroom and scheduling meetings to discuss the teacher's work. The assistance of a mentor can be particularly helpful at this time. Incorporating a mentor in the process, however, does not relieve you of your responsibilities. It is important to remember that the teacher needs help, and the administrator's job is to offer resource assistance and make honest assessments of the teacher's progress.

Deciding whether to drop the process after the initial diagnosis or to shift gears and continue on to the first step in Phase 2 is sometimes difficult for an administrator. A few probing questions that deal with performance, management effort, and contamination of the system can help here. See the job performance evaluation questions in Figure 9.3.

Figure 9.3 Job Performance Evaluation

Name of Employee: _____

Circle the appropriate response:	Unsatisfactory	Marginal	Satisfactory
What is this teacher's current performance level?	1 2	3	4 5

Management effort:	More than Average	Average	Less than Average
How much of your management time does it take to enable the individual to function at his or her most effective level? (Is this person a resource for the school or a drain of energy and/or other resources?)	1 2	3	4 5

Contamination:	Negatively	Mixed Bag	Positively
In what way does the individual's behavior (verbal and nonverbal) affect the system? (Does this person give healthy stimulation to the school or cause trouble?)	1 2	3	4 5

If your total rating for the individual is below 9 points, you are quite likely dealing with a marginal employee. If sufficient progress is demonstrated and if the answers to the above questions warrant it, the process stops here. If not, go on to Phase 2.

All states specify dates by which probationary teachers must be served with a notice of intent not to renew their contracts. In these cases, teachers generally receive 60 or 90 days' notice for improvement of instructional deficiencies and 45 days for charges of unprofessional conduct. If sufficient improvement does not occur during Phase 2, the teacher does not receive a contract for the following year, and the process is terminated. In some cases, this notice can be issued immediately following the second step in Phase 1 (assessment of the deficiency), and the third step (professional development) becomes the 60- or 90-day period for improvement. These dates and notice requirements differ from state to state, so we recommend you consult the state statutes, your district's policies and procedures, your human resources administrator, and your district's legal counsel.

Phase 2: The First Formal Plan for Improvement

This phase is more structured and formal than Phase 1, and the requirements for keeping accurate records and maintaining a "helping" attitude are even more important. The length of time devoted to improvement plans will vary from case to case. Probationary teachers seldom require more than the 60- or 90-day period as specified by law. Tenured teacher cases may require a full year or more of improvement efforts and case building before dismissal is sought. This is particularly true in cases where the teacher's file contains inadequate documentation or if deficient behavior has been ignored by past supervisors.

The Superintendent's Office and Legal Counsel

Informing the superintendent and legal counsel is advised at this time. Nothing rankles central office administrators more than being informed at the last minute that you want to present a dismissal decision to the board of education. Informing the central office from the beginning will prevent surprises and help ensure cooperation. The same is true for legal counsel. Keep the lawyers informed, and allow them to give advice on due process, documentation requirements, timelines, and so on. Your district may have a designated position for dealing with these matters. If so, keep these people very well informed. But a caution—don't just turn it over to them. Stay in close communication to ensure that the process moves forward and that all requirements are met. Missing just one detail could cause the case to be thrown out later in the process. Technicalities may be a nuisance to follow, but any one of them can make or break the case.

Independent Evaluators

Gaining the cooperation of one or more independent evaluators is important for two reasons: First, the second opinion(s) will help you confirm, rethink, or possibly disconfirm your findings, and second, they will add substantial credibility to your case. The independent evaluators can be trained teacher evaluators (retired administrators) from within your district or trained evaluators from other organizations such as other school districts, universities, regional labs, or the like. Do not use a teacher to perform this function. Teacher mentors should participate in the resource assistance stage, but not in the decision-making stage. This would not be fair to the mentor or the teacher to be evaluated. Regardless of where independent evaluators come from, they will strengthen your case, whether it is to terminate the process, redirect it toward other deficiencies, or confirm the importance of continuing the process.

The teacher must be informed of the responsibility to develop a performance improvement plan. The mentor or peer assistant (described in the following paragraph) and administrator may assist the teacher, but it must be clear that development of the plan is primarily the teacher's responsibility. The plan should include objectives that state what is to be accomplished, outcomes desired, and the method of measuring performance. The plan should also include the remediation activities, reasonable timelines, deadlines, and assistance needed.

The Mentor or Peer Assistant

The function of a mentor or peer assistant is to assist the teacher in improvement efforts. Mentors or peer assistants do not evaluate teachers. The mentor should be capable of modeling the teaching techniques designated to improve the deficiencies indicated in the performance improvement plan. The mentor also must agree to allow the teacher to observe his or her classes, observe the teacher's classes, and meet and confer with the teacher to discuss performance. The role of the mentor should be specified in the performance improvement plan. This is called the peer assistance and review plan in some states. At this stage, all supervision should be direct; that is, the marginal or incompetent teacher needs to be told the specific problem(s), what the research says about this problem, and what to do to improve. Teacher evaluation is the responsibility of the administrator—either the principal or another administrator in the district. The mentor's role is to aid the teacher's improvement efforts.

Reviewing and Validating
the Performance Improvement Plan

Reviewing and validating the performance improvement plan is your responsibility. Use the following questions to accomplish this task:

- Does the plan flow from the written deficiencies?
- Do the activities fit the performance problems the teacher is experiencing?
- Are the performance improvement objectives, activities, and evaluation methods aligned?
- Is the plan challenging, realistic, worthwhile, and achievable?
- Given the assumption that the teacher possesses the potential, are the activities likely to improve the teacher's performance?
- Is the timeline reasonable?

Observations

Schedule observations to assess and record progress in overcoming deficiencies. A frequent mistake made at this point is the administrator accepting responsibility for the teacher's improvement. Statements such as "We're going to work on this together" put the monkey on the administrator's back. The administrator's monkey (responsibility) is to provide services and assistance. It is the teacher's responsibility to improve. No one can improve for that person—only the individual can do it. Statements such as the one above generally are made when the administrator feels uncomfortable and wants to soften the impact on the teacher. The situation is difficult for the teacher; this fact must be accepted. Communication from the administrator must be direct, forthright, and honest. Anything less will ultimately make the process more difficult for the teacher and the school district.

Signed Documents

Finally, both the teacher and the administrator must sign the performance improvement plan and each get a copy. Copies must also be sent to the teacher's personnel file, the building administrator's supervisor, and legal counsel. The teacher may choose to also give a copy to the mentor. The teacher is free to distribute this information. You should not, however, give the plan or any other information regarding the teacher and the case to anyone other than school district administrators and legal counsel. If you are unsure how to respond to requests for information, seek the legal counsel's advice.

Follow the plan, and make changes only when the teacher agrees. Keep accurate and complete records. A school administrator should be in the classrooms on MBWA missions frequently, at least 10 times a week for 2- to 30-minute segments. These visits are now part of the formal teacher evaluation plan, not the walk-through process. Using an independent evaluator—a highly skilled retired administrator, an administrator at another building, or an assistant principal—and a mentor is advised at this time but does not reduce the necessity for MBWA visits.

Following the completion of the performance improvement plan, the teacher should be given the opportunity to try out the skills in question with the mentor teacher before the administrator conducts another formal evaluation. Cases have been lost when it has been shown that the teacher was evaluated prior to completion of the plan.

During the monitoring and evaluating phase, the administrator should assure the following:

- Supervision is ample in scope and amount. In other words, the administrator must practice frequent MBWA with this teacher. Close, helpful, and honest supervision is required.
- Evaluation data and notes are complete, well documented, and properly recorded.
- Assistance is provided per the performance improvement plan and properly documented.
- The teacher is treated fairly and equitably. The principal must be helpful and above all conduct the process in a highly professional manner.

Even though this stage of the process is designed to remedy the teacher's deficiencies, the administrator must anticipate the possibility that the teacher will not demonstrate adequate improvement and must prepare accordingly. The preparation must include the development of a pattern of inadequate performance. The demonstration of a pattern of inadequate performance sustained over a period of time is necessary to prepare for a dismissal hearing on the basis of technical, bureaucratic, productive, or personal failure. Single examples of ethical failure, such as molestation, physical abuse, and other criminal activities, are exceptions. In general, however, unsatisfactory performance must be shown as a pattern of recurring instances rather than a single egregious incident. The importance of a demonstrable history of inadequate practices has a long history and is summarized by a court as follows:

> Proof of momentary lapses in discipline or of a single day's lesson gone awry is not sufficient to show cause for dismissal of a tenured teacher. . . . Yet, where brief instances and isolated lapses occur repeatedly, a pattern of behavior emerges which, if serious enough, will support the dismissal of a tenured teacher. Where the school board fails to show that the example of conduct constitutes a pattern of deficiency, then dismissal cannot be permitted. (*Board of Education v. Ingels,* 1979, pp. 71–72)

The most commonly used sources of evaluation information are the supervisor's evaluations based on classroom observations, anecdotal notes from informal observations, complaints from parents and students, and evaluations from students. Parent and student evaluations must serve as supportive evidence, not as primary support for the major charge of incompetence or unsatisfactory performance. The strongest evidence of a teacher's incompetence is the supervisor's evaluation. (See Chapter 10. Also see Summative Teacher Performance Evaluation document in Resource C at the end of this book.)

Phase 3: Official Corrective Action

By the time Phase 3 begins, news of the teacher's performance and tenuous employment with the district is buzzing about the school and community. It is essential at this point that you, the supervising administrator, review the requirements for due process afforded the teacher. Chapter 10 addresses these important legal details along with the protocols for building effective supporting documents.

These are very trying times for the teacher, the administrator, and everyone else involved. The official notification given in this phase requires board action and is therefore public information in most states, although details of the actual charges are generally private and confidential information. Regardless, the board action frequently does result in exposure in the media. We have experienced this situation firsthand. In one instance, official notice of the board's charges against a teacher appeared in the local paper resulting in calls to district leaders and an editorial in the local paper. It is reasonable to assume that the possibility of dismissal will disappoint and anger a teacher. These emotions may be manifested in charges that the evaluations are invalid; general irritability; failure to cooperate; and attempts to rally support from faculty, community, and the teachers association. Resenting the teacher's anger complicates the situation and is ill-advised. Administrators must understand the origin of the stress, be compassionate, and remain firm and professional in their decision to follow through with the process. Administrators must also be practical. When teachers are found to be incompetent for any reason, they should be removed from the classroom. This can be accomplished through paid leave and reassignment to another job. In all cases, keep a clear and objective head, and stay in touch with the central office and the district's legal counsel. Doing otherwise could result in losing the case.

Notice to Improve

At this step, official notice to the board of education of intent to recommend dismissal if specific improvements are not made must be given to the teacher. The notice should be delivered by certified mail or by hand. If delivered by hand, a witness should be present to sign a document saying that the notice was received by the teacher, that the teacher refused to accept it, or whatever else may have occurred. This letter or official memorandum should be signed by the superintendent and approved by legal counsel to ensure compliance with the law. The notice should state that a plan of corrective action (performance improvement plan) is being instituted because performance deficiencies have persisted through previous phases despite efforts by the administration to correct them. Official stationery should be used. Each individual state's statutes specify unique timelines and documentation requirements, which must be meticulously observed. All notification documents should be developed in close consultation with the district's legal counsel.

Carrying out the plan requires a good deal of time. Allowance for this demand must be planned and scheduled on the calendar in permanent ink. This is not something that can be stacked on top of everything else on the calendar; some other activities must be reassigned or postponed.

Stepping up the supervision schedule may be interpreted and claimed by the teacher to be harassment, but the practice does have support in case law. That is, the courts have interpreted additional attention (observations and consultations) as helpful.

The Final Decision

The decision to recommend dismissal must be made on "performance" in relation to the deficiencies cited in the notice. This is another hard decision, but maintaining an awareness of the fact that the purpose of this exercise is to ensure that only completely competent teachers are in contact with students makes it rational, if not easier. It is our experience that the majority of these cases are referred to the fourth phase for termination if not resolved at this level via a cash settlement or other method of induced exit. This is not unexpected or unreasonable in light of the contention that only 10 percent of the teachers found to be incompetent ever achieve competency. Not everyone employed by a school district as a teacher is destined to be a competent teacher. Teaching takes a special person with special skills. It is an insult to the profession to think that anyone can or should teach in the public schools.

Phase 4: The Termination Process

Administrators have two responsibilities in Phase 4: (1) to assist in preparation for the hearing and (2) to participate in the hearing. The latter can be very taxing and requires excellent preparation. The principal and all other personnel who may be called as witnesses should review all documentation and be very familiar with the charges, board policy, state statutes, and personnel contracts.

The official notice of intent to terminate should be written by the district's legal counsel. Statement of the intent, the charges, and the timeline will be included along with necessary documentation such as the evaluations and statutes. Other requirements as stated in the first step in Phase 3 apply here also.

Preparing for the hearing involves development of the evaluation summary. The person assigned to this task varies from district to district. In large districts, the director of human resources usually performs this function. In smaller districts, the superintendent or assistant superintendent may draw the duty. Legal counsel will give direction for determining the contents and format of the summary and may also be called upon to write it. It is important to work closely with legal counsel in this effort to ensure the file is interpreted correctly. You should insist they justify their interpretations. Do not give them carte blanche authority. Use them as advisers. The administration is responsible for the district and the outcome of the hearing.

Remember, timelines and deadlines for issuing notices vary from state to state, but the four-phase process in the case of a tenured teacher may take 2 to 3 full years. Meeting each deadline in the process is a must. Being late or not complying with a requirement will likely result in termination of the process and loss of the case. Timelines may be obtained from the state administrator's association, state school board association, district personnel office, or the district's legal counsel. Each administrator should keep a timeline in his or her office.

A hearing officer (judge, board president, or the like) runs the hearing. The district's legal counsel organizes and presents the case for the district; the school administrator supports legal counsel, offers advice when appropriate, and will serve as a key witness and arrange for other key witnesses as appropriate. The latter is a difficult, time-consuming task. This preparation requires careful review of all documentation, timelines, policies, and statutes. The major points need to be committed to memory, because when on the stand, there is little time or allowance for reflection and fact finding.

If the decision of the hearing office is in favor of the district, the teacher may have the right to an appeal, depending on state law. If appeal is a possibility, the school administrator, the legal counsel, and the personnel director or another central office administrator should begin preparing for an appeal. Transcripts of the hearing, testimony of witnesses, arguments posed by the defense, and the district's arguments must be reviewed and evaluated for strengths and weaknesses if there is an appeal. In many states when an appeal is initiated, the hearing is a review of the transcript from the initial hearing and no testimony is heard. When an appeal occurs, the case can last considerably more than a year—in some cases as long as 3 years. Since the process can be arduous, it is important that the administrator keep the following points in mind.

Points to Keep in Mind When
Dealing With Unsatisfactory Teachers

1. The administrator's primary goal is putting only competent teachers in contact with students so that they have the very best chance of learning.

2. When teacher deficiencies are detected, the first responsibility of the administrator is to provide resource assistance to the teacher. Personal or ethical failures such as child abuse are exceptions to this rule. In these cases, the teacher must be at least temporarily barred from the

classroom. Statutes may require this, especially when the teacher presents a danger to the students.

3. Know the due process requirements, both procedural (e.g., rights to a hearing and notice) and substantive (fairness of the law). See Chapter 10.

4. Make sure you have the support of your supervisor.

5. Due process provisions may be found in each state's statutory laws and regulations, school board policies, state personnel commission policies, the negotiated agreement, and case law. Be familiar with these provisions.

6. Know whether or not board policy grants "just cause" provisions to nontenured teachers. These provisions may put the district in the position of being required to conduct the entire four-phase process as opposed to only Phases 1 and 2.

7. Know the law, the collective bargaining agreement, and district policies.

8. Tougher and more thorough evaluations and supervision are required as the four-phase process proceeds.

9. Compile only accurate and appropriate information.

10. Schedule adequate time for supervisory visits and other responsibilities related to the four-phase process.

11. Keep comprehensive and accurate records of all activities and contacts regarding the process.

12. Keep the central office administration and legal counsel well informed.

13. Allow the teacher reasonable time for improvement.

14. Be consistent and fair in dealings with the teacher, and maintain a professional demeanor throughout the process.

15. Seek and scrutinize advice from legal counsel.

16. Develop a support group to help you, the supervising administrator, through the process.

17. Keep only the information you have shared with the teacher in the personnel file. Other information is not admissible in court. Information accumulated during the hiring process (e.g., placement papers, rankings, reports, notes from identifiable examination or promotion committees) or notes used for planning/conducting the four-phase procedure are not subject to review by the teacher.

18. When the going gets tough, remember that there is more to lose through substandard evaluations and substandard supervision than there is in angering some teachers and others who may support the teacher in question (such as parents, friends, and politicians).

AVOIDING OR DEALING EFFECTIVELY WITH GRIEVANCES

Most school districts have grievance policies on file. The best way to avoid grievances and to win them when they do arise is to play by the book and follow the rules. Any time your actions are not consistent with district policy, the bargaining agreement, and laws, you are giving employees legitimate cause to file a grievance. Certainly the topics addressed in this chapter are volatile and more prone to grievances than many other topics. The following guidelines will help you avoid grievances and deal effectively with them when they do occur.

- Be intimately familiar with and follow provisions of the bargaining agreement, state laws, and all board policies. In general, a grievance must be related to a specified violation of the provisions of the bargaining agreement.

- Accept the fact that teachers and other employees have the right to have grievances.
- Work with the district administrator responsible for collective bargaining in an attempt to settle grievances at the lowest level, possibly before the grievance is filed. This does not mean you should give away the store, but mistakes do happen. When they do, admit it and get on with school business. If the grievance is not well-founded, explain your reasoning and attempt to convince the employee.
- Be sure teachers believe they can have time with you to discuss matters of concern. This will help head off grievances.
- Talk with other administrators about the problem; they may have good advice.
- Follow the grievance policy to the letter.
- Don't hear a grievance unless the teacher can cite the part of the contract provision(s) allegedly violated.
- Alert your supervisor to the possible grievance.
- Do not allow friendship, past employee experiences, or gender to influence your decisions.

In the next chapter, we focus on the administrator's responsibility to protect the teacher's rights to due process, as well as important details of building a file to support termination.

10

Ensuring Due Process and Building the File

Nor shall any state deprive any person of life, liberty, or property, without due process of law.

—Due process clause of the 14th Amendment of the U.S. Constitution

As we discussed previously, navigating through the due process procedures to dismiss a marginal or incompetent teacher is difficult (see Chapter 9, Figure 9.2). It is filled with legal and procedural potholes. The good news is that all of these can be avoided. The key is to develop expert documentation fully compatible with the state laws, the relevant district policies, and the negotiated agreement. Keeping faith in the conviction that only competent teachers should be in the schools is absolutely crucial.

In our work with hundreds of school principals and central office staff, we have heard the old refrain "We can't get rid of a bad teacher because of the teacher tenure law." Let's be very clear: This statement is dead wrong. Dismissing a tenured, but incompetent teacher is tedious and to a certain extent difficult—but far from impossible. Teachers are being dismissed for cause in every state every year.

WHY TENURE?

There was a time in public education when tenure did not exist and teachers served at the pleasure of school boards. For example, in the 1920s, more than half of the teachers in Wyoming were new to their positions. Board power to dismiss and discipline teachers was unchecked, and teachers were dismissed for various and sundry pretexts unrelated to teaching competence or morality issues (Lebeis, 1939). Bridges (1990) recounts that teachers were released for numerous invalid reasons including the following:

- To make room for friends and relatives of board members
- To save money by reducing the number of teachers, thus increasing the workload of others
- To secure the welfare of the community by refusing to employ teachers who were married or had children

- To save money by dismissing experienced, higher-paid teachers and replacing them with less experienced and lower-paid teachers
- To punish those who were disloyal to the administration

Times have changed. By standards of common sense and morality, arbitrary and capricious reasons for dismissal were wrong and led teachers associations to press for tenure legislation. The first tenure law was passed in New York early in the 20th century, and by the end of World War II, most states had passed laws that guaranteed teachers everything from special free speech protection to strict due process for disciplinary matters and tenure rights. By the early 1960s, nearly all states gave extensive tenure provisions to teachers. Challenges to the constitutionality of tenure laws were heard and rejected by the Supreme Court, blunting the ability of school boards to arbitrarily or capriciously dismiss teachers.

Tenure is America's way of saying that teachers (and, in some states, administrators) have what is called a "property interest," the teachers' right to their jobs beyond the current contract. Such jobs cannot be taken away without proving just cause and following required due process procedures.

Probationary teachers' property interests are limited or nonexistent in some states. In most cases, probationary teachers have a right to their jobs for the current contract year but not beyond, as in the case of tenured teachers. Tenure gives strong and well-defined rights to due process but is not guaranteed employment. Court cases have proved that competency in teaching is required. Nevertheless, tenure does make dismissal tedious simply because all due process requirements must be met and documented. Hence, due process is frequently addressed as "a pain." It seems to hinder administrators in pursuit of one of their important tasks: providing students with fully competent teachers. Due process can be burdensome. It takes precious time. But due process is one of the hallmarks of our civilization. It is a compassionate society's attempt to ensure that those being dismissed are protected from arbitrary prejudices, vendettas, and other unethical motives for termination of employment.

Principals with sound reasons for dismissing a teacher and with evidence of compliance with all due process requirements are likely to win. Those who do not follow due process requirements are likely to lose, on the technical or ethical grounds set forth in the due process requirements. The purpose of this chapter is to provide necessary background information and legal requirements regarding due process.

DUE PROCESS

Two categories of due process are crucial to successful teacher dismissal and frequently affect the outcome of court dismissal cases:

- *Substantive due process* requires school administrators to provide valid reasons and substantial supporting evidence for termination. Substantive due process is sometimes called *just cause*. Charges that are not valid and not accompanied by substantial supporting evidence do not stand up in a hearing.
- *Procedural (statutory) due process* requires school administrators to follow documented statutory or constitutional procedures stipulating proper notices, hearings, and unbiased decision makers. Failure to follow any one procedural due process requirement can result in losing the dismissal case.

Actions typically required by these due process categories include the following:

Substantive Due Process

1. Define competencies by providing written and oral standards of performance.

2. Specify data-gathering procedures and provide evidence and documentation.

3. Specify opportunities available for improvement, and provide resource assistance in conjunction with opportunities for improvement.

Procedural Due Process

1. Provide notice of deficiencies/procedures/rights.

2. Notify teacher of opportunity for a hearing.

3. Provide a neutral, unbiased decision maker, and notify teacher of hearing process rights including the right to legal counsel, to examine witnesses, to call witnesses to testify, and to examine written records.

4. Follow state statutes and local policies and procedures including timelines.

Guidelines for Ensuring Substantive Due Process

Substantive due process guidelines for increasing the likelihood of success in teacher dismissal cases are presented below.

Substantive Due Process Guideline 1:
Defining Teacher Competencies

Competency must be defined. Defining competencies is a difficult chore, but research over the past 10 years has offered valuable and definitive descriptions of teacher behaviors that result in learning. There is no universally accepted definition, and courts accept a school's or school district's definition if it is reasonable and formally adopted by the board. Definitive and reasonable standards of performance help ensure that the stated charges and deficiencies will be clear, accurate, and substantive. Standards are the reference points for measuring teachers' performance. Without predetermined standards, conclusions about competency are arbitrary and unfair to the teacher in question, the students, and the profession. Conclusions determined to be arbitrary in court sully the name of education and create terrible public relations for school administrators.

Detailed descriptions of skills and indicators of the roles and responsibilities of teaching should be present in job descriptions and evaluation instruments. The list of skills should be based on expert advice and respected research findings. Table 10.1 outlines the performance areas, criteria, and indicators that constitute a typical school district's teaching standards. All teachers should receive copies of their job descriptions and evaluation instruments, along with related procedures, policies, and job performance expectations. This is required by law in many states.

(Text continues on p. 224.)

Table 10.1   Teacher Evaluation Performance Areas, Criteria, and Indicators

(The indicators listed below with an asterisk are considered essential to professional proficiency.)

I. Effective Lesson Planning

A. Demonstrates Effective Instructional Planning Skills

- *Uses instructional objectives congruent with district curriculum and state standards
- *Can write or verbalize learning behavior for the intended objective
- *Selects topics and activities congruent with instructional objective
- *Plans instruction to accommodate varying levels of ability
- *Writes daily lesson plans in a form comprehensible to administrators or substitutes
- Plans formative and summative evaluation procedures
- *Has developed and follows course or unit outlines for prescribed curriculum
- Assists students in defining realistic self-development goals
- Can write a five-step lesson plan
- Plans for use of high-interest media and activities
- Plans instruction to accommodate varying learning styles
- Plans for development of critical thinking, including objectives at all levels of Bloom's Taxonomy

B. Selects Appropriate Objectives

- *Selects objectives at correct levels of difficulty for all students
- *Chooses materials and instructional methods appropriate to students' abilities and interests
- *Selects accurate and up-to-date information for lessons
- *Adjusts objectives for special needs students
- *Utilizes task analysis in developing lesson plans.
- *Incorporates lesson objectives from all levels of Bloom's Taxonomy

C. Assesses Student Learning

- *Has and uses a plan for assessing student learning
- *Utilizes reliable and valid assessment instruments and procedures
- *Systematically collects assessment data
- *Uses assessment data for program evaluation and modification
- *Can provide evidence of student progress
- Maintains written records of pertinent progress data for all students
- Can describe the strengths and weaknesses of the instructional program
- Discusses graded work with individual students and small groups, assuring their recognition of ways of improving performance or overcoming difficulties
- Shares diagnostic data with individual students, helping them to set specific, realistic learning objectives
- Has and uses a plan to assess student attitudes

II. Effective Classroom Management

A. Establishes and Reinforces High Standards for Student Discipline

- *Manages discipline in accordance with school procedures, school board policies, and legal requirements
- *Defines limits of acceptable behavior and consequences of misbehavior, and communicates these to students and their parents

(Continued)

Table 10.1 (Continued)

- *Attends to disruptions quickly and firmly
- *Demonstrates fairness and consistency in handling student problems, always maintaining the dignity of individuals
- *Uses a behavior management system based on sound theory and research
- Posts classroom rules
- Uses voice control, cues, hand signals, eye contact, and other techniques to establish desired behavior
- B. Maximizes Student Time-on-Task
- *Schedules learning time in accordance with district policy
- *Efficiently manages time by starting class and lessons promptly
- *Ensures that students are engaged in task-relevant activities
- *Ensures that a high percentage of students are on task at all times
- *Minimizes the time spent on administrative tasks

III. Effective Teaching Practices

A. Teaches to the Objective

- *Uses models, explanations, information, questions, activities, and responses that are congruent with the objectives
- *Reinforces student responses that are congruent with objectives
- *Provides practice that is congruent with objectives
- *Refrains from losing focus on the objective through digression or irrelevant information

B. Monitors and Adjusts Instruction

- *Elicits overt behavior from the whole group or individuals to monitor understanding
- *Reteaches or alters instruction based on monitored student behavior
- *Alters the pace of instruction based on monitoring
- Circulates to monitor level of understanding
- Provides alternative activities for special needs students
- Uses formative evaluation techniques for monitoring

C. Communicates and Reinforces High Expectations for Student Achievement

- *Bases expectations on observed student needs and potential
- *Provides encouragement and response opportunities for all students
- *Uses techniques such as delving and proximity to ensure equitable response opportunities
- *Projects an attitude that all students can learn
- *Maintains clear and reasonable work standards and due dates
- Promotes personal goal setting
- Provides gifted and talented students with higher-level work rather than greater quantity
- Takes time to write supportive comments on report cards and student work

D. Demonstrates the Ability to Motivate Students

- *Expresses genuine interest and enthusiasm about subject matter
- *Utilizes novelty and relevance to interest students
- *Provides specific and immediate feedback to motivate students
- *Strives for success by providing support and corrective feedback
- *Utilizes a variety of active participation strategies
- Exhibits a high degree of energy and vitality
- Invests time to decorate classroom to reinforce goals

E. Effectively Reinforces Learning Through the Use of Appropriate Practice

- *Prepares students to perform assignments independently and successfully
- *Introduces new concepts and vocabulary found in assignments
- *Provides feedback on assignments within a reasonable period of time

(Continued)

Table 10.1 (Continued)

- *Communicates the specific purposes of assignments
- *Follows school and district homework guidelines
- Maintains a schedule for the intermittent review of key concepts

F. Demonstrates Effective Lesson Presentation Skills

- *Presents ideas sequentially and clearly
- *Gives easily understood directions
- *Checks for understanding
- *Provides feedback on correctness of classroom work
- *Uses an array of question types
- *Reviews previously learned concepts or skills that are essential prerequisites for new learning
- *Leads students to summarize main points of lessons
- Posts or writes important information for students

IV. Positive Interpersonal Relations

A. Demonstrates Effective Interpersonal Relations

- *Refrains from exhibiting defensiveness, hostility, or anger in student or parent conferences
- *Initiates parent contact for students with problems
- Uses active listening techniques
- Provides written expectations for homework and discipline to students and parents
- Provides parents with written overviews of courses

B. Demonstrates Effective Interpersonal Relations With Colleagues, Administrators, and Other Support Personnel

- *Refrains from chastising or belittling other employees
- *Treats other employees respectfully and courteously
- *Cooperates with support personnel
- Shares ideas with colleagues
- Maintains an optimistic and positive attitude in dealings with others

C. Demonstrates Good Interpersonal Skills When Relating to Students

- *Makes time for student conferences
- *Uses discretion in handling confidential information

- *Demonstrates patience and interest when speaking with students
- *Demonstrates an authentic concern for the welfare of students
- Uses names in a warm and friendly way when addressing students
- Uses active listening skills when conferring with students

D. Actively Uses Techniques to Promote Student Self-Esteem

- *Provides opportunities for all students to achieve recognition for academic success
- *Provides positive, constructive feedback and avoids sarcasm
- *Refrains from shouting or exhibiting hostility
- Shows sensitivity to physical and emotional needs of students
- Encourages students to monitor their own progress
- Reinforces student self-control

V. Professional Responsibility

A. Demonstrates Employee Responsibility

- *Responds appropriately to parental concern
- *Provides timely and accurate data requested by the administration
- *Maintains teaching tools and equipment in good condition
- *Demonstrates responsibility for student behavior in all aspects of campus life
- *Models appropriate behavior at school functions
- *Adheres to school and district policies and procedures
- *Utilizes appropriate channels for resolving concerns
- Demonstrates a positive and constructive attitude

B. Pursues Professional Growth

- *Selects growth activities relevant to school and district programs
- *Stays informed of current professional practices and research
- *Demonstrates an openness to professional improvement
- Provides a rationale for growth activities as requested

Source: Frase & Hetzel (1990, pp. 182–188).

The performance areas, criteria, and indicators described in Table 10.1 should be aligned with a summative teacher performance evaluation. A summative evaluation report document tied to the performance indicators outlined in Table 10.1 can be found in Resource C at the end of this book. A document of this sort can be developed for your district and used to guide the principal or other evaluator observing teacher performance. All of these areas, criteria, and indicators must, of course, be linked to adopted board policy.

Dismissal cases are frequently lost when the charges are vague or arbitrary. Charges of incompetence are best derived from the district's performance standards. Caution must be taken that these are proper as defined by board policy, the teacher contract, and state statutes. Court cases provide clues to five criteria useful in establishing these standards. Following is a checklist of criteria you can use to assess your school's teacher performance standards.

CHECKLIST FOR ASSESSING
TEACHER PERFORMANCE STANDARDS

Are the performance standards for teachers	YES	NO
Substantive and comprehensive?	_____	_____
Clear, concise, and specific?	_____	_____
Fair, attainable, and ascertainable?	_____	_____
Related to board policies, procedures, and job requirements?	_____	_____
In conformance with state statutes and regulations?	_____	_____

For your performance standards to stand up in a hearing, you must be able to answer yes to all these five questions. These criteria are not difficult to achieve, but they must be attained. They are crucial to success in teacher dismissal cases. Each is discussed below.

1. **Substantive and comprehensive.** First, performance standards must be adopted by the governing board and they must be substantive and comprehensive. Performance standards must not deal with trivialities or represent a severely limited aspect of teaching. Substantive and comprehensive standards address teaching techniques, classroom management, interpersonal relations, and curriculum management and organization.

2. **Clear, concise, and specific.** Possibly the most common weakness in teacher dismissal cases is the lack of specificity and conciseness of charges, and charges can only be as specific and concise as the performance standards.

3. **Fair, attainable, and ascertainable.** Many administrators are concerned that they cannot succeed in dismissing the weak tenured teacher. This is not the case when standards of performance are fair, attainable, and ascertainable. In other words, the performance standards must make sense and be reasonable.

4. **Related to board policy and procedures and job descriptions.** Board policy and procedures as well as specific job requirements such as the following should be included in the list of competencies:

   - Following district-adopted curriculum (*Stamper v. Board of Education*, 1986)
   - Completing course work to meet district accreditation program standards (*Feldusen v. Beach Pub. School Dist.*, 1988)
   - Obtaining acceptable scores on a test (*York v. Bd. of School Com. of Mobile County*, 1984)
   - Student achievement (learning) as defined by an objective measure such as norm-referenced tests

5. **In conformance with state statutes and regulation.** Finally, standards of performance should incorporate district expectations for the job and must also conform to state statutes. The standards should be included in job descriptions and teacher evaluation procedures and be communicated to all teachers. Standards may be distributed with employment application forms and during orientation sessions with teachers. Principals or other officials should review the evaluation process and performance expectations with teachers each year.

School system personnel must not only define competence, but must also specify the way it is measured. A well-defined procedure for gathering evidence, such as having trained, reliable evaluators who are responsible for gathering and documenting such evidence, is critical. Documentation in the form of memos and other required forms (e.g., observation records, conference minutes) establishes substantial evidence and is a prerequisite to successful dismissal cases.

Substantive Due Process Guideline 2:
Data-Gathering Procedures and Documentation

Teacher evaluation guidelines must specify data-gathering procedures, including observation data collection sheets, anecdotal forms, written descriptions of conferences, summative data forms, and job target forms, and administrators must gain proficiency in the preparation of written documentary evidence (see Figure 10.2). The following five criteria can be used for assessing your skills in preparing evidence and documentation. Evidence and documentation must conform to the following:

1. **Be frequent and cumulative, with follow-up observations to determine improvement.** Court cases illustrate the need for frequent and cumulative evidence of a behavior pattern. Dismissals based on single incidents of technical failure seldom find support in court.

2. **Be specific and supportable.** Not only does a pattern of incompetence need to be substantiated, but also the evidence must be specific and supportable. For example, courts have supported the following charges:

- *Poor lesson planning*—The lesson plans provided by the teacher lacked objectives, materials, and motivation strategy.
- *Inability to get students to participate* actively in class presentations—Of the 24 students, 15 were not attending to the teacher. The same three students responded to each question asked by the teacher.
- *Maintaining improper pace* in presenting information—Students continually asked the teacher to slow down and said they were confused. Four students asked when they could get on to the next lesson because they had learned this stuff last year.
- *Lack of preparation for instruction*—No lessons plans were present on (give dates). Lesson plans provided on (give dates) lacked objectives or designation of materials to be used. Materials needed for the class (paper, books, bulletin board, math manipulative materials, and so on) were not present in the classroom.
- *Inadequate reinforcement of learning*—The teacher went on to the next subject (lesson) without providing follow-up (closure activity or homework).
- *Improper sequencing of activities during instruction*—Teacher began the lesson by directing students to "do" the exercise on page 10. After 10 minutes, teacher addressed students' confusion regarding how to do the exercise on page 10. Then the teacher explained how to do the exercise on page 10.
- *Failure to maintain classroom discipline*—Nine children chattered during teacher's presentation regarding topics unrelated to the lesson. Four children sat on their desks during the teacher's presentation. Six students were out of their seats while the teacher

gave directions. Of 23 students, 15 were not attending to the teacher's directions and were involved in activities unrelated to the lesson.

3. **Be from independent data sources.** Identical or similar data obtained from more than one source strengthen the case. Independently gathered data make it difficult for the teacher to charge that there was a personality clash or personal bias.

4. **Be credible and noncontradictory.** Evidence must be credible and noncontradictory. Believable, noncontradictory evidence from independent data sources is highly credible in court. Although you are responsible for the burden of proof, you need not bear the entire burden of collecting the data. In fact, your case will be greatly strengthened with the use of other evaluators. Call on other evaluators (expert retired administrators, principals, assistant superintendents, assistant principals) in your and other school districts. Collecting similar evaluation results from other evaluators (independent data sources) is the smart thing to do. Check your pride. Are you willing to call on others to strengthen your charges and test their accuracy? If you lean toward wanting to do it all by yourself, remember that evaluations from others will help you achieve your mission, which in this case is freeing the students in your school from incompetent teachers. If other trained observers disagree with your conclusions, maybe you are not on the right track. Our experience has shown that the accuracy of charges is strengthened by other trained evaluators.

5. **Be in support of dismissal as a reasonable consequence.** A final aspect of substantive due process is that the behavior must warrant the penalty of dismissal. Teacher evaluation procedures must delineate approved means for gathering and reporting data. Anecdotal approaches such as scripting the actual words of the

teachers and students and descriptions of teacher and student behavior and classroom climate are recommended. These data help districts win cases. Table 10.2 presents a list of typical sources for documentation.

Table 10.2   Sources for Documentation

Board Policies
Faculty Handbooks
Work Rules/Job Descriptions
Education Code, Government Code, Penal Code
Parent/Guardian Complaints
Student Complaints
Student Grades
Student Disciplinary Referrals
Substitute Evaluations
Oral Conferences, Employee Counseling
Written Conference Summaries
Incident Reports (Site File)
Written Reprimands
Direct Observation
Goals and Objectives
Classroom Observation
Performance Evaluations
Photographs
Employee-Prepared Material
Bargaining Contract

Copies of observation forms used by administrators in evaluation should be included in the documentation. It is important to document that *notification,* as well as descriptions of the required behavior change(s), are provided to the teacher.

Documents describing performance standards are critical in dismissal cases. Performance standards are used as minimum job performance standards as well as growth targets for teachers functioning satisfactorily. As much as we deplore checklists for evaluating teachers, we admit they can be indispensible in a dismissal proceeding. To be useful as a dismissal document, standards must be incorporated into a summative rating scale that reflects the full range of performance as illustrated in the following example:

M = Meets and/or exceeds district standards

P = In process

I = Unsatisfactory, not acceptable

Districts frequently use "needs improvement" rather than unsatisfactory or unacceptable. This rating fails to communicate the message accurately by downplaying the severity of the teacher's poor performance. Hearing commissions and judges do not interpret "needs to improve" as a severe problem. A rating of "unsatisfactory" cannot be misinterpreted.

The middle standard, "in process," is useful for people beginning to improve their performance but not yet meeting standards (e.g., a beginning teacher). The "meets and/or exceeds" rating is used mainly to discriminate between the satisfactorily functioning teacher and one in remediation. Such a rating, however, does not distinguish between superior and average performers. Teacher associations are generally loath to allow use of these categories because they are typically used to discriminate between teachers based on their performance in merit pay programs. Unless you are going to implement a merit program, we suggest that you avoid using categories that discriminate between average and superior classroom performers.

Although the summative rating scale of performance standards is necessary for all teachers, it is not an adequate guide for improvement of teaching. Additional evaluation processes such as a performance improvement plan must be included in teacher evaluation procedures for this purpose.

As principal and chief executive officer of your school, you must be competent in gathering data and documenting evidence. How do you rank yourself in these areas? As okay?

Lacking in confidence to do a top-notch job? Highly skilled? Competent? Depending on the situation, you may find that all of these fit you. If that's the case, you're having trouble seeing the big picture or you lack confidence. Here's a question that should give you a very accurate answer:

> Do I have sufficient confidence in my instructional, teacher observation, and documentation skills to hold up well in a cross-examination by experts?

If you do not respond with a hearty and confident *yes!* you're not ready to do the job that must be done.

Substantive Due Process Guideline 3:
Remediation and Resources

A third area that must be considered to meet substantive due process requirements includes remediation and resources. Teachers must be provided with the time (a remediation period) and the resources (i.e., opportunities for remediation) to remove the deficiencies. Guideline 3 addresses these issues.

Evaluation procedures should specify a period of time to improve: Forty-five working days is usually considered appropriate. In addition, adequate resources must be made available to the teacher to assist in eliminating the deficiencies. Comprehensive written evidence that time and adequate resource assistance were provided must be maintained. Three requirements, derived from court cases, apply to this guideline:

1. **Provide a reasonable time to improve.** It is not only reasonable but necessary that teachers be given *time to improve* when inadequate performance is the issue. A minimum recommended time period is 45 working days; however, more time could be provided if there is documented evidence that the teacher has improved and that additional time is likely to lead to further improvement. Remember that you and the district *must* provide the teacher time to improve. When the teacher

is not extended that right, and the teacher's legal counsel discovers this infraction, the district's case is likely to fail.

2. **Provide opportunities to improve, and make available resource assistance that matches the teacher's deficiencies.** School administrators have the legal obligation to *provide resource assistance.* The recruiting and induction process represents an investment by the district, and, for both moral and economic reasons, district personnel should determine whether deficiencies can be remediated before proceeding with the dismissal process.

3. **Provide adequate resource support.** A variety of resource assistance measures relative to the identified incompetency need to be made available. Workshops, readings, observation of proper classroom performance, critiques and guidance from a mentor teacher in the deficient teacher's classroom, observations with the principal, and conferences regarding deficiencies are just a few of the resources that can be made available to teachers.

The offer of resource assistance should be documented in a performance improvement plan. It is important that this plan not list resources the teacher is supposed to use, but rather resources made available to the teacher. The goal is for the teacher's behavior to change, not to use all the resources listed. Sometimes teachers in remediation confuse these two ideas and think that if they use all resources made available they will retain their jobs. Principals should be advocates for the teachers in providing necessary resources. Improvement in teaching performance is the goal, however, and must continually be the focus.

Staying Legal With Substantive
Due Process Requirements

Table 10.3 lists 16 questions you should ask yourself, to check your understanding of substantive due process. The questions listed under Guideline 1 above should be applied to all teachers in the school district. Questions for Guidelines 2 and 3 apply more directly to those teachers you suspect are marginal or inadequate. Use these questions to help you keep track of substantive due process requirements. Check them off as you complete them, and mark your calendar to accomplish those not yet completed.

Table 10.3   Understanding Substantive Due Process—A Self-Check

Substantive Due Process Guideline 1: Standards of Performance

Are the standards of performance	*YES*	*NO*
a. provided in board policy, teacher handbooks, job descriptions, and teacher evaluation instruments?		
b. based on research findings and/or expert advice?		
c. adequate, substantial, and comprehensive?		
d. clear, concise, and specific?		
e. attainable and ascertainable?		
f. related to job requirements and board policy and procedures?		
g. in line with state statutes and regulations?		

Substantive Due Process Guideline 2: Evidence and Documentation

Is your evidence and documentation	*YES*	*NO*
a. based on frequent (once per week minimum) observations?		
b. specific and supportable?		

(Continued)

Table 10.3 (Continued)

c. derived from independent sources (more
than one observer)?   _____   _____

d. credible and noncontradictory?   _____   _____

e. substantive enough to warrant dismissal?   _____   _____

**Substantive Due Process Guideline 3: Opportunities to Improve and
Resource Assistance**

Did you   YES   NO

a. provide the teacher with reasonable time to
improve?   _____   _____

b. make a variety of resources available that
match the teacher's deficiencies?   _____   _____

c. document the offer of resources in the
professional development plan or
elsewhere?   _____   _____

d. document your suggestion to use the
resources?   _____   _____

Guidelines for Ensuring
Procedural or Statutory Due Process

The courts have specified several procedures that must be
followed to ensure that a person's property right (right to a
livelihood) has not been denied. Courts have upheld these
rights for tenured teachers. The guidelines for meeting procedural due process are described below.

Procedural (Statutory) Due Process Guideline 1:
Notice of Deficiencies, Procedures, Rights

Two notices are required. The first, as discussed earlier, is
that all teachers must be informed of performance standards.

This type of notice is required in dismissal cases, and many states require districts to inform all teachers of this. The second notice required under procedural due process informs teachers of deficiencies and required changes.

Written administrative guidelines for dismissal delineate steps for developing the written notice, how to formulate the statement of deficiencies, timelines regarding the notice, and samples of written notices and how these are linked to the evaluation instrument. It is also suggested that written guidelines for conducting the conference in which notification is given and access to legal counsel be available for administrators to consult. Unfortunately, many dismissal cases never come to court because proper notice of deficiencies was not given.

Four criteria for assessing your adherence to Procedural Due Process Guideline 1 follow:

1. **Multiple warnings.** The necessity for multiple warnings has been demonstrated in court. It's really quite simple: When proof can be shown that warnings were given, courts have found in favor of the district. When proof cannot be shown, court rulings are in favor of the teacher.

2. **Written notices of deficiencies.** Notice of deficiencies must be in writing. It is suggested that the written notice include both the inappropriate behaviors and the desired behaviors. Include the following in the notice:
   - Guidelines for just cause (substantive due process)
   - The length of time provided for improvement to take place
   - Resource assistance to be provided or made available

   Sometimes principals separate the written resource assistance from the notice as part of a performance improvement plan (see Chapter 9).

3. **Warnings and notices closely related to the written formal evaluation process.** Following the remediation

period, if the teacher has not improved to a satisfactory level, notice must be given for dismissal or nonrenewal of contract, whichever applies. Both notices should be given following appropriate board action. In most cases, attorneys will advise the use of case numbers in board action rather than the teacher's name. It is further recommended that both dismissal and nonrenewal notices include the following:

- The written summative evaluation form
- The list of performance standards
- The statement of deficiencies (see Chapter 9 for further specifics)

These should be attached to the notice along with appropriate board policies, procedures, and other written directives.

4. **Follow timelines meticulously.** Often, cases are lost because district policy or state statutes that establish timelines for giving notices are not followed. Deliver a notice 2 days late, and you lose the case. Why? Because you did not meet a procedural due process requirement. This is where due process may seem to be excessive protection for teachers. Maybe so, but the requirements are clear and actually easy to meet. It's simply a matter of knowing you have to do it, scheduling it, and then doing it. The bottom line is this: Be on time with notices for tenured or probationary teachers, or both the students and you lose.

Deadlines for serving notices sometimes pass before we identify an incompetent teacher. Don't panic, but don't serve the notice. It's too late for this year. In this situation, administrators frequently just drop the finding or decide to "wait until next year" to notify teachers of deficiencies. This action is not justified from either a child advocacy or a teacher advocacy perspective. The child has a right to be taught by a competent teacher, and efforts to make the teacher aware of deficiencies and to make resources available should begin immediately.

Procedural Due Process Guideline 2:
The Right to a Hearing, Proper Notification

A second procedural due process right for most employees is the right to a hearing. Hearings are required before termination of tenured teachers because they have a property interest in the job.

Both district policy and the teacher evaluation procedures should delineate the process regarding the right to a hearing and conduct of a hearing. Court cases are clear about hearings. Administrators are responsible for

- providing a hearing to all those who have such right;
- providing a pretermination hearing in which the employee is given reasons for dismissal and the right to refute;
- providing a timely hearing for a proposed dismissal.

Although all tenured teachers have a right to a hearing, nontenured teachers typically do not. Such rights may be extended to them by the board or a negotiated agreement, however. Check these documents to determine whether additional rights have been established.

The courts have provided tenured teachers the right to a pretermination hearing to inform them of the charges and allow them an opportunity to refute them. The timeline of a hearing is important. Usually, there are written guidelines on the length of time a teacher has to appeal the dismissal. These timelines should be stated in policy and procedures as well as in the notice given to the teacher. Adhering to these timelines is crucial to dismissing an incompetent teacher.

The right to a hearing must be spelled out in detail in writing to the teacher. Such rights are usually given in the notice of dismissal with accompanying policy and teacher evaluation procedures guidelines. It is important to document that the teacher has been told of the his or her rights to a hearing both in the written notice and in a written summary of the conference in which this right was discussed with the teacher.

Procedural Due Process Guideline 3:
Formal Hearing Rights

Teachers have numerous rights within the hearing itself. Six are discussed below.

1. **Right to an unbiased hearing officer.** First and foremost, the teacher has the right to an *unbiased hearing officer.* District charges have been overruled by courts when it was shown that the board (hearing officers) held bias against the teacher. This is a sobering thought, since principals and superintendents generally share information regarding marginal teachers with the board so that boards are not caught by surprise when charges are issued. If the board is to serve as a hearing body, however, it is vitally important that the board only be apprised of legal, board policy, and collective bargaining agreements regarding the case. Sharing information regarding charges or situations relative to the charges with the board or individual board members may serve to "bias" them. This process varies from state to state. Some states provide an administrative judge or hearing officer to hear the case.

2. **Right to present evidence orally or in writing.** Teachers have a right to present evidence regarding their defense either orally or in writing. The teacher must be informed of these rights.

3. **Right to examine data.** Defendants have a right to examine data. In fact, employees have a right to examine their files and all information included therein, excluding information and ratings by identifiable personnel gathered during the hiring process. So the rule is that teachers have the right to examine information regarding them

and their case before, during, and after hearings. Failure to allow such examination could easily result in dismissal of the case on the grounds that the district prevented the teacher from exercising due process rights.

There are many criteria to be followed when conducting a hearing. These rights should be written in state statutes, board-adopted policy, the teacher contract, and teacher evaluation procedures. All administrators need to be apprised of these rights, and a person in the district should be designated to ensure that the rights are extended to teachers. So that you have nothing to hide, let the teacher (or other employee in question) examine the data. If you do, you can win the case. If you don't, you are likely to lose.

4. **Right to cross-examine witnesses and call witnesses.** The teacher has the right to confront and challenge all evidence against him or her, including written documents and testimony of adverse witnesses.

5. **Right to official written record of the hearing.** The teacher has the right to receive written record of the hearing, and you or the hearing officer is obliged to supply it.

6. **Right to appeal.** Tenured and probationary teachers have a right to appeal the verdict, as provided by state law.

Procedural Due Process Guideline 4:
Statutes, Board Policies, and Procedures

State statutes, board policies, and collective bargaining agreements often go beyond the constitutional requirements of due process. You, your superintendent, and/or your legal counsel should scour these documents for additional due process (substantive and procedural) provisions. It is important to remember that, as long as due process provisions remain on the books, *you must follow them* if you expect to be successful in weeding incompetent teachers out of your school.

Districts should incorporate all statutory and board policy requirements into their written teacher evaluation procedures and require that they be followed. As a principal, it is your responsibility to make sure that this is done. If a case you generated is lost due to failure to follow a due process requirement, you have no one to blame. It actually may have been the superintendent's fault, but saying so will appear to be scapegoating. Not only do you lose the case and the teacher stays in the classroom and on the payroll, but you also look foolish for projecting blame. The solution is to keep close contact with central office administrators in charge of such matters and demand that legal counsel be briefed and questioned frequently. Including the statutory provisions and board policy in the evaluation procedures may require negotiations with the teacher association or union.

Staying Legal With Procedural Due Process

A monitoring checklist is provided below in Table 10.4 to help you keep track of procedural due process requirements. All of the items in this checklist apply to teachers identified as marginal or inadequate. At the first sign that a teacher in your school may be marginal, refer to this list for things to be done. Some of these may seem inconsequential. To the contrary, noncompliance with any one of them can result in you and your school district losing a case. We hope that all items will be marked yes. If not, make your plan for getting them done and on time.

Table 10.4   Understanding Procedural Due Process—A Self-Check

Procedural Due Process Guideline 1: Standards of Performance		
Have the following timely and multiple notices been accomplished?	YES	NO
a. Intent to terminate and process to be followed?	_____	_____

b. Efficiencies and required changes? _____ _____

c. Notices and deficiencies tied to
evaluation process? _____ _____

d. Notices for a and b given on time and
more than once

For a and b? _____ _____

For a? _____ _____

For b? _____ _____

Procedural Due Process Guideline 2: Evidence and Documentation

Have the following been completed?   *YES*   *NO*

a. A pretermination hearing? _____ _____

b. A hearing per statutes and policy for
proposed dismissal? _____ _____

c. Statutory and policy timelines? _____ _____

d. Rules for hearing followed

For a and b? _____ _____

For a? _____ _____

For b? _____ _____

Procedural Due Process Guideline 3: Hearing Rights

*Have the following teacher rights been explained
and assured?*   *YES*   *NO*

a. Right to an unbiased hearing officer? _____ _____

b. Right to present evidence orally and in
writing? _____ _____

c. Right to examine data? _____ _____

d. Right to call witnesses and cross-
examine? _____ _____

(Continued)

Table 10.4 (Continued)

e. Right to a record of the hearing?   _____   _____

f. Right to appeal?   _____   _____

Procedural Due Process Guideline 4: Notice of Deficiencies

Have the following regarding statutory and policy requirements been completed?	*YES*	*NO*
a. Included in the teacher evaluation procedures?	_____	_____
b. Presented to all employees in teacher contracts?	_____	_____

DOCUMENTATION AND FILE BUILDING

To prevail in a dismissal case, you must be prepared with evidence to support your charges. This evidence is housed in the teacher's personnel file. Simply "knowing" that a teacher is incompetent and supplying personal testimonial to that effect are insufficient. All meetings, evaluations, and communiqués (e.g., directives) that take place during the four-phase progressive discipline process must be documented in writing. This documentation is the substance of your case and must be kept in the teacher's file. Don't allow yourself to "slip" it into a side drawer or "secret" file without also placing it in the teacher's personnel file; such practices are against the rules, and the documents cannot be used as evidence. Items such as the evaluation/observation schedule and working notes may be kept in the principal's file and are not subject to review by the teacher.

Writing complete memoranda takes some practice. There are four characteristics of a well-written disciplinary memo:

1. It is clear, direct, and relevant to the teacher and the issue at hand.

2. Content is based on factual information, not conclusions.

3. Content is detailed and specific.

4. Content contains no sarcasm, innuendo, or statements that signal a personality conflict.

5. All written content should be free of typographical, semantic, and grammatical errors. Written documents will be reviewed by a hearing officer. Criteria 2, 4, and 5 above require little interpretation. Fact is fact, and conclusion, sarcasm, and innuendo are easy to spot, as are typographical, semantic, and grammatical errors. Consequently, we will not discuss these criteria further. On the other hand, requirements 1 and 3 are not as easy. These are addressed below.

Criterion 1: Clear, Direct, and "to the Point" Versus Veiled and "Sugarcoated"

Education is a helping profession, and we're proud of it. As a result, some of us are very reluctant to "write it like it is." Instead, we are known for beating around the bush, equivocating, mollycoddling, and practicing other forms of avoidance behaviors. We like to think that being nice will help soothe the teacher's feelings and help him or her to improve. The opposite is true. Being frank, to the point, and polite is helpful because the teacher receives an honest message and can then deal with it. Veiled messages are difficult to interpret and leave the teacher in a quandary, unsure of what the problem really is, and without an opportunity to improve. Problems must be met head-on. We must face the brutal facts. Consider the case of a teacher who is experiencing problems maintaining classroom discipline. The veiled and indirect message might be this: "Could benefit from additional workshops in classroom discipline." The problem here is that nearly all teachers can benefit from additional study, so what is different about this teacher? The difference is that this teacher's current practice is *inadequate*. As we discussed earlier in this chapter, this deserves a direct and clear statement such as this: "Classroom discipline is inadequate." We cannot expect teachers to improve their performance unless we give direct and clear information about their deficiencies and suggest strategies for improvement.

Criterion 3: Detailed and Specific Content

For the message to be effective, you must document forthrightly. The following is a set of very useful guidelines. They have been proved effective over time—follow them:

- Be specific rather than general. Precision and directness are paramount.
- Be clear and direct rather than circumspect. Bureaucratic, humanistic generalities are fatal. Plain English should be used. Remember—this will be read by a hearing officer.
- Set forth the facts forming the basis for the conclusion: Include names of witnesses, dates, times, and all other relevant facts. Avoid general summaries, conclusions, and judgments without the supporting facts.
- Remember, it is not what you know that counts but what you can prove. This means you must review all documents for typographical, semantic, and grammatical errors and correct them. If it isn't written, you can't prove it happened (Marquand, 1997).

Once we have a direct and clear statement such as the one above, the next step is to make it detailed and specific. Making detailed statements is simply a matter of practice. Consider the teacher who is experiencing classroom discipline problems. Typical detailed and specific statements follow in Figure 10.1.

Figure 10.1   Sample Memo Language to Teacher About
                   Observed Inadequate Classroom Discipline

Concern: Classroom Discipline Is Inadequate

Your classroom discipline during September, October, and November
has been inadequate as illustrated below and described in your formative evaluations for the same dates.

Inadequate Practice	Date
1. Six students were talking while you gave directions.	9-21-12
2. Two students were in the sleeping posture during class.	9-25-12
3. Five students were out of their seats and not attending to the lesson.	9-28-12

After specifying and communicating the problems, the
next task is to direct the teacher to resources and activities
that may help remedy the problems. Understanding the difference between a suggestion and clear direction is important at this point. The following is a list of clear directions
to teachers.

1. Complete the following by Friday, October 26, 2012:

   (list tasks)

2. Attend the Friday, October 26, classroom management
   workshop at the county office, and on Monday, October
   29, submit to me the learned techniques you plan to
   institute to address the problems of classroom management I discussed with you.

3. Submit to me every Monday morning by 7 AM your lesson plans for maintaining adequate classroom management as outlined in our teacher handbook.

In contrast, the following "directions" are merely suggestions or questions, rather than clear directions:

1. It is clear that you are a fine teacher, but you're having a little difficulty right now. Why don't you read Marzano's new book?

2. I insist that you consider the following practices:

(list practices)

The Formal Disciplinary Memo

Disciplinary memos must contain specific items of information. They should be neat, errorless (including spelling, punctuation, and grammar), and typed on your school's letterhead. The memo also should be clearly written and free of confusing educational jargon. The FRISK (Andelson, 2001) model for developing documentation is very helpful and has proven effective in court cases. FRISK is an acronym for Facts, Rules, Impact, Suggestions, and Knowledge. The following table presents the crucial elements of FRISK-style documentation.

Table 10.5   FRISK Checklist for Writing a Disciplinary Memo

Heading of Memo	*(FACTS)*

1. Who is it directed to?

2. Who prepared it?

3. The date prepared

4. The subject

Necessary Information to Be Included in Body of Memo

5. When did it happen?

6 Where did it occur?

Heading of Memo	*(FACTS)*
7 What happened?	
8. Why did it happen? (employee's explanation)	
9. What is wrong? Or what rule was violated?	**(RULES)**
10. Impact: What is the actual impact of the violation on the instructional program?	**(IMPACT)**
11. Visibility and notoriety of conduct	
12. What should the employee do (directives, resource assistance, suggestions, remediation plan)?	**(SUGGESTIONS)**
13. What will happen if they do not follow directives in item 12?	**(KNOWLEDGE)**
14. Right to respond to memo placed in personnel file	

It is crucial to include all of these elements in any communiqué to a teacher in question. These include letters of reprimand, conference summaries, performance notices, and directives. The worksheet presented in Table 10.6 is from the 2001 FRISK Manual (Andelson, 2001). It serves as a handy reminder of critical elements to address in communiqués to marginal teachers.

Giving directions for corrective action is the principal's responsibility. As we stressed earlier in this chapter, the statements must be very direct and clear. Here are a few unacceptable leadoff phrases:

- Please respond by . . .
- I think you should . . .
- You must be concerned about . . .

Table 10.6   Sample FRISK Worksheet and Reference Guide

Components	Notes (Use this column for writing your questions, observations, and "to do" list.)
FACTS "What did the employee do?" • Be specific. • Be explicit. • Be accurate (do not embellish).	Pinpoint the specific conduct, and describe the conduct in complete and explicit terms. If necessary, supplement general statements with specific examples to provide a proper factual foundation.
RULES "What should the employee have done?" Include the standard, authority, or mandate that the employee is expected to follow.	Include the rule, authority, or expectation relating to the deficient performance, such as board policies or administrative regulations, labor contract provisions, adopted curriculum, administrative directives, education code sections, recognized professional standards, *and* include prior same-rule violations.
IMPACT "What is the negative impact or possible impact of the employee's conduct on the district or school or student, etc.?"	Include facts that describe the negative or adverse effect of the employee's conduct on the district, other employees, students, and parents.
SUGGESTIONS/DIRECTIONS "What do you want the employee to do to improve the deficient performance?" • Give clear and unequivocal direction. • Give suggestions to assist.	Include clear and unequivocal directions on the proper conduct you expect the employee to follow, the timelines and the consequences if the employee fails to comply, *and* include suggestions for improvement.

KNOWLEDGE	Include language notifying the
"Does the employee have knowledge of the document and the right to respond?" • Specify date for response.	employee of the right to file a response to a derogatory document prior to the document's placement in the personnel file.

Source: Andelson (2001), *FRISK Documentation Model,* Cerritos, CA: Atkinson, Andelson, Loya, Ruud, & Romo. Reprinted by permission from S. Andelson.

Compare these to the following acceptable, clear leadoff phrases. Note the highly directive presentation and the clarity:

- Return the . . . to me by 10 AM on May 10, 2012.
- Turn in your complete improvement plan to me by . . .
- I will be in your classroom at 9 AM on May 14, 2012. This is your mathematics instruction hour. Please use the [specific] instructional technique as presented in our April 2 professional development program. I will conduct a formal observation consistent with the teacher contract provisions.

The Phase-3 Decision

Following documentation and provision of resource assistance, you must decide if the teacher has improved sufficiently to meet requirements or not. The decision to stop the process or to move on to Phase 3 is described in detail in Chapter 9 and Figure 9.2. This process, including official board action and notification, must be made on the basis of the extent to which improvement in performance has been achieved and documented, not perceptions of the degree to which the teacher has "tried." Trying is important, but it is a distant second to actually demonstrating competence in using strategies that result in student learning. If sufficient improvement has not been made as stated in the performance plan, the decision to move to Phase 3 must be made. It is crucial that the principal and district meet all obligations—such as meeting deadlines and providing assistance to the teacher.

The Phase 3 decision should be discussed with the appropriate district administrators and reviewed by legal counsel before presenting an official communiqué to the teacher.

Determining Access to Personnel Files

Personnel files are confidential. Only the teacher and authorized administrators are granted access to the file. Laws regarding use of files vary from state to state, but common elements are as follows:

- Notice, either verbal or written, must be given to the teacher prior to placing derogatory information in the file.
- The teacher must be informed of his or her right to respond to such information before it is placed in the file.
- The teacher must have the opportunity to gather information in his or her defense prior to reaching a decision regarding the teacher's employment status.
- Information must be sufficiently current so that the teacher has a reasonable chance to refute it.

Teachers have the right to inspect their personnel files in the presence of an administrator with the following exceptions:

- Information gained during the hiring process
- When the request is to review the files during a time the teacher is required to render service

Confronting the failure of a teacher to perform adequately is uncomfortable. However, it is essential to the success of a school. Our experience over the years tells us that the vast majority of teachers support and appreciate strong, committed, professional leaders who demand excellent teaching. Moreover, they applaud the leader who takes action when action is required. The key is to do it right. Follow the rules, and maintain a professional posture. The reward is a more effective school.

ALTERNATIVES TO THE DISMISSAL PROCESS

Alternatives to conducting all four phases of the progressive process are presented below, but none includes the option of leaving an incompetent teacher in the classroom. They all accomplish the required end of removing the incompetent teacher from contact with students.

Reassignment

Large districts may have non-classroom positions for which the incompetent teacher is qualified and can perform adequately. This is another example of the "dance of the lemons." The education profession and students have suffered from its use with incompetent teachers and administrators. If the teacher's skills and abilities match those required by the position, the reassignment is valid. If it is a way of avoiding biting the bullet, it is not valid. Reassigning incompetent teachers and administrators to new positions where their performance also is inadequate has given this alternative a black eye. Use only where appropriate.

A Settlement or Buy-Out

Terminating a tenured teacher or dismissing a temporary teacher costs money and taxes the energy of personnel. A settlement can serve both the teacher and the district. Teachers gain severance funds and/or other benefits and avoid the embarrassment of going through the process and having a record of the process in their personnel files.

Recent tenure dismissal cases have cost districts up to as much as $300,000 apiece. Reeder (2005) reported that the average cost of a teacher dismissal in Illinois between 2001 and 2005 was $219,504. Buy-outs, on the other hand, typically cost around $40,000.

Buy-outs can take many forms. The teacher may simply resign for a price or may take early retirement in the form of a tarnished golden handshake. Teachers seldom want to choose the termination process, have their names in the paper, and have the charges in their files. This is particularly true in the case of nonrenewal of nontenured teachers where there is little or no hope that they could win the case. To avoid the charges and keep the files clean, resignation or a settlement in exchange for a resignation are good alternatives.

First, settlement in exchange for a resignation does not require the extensive efforts involved in the dismissal procedure and therefore requires much less time. Second, this option is useful in cases where the district's argument is valid but, for whatever reason, may be in jeopardy at the hearing level, or where the district would prefer to avoid the publicity generated by the process. Third, teacher associations are publicly critical of the administration but privately supportive of the arrangements in 88 percent of the cases (Scott, 1991).

The buy-out alternative may appear to be the "wimp's" way out, but it is not. It is, in most cases, the smart way out. Granted, giving benefit to an incompetent who refuses to improve or cannot improve is unseemly. However, saving the district large amounts of money, saving yourself and many others large amounts of time, avoiding time- and money-consuming confrontation with the teacher association, and still terminating employment of the teacher are respectable advantages. Buy-out can be the smart alterative.

It is reasonable to expect that any administrator reading this chapter has contemplated these weary queries: Is it worth it? Does it work? Can we really dismiss incompetent but tenured teachers? Today, the answer is yes. Managing the marginal or incompetent teacher takes time, taxes emotions, induces psychological stress, and engenders feelings of self-doubt and guilt on the part of both the administrator and the teacher. It is no wonder that many principals have avoided confronting these teachers. But yes, it can be done and it is worth it, for many good reasons. Weeding out the incompetent teachers will have an immediate impact on the quality of the school, such as in improved test scores, and will result in greater respect from the public. The teacher is the most important factor in the education process, and it is the MBWA administrator's responsibility to put the very best teachers available in contact with students.

Epilogue

Accepting Your Fate or Creating Your Destiny

The Choice of Leadership

A n ancient Eastern proverb declares that man can accept his fate or create his destiny. So can schools. Leadership is a choice between waiting for problems or pursuing goals, between being passive and reactive or being proactive and creative. School Management by Wandering Around is an approach to leadership based on the belief that leadership is visionary, goal focused, and people centered. It assumes improvement to a school, a classroom, or a personal leadership attribute is a lifelong journey. It is not aimless meandering. Rather, it is purposeful involvement with people to promote school improvement.

MBWA is both diagnostic and prescriptive. Wandering around provides living data about who and what needs strengthening and support. Prescriptively, it is an opportunity to model desired behavior and reinforce people doing things right. MBWA isn't as much an open-door philosophy as a window into the classroom, school, and community. It is leadership that creates opportunity by searching out needs and creating alternatives rather than waiting for problems and hoping for solutions. It is precisely what is needed to tackle the challenges facing the public schools of the 21st century.

MBWA school administrators know that tomorrow will come, and rather than wait for events to dictate what tomorrow brings, they initiate action to create the future they want. The choice is always theirs to make. Children can learn, teachers can teach, and principals can lead, if they choose to do so.

Resource A

Elementary School
Parent Survey

Several areas of interest have been identified in the question-naire below. We would like to have an indication of your feel-ings about these areas and the importance you attach to them. In the center of the page is a series of statements. Please indi-cate your agreement or disagreement that each statement is true of _____ School *today* by marking the scale to the left. On the right of each statement, please indicate the impor-tance you attach to it. Each statement should have two responses. Space has been provided for your comments and suggestions below each section.

Please circle the grade(s) that your child/children attend.

K   1   2   3   4   5   6

A Strongly Agree

B Agree

C Disagree

D Strongly Disagree

E Lack Info to Respond

1 Very Important

2 Important

3 Somewhat Important

4 Not Important

DO I AGREE OR DISAGREE WITH THIS STATEMENT?

HOW IMPORTANT IS THIS AREA TO ME?

COMMUNICATION:		
A B C D E	1. The school communicates clearly its rules and standards of behavior to parents.	1 2 3 4
A B C D E	2. The school keeps parents informed of school activities.	1 2 3 4
A B C D E	3. Students have the opportunity to communicate their interests and concerns to teachers.	1 2 3 4
A B C D E	4. Teachers keep students informed of their progress.	1 2 3 4
A B C D E	5. Parents are encouraged to discuss their children's problems with teachers.	1 2 3 4
	6. The following types of communication between home and school work well to keep parents informed:	
A B C D E	(a) What-to-Expect-Night	1 2 3 4
A B C D E	(b) Teacher Notes and Phone Calls	1 2 3 4
A B C D E	(c) Report Cards	1 2 3 4
A B C D E	(d) Parent–Teacher Conference	1 2 3 4
A B C D E	(e) Open House	1 2 3 4
A B C D E	(f) The Thursday Bulletin	1 2 3 4

Comments:

_____

_____

_____

_____

_____

**DO I AGREE OR DISAGREE   HOW IMPORTANT IS
WITH THIS STATEMENT?   THIS AREA TO ME?**

STUDENT BEHAVIOR		
A B C D E	1. Students in our school are generally respectful of each other.	1 2 3 4
A B C D E	2. Most students and teachers in our school maintain good working relationships.	1 2 3 4
A B C D E	3. Our school is doing a good job of helping my child understand his/her responsibilities as a student.	1 2 3 4
A B C D E	4. Our school helps my child to understand and get along with other people.	1 2 3 4
A B C D E	5. Discipline is not a serious problem in our school.	1 2 3 4
A B C D E	6. Our school places appropriate emphasis on the social development of my child.	1 2 3 4
A B C D E	7. My child looks forward to school each day.	1 2 3 4
A B C D E	8. The overall morale of students in our school is good.	1 2 3 4
A B C D E	9. School rules and regulations affecting my child are reasonable.	1 2 3 4

(Continued)

257

(Continued)

Comments:
_____
_____
_____
_____
_____

**DO I AGREE OR DISAGREE
WITH THIS STATEMENT?**

**HOW IMPORTANT IS
THIS AREA TO ME?**

CURRICULUM		
	1. The following curricular areas are meeting our students' needs:	
A B C D E	(a) Spelling	1 2 3 4
A B C D E	(b) Grammar	1 2 3 4
A B C D E	(c) Written Composition	1 2 3 4
A B C D E	(d) Creative Writing	1 2 3 4
A B C D E	(e) Reading	1 2 3 4
A B C D E	(f) Social Studies	1 2 3 4
A B C D E	(g) Science	1 2 3 4
A B C D E	(h) Mathematics	1 2 3 4
A B C D E	(i) Foreign Language	1 2 3 4
A B C D E	(j) Physical Education	1 2 3 4
A B C D E	(k) Music	1 2 3 4
A B C D E	(l) Art	1 2 3 4
A B C D E	(m) Library	1 2 3 4
A B C D E	(n) Computer	1 2 3 4

	2. Students with special needs are receiving appropriate services in the following areas:	
A B C D E	(a) Health	1 2 3 4
A B C D E	(b) Counseling	1 2 3 4
A B C D E	(c) Resource/Learning Problems	1 2 3 4
A B C D E	(d) Speech and Language	1 2 3 4
A B C D E	(e) Challenge/Gifted	1 2 3 4
A B C D E	3. Children have adequate equipment, materials, and supplies available at school.	1 2 3 4
	4. The school devotes appropriate time to cultural enrichment through	
A B C D E	(a) Assemblies.	1 2 3 4
A B C D E	(b) Field Trips.	1 2 3 4

Comments:

_____

_____

_____

_____

_____

DO I AGREE OR DISAGREE WITH THIS STATEMENT?   **HOW IMPORTANT IS THIS AREA TO ME?**

TEACHERS AND INSTRUCTION		
A B C D E	1. Teachers in our school are concerned about my child as an individual.	1 2 3 4

(Continued)

(Continued)

A B C D E	2. Our teachers appropriately emphasize developing critical thinking skills, i.e., problem solving, estimating, analyzing, etc.	1 2 3 4
A B C D E	3. Our teachers are competent.	1 2 3 4
A B C D E	4. Our school provides my child with opportunities to reach full potential.	1 2 3 4
A B C D E	5. Our school places proper emphasis on grading.	1 2 3 4
A B C D E	6. Our school pursues innovative instructional methods.	1 2 3 4
A B C D E	7. It is easy to make appointments to see teachers in our school.	1 2 3 4
A B C D E	8. My child receives the personal attention needed in the classroom from his/her teachers.	1 2 3 4
A B C D E	9. Homework assignments are meaningful.	1 2 3 4
	10. The amount of homework is	
A B C D E	(a) Too much.	1 2 3 4
A B C D E	(b) Too little.	1 2 3 4
A B C D E	(c) Enough.	1 2 3 4
A B C D E	11. Teachers utilize a variety of methods to teach students.	1 2 3 4

Comments:

_____

_____

_____

_____

_____

DO I AGREE OR DISAGREE WITH THIS STATEMENT?		HOW IMPORTANT IS THIS AREA TO ME?

ADMINISTRATION		
	1. Class size is	
A B C D E	(a) Too large.	1 2 3 4
A B C D E	(b) Too small.	1 2 3 4
A B C D E	(c) About right.	1 2 3 4
A B C D E	2. Custodial service is adequate.	1 2 3 4
	3. The school is well-maintained with regard to	
A B C D E	(a) Buildings.	1 2 3 4
A B C D E	(b) Grounds.	1 2 3 4
A B C D E	(c) Equipment.	1 2 3 4
A B C D E	4. The present bus service meets the needs of students.	1 2 3 4
A B C D E	5. The principal continually strives to improve the effectiveness of our school.	1 2 3 4
A B C D E	6. The principal is available to listen to parent concerns.	1 2 3 4
A B C D E	7. The principal is visible.	1 2 3 4
A B C D E	8. Students perceive the principal in a positive light.	1 2 3 4
A B C D E	9. The PTA is an effective parent organization.	1 2 3 4

(Continued)

(Continued)

Comments:

_____

_____

_____

_____

_____

Source: From *School Management by Wandering Around*, by L. Frase and R. Hetzel, 2003, Lancaster, PA: Technomic Publishing Company. Copyright by Scarecrow Press, Inc. Reprinted with permission.

Resource B

Secondary School
Parent Survey

1. Students in our school are generally respectful of each other.

   A. Strongly Agree

   B. Agree

   C. Don't know

   D. Disagree

   E. Strongly Disagree

2. Most students and teachers in our school maintain good working relationships.

   A. Strongly Agree

   B. Agree

   C. Don't know

   D. Disagree

   E. Strongly Disagree

3. Substance abuse in our school is not a serious problem.

   A. Strongly Agree

   B. Agree

   C. Don't know

D. Disagree

E. Strongly Disagree

4. Decisions made by our school reflect the concerns of parents.

   A. Strongly Agree

   B. Agree

   C. Don't know

   D. Disagree

   E. Strongly Disagree

5. Our school is doing a good job of helping my child understand his/her responsibilities as a student.

   A. Strongly Agree

   B. Agree

   C. Don't know

   D. Disagree

   E. Strongly Disagree

6. Teachers in our school are concerned about my child as an individual.

   A. Strongly Agree

   B. Agree

   C. Don't know

   D. Disagree

   E. Strongly Disagree

7. Our school helps my child understand and get along with other people.

   A. Strongly Agree

   B. Agree

   C. Don't know

D. Disagree

E. Strongly Disagree

8. Discipline is not a serious problem in our school.

    A. Strongly Agree

    B. Agree

    C. Don't know

    D. Disagree

    E. Strongly Disagree

9. Reports from our school concerning my child's progress are helpful.

    A. Strongly Agree

    B. Agree

    C. Don't know

    D. Disagree

    E. Strongly Disagree

10. Theft is not a serious problem in our school.

    A. Strongly Agree

    B. Agree

    C. Don't know

    D. Disagree

    E. Strongly Disagree

11. Our school places appropriate emphasis on the social development of my child.

    A. Strongly Agree

    B. Agree

    C. Don't know

    D. Disagree

    E. Strongly Disagree

12. Our school's physical plant is well-maintained.

    A. Strongly Agree

    B. Agree

    C. Don't know

    D. Disagree

    E. Strongly Disagree

13. Our teachers appropriately emphasize developing critical thinking skills, that is, problem solving, analyzing, and so on.

    A. Strongly Agree

    B. Agree

    C. Don't know

    D. Disagree

    E. Strongly Disagree

14. Our teachers are competent.

    A. Strongly Agree

    B. Agree

    C. Don't know

    D. Disagree

    E. Strongly Disagree

15. Our school provides my child with opportunities to reach full potential.

    A. Strongly Agree

    B. Agree

    C. Don't know

    D. Disagree

    E. Strongly Disagree

16. Cheating is not a serious problem in our school.

    A. Strongly Agree

    B. Agree

C. Don't know

D. Disagree

E. Strongly Disagree

17. Our school places proper emphasis on grading.

    A. Strongly Agree

    B. Agree

    C. Don't know

    D. Disagree

    E. Strongly Disagree

18. Our school pursues innovative instructional methods.

    A. Strongly Agree

    B. Agree

    C. Don't know

    D. Disagree

    E. Strongly Disagree

19. Our school's extracurricular activities program is sufficient to meet the needs of my child.

    A. Strongly Agree

    B. Agree

    C. Don't know

    D. Disagree

    E. Strongly Disagree

20. Student participation in extracurricular activities is an important aspect of education at our school.

    A. Strongly Agree

    B. Agree

    C. Don't know

    D. Disagree

    E. Strongly Disagree

21. The services provided by our school's counselors are supportive of my child's present needs.

    A. Strongly Agree

    B. Agree

    C. Don't know

    D. Disagree

    E. Strongly Disagree

22. Our school's health services are adequate.

    A. Strongly Agree

    B. Agree

    C. Don't know

    D. Disagree

    E. Strongly Disagree

23. Transportation services provided by our school meet my child's needs.

    A. Strongly Agree

    B. Agree

    C. Don't know

    D. Disagree

    E. Strongly Disagree

24. Vandalism is not a serious problem at our school.

    A. Strongly Agree

    B. Agree

    C. Don't know

    D. Disagree

    E. Strongly Disagree

25. My child looks forward to going to school each day.

    A. Strongly Agree

    B. Agree

C. Don't know

D. Disagree

E. Strongly Disagree

26. The overall morale of students in our school is good.

    A. Strongly Agree

    B. Agree

    C. Don't know

    D. Disagree

    E. Strongly Disagree

27. It is easy to make appointments to see teachers in our school.

    A. Strongly Agree

    B. Agree

    C. Don't know

    D. Disagree

    E. Strongly Disagree

28. The principal continually strives to improve the effectiveness of our school.

    A. Strongly Agree

    B. Agree

    C. Don't know

    D. Disagree

    E. Strongly Disagree

29. The principal is available to listen to parent concerns.

    A. Strongly Agree

    B. Agree

    C. Don't know

    D. Disagree

    E. Strongly Disagree

30. My child receives the personal attention needed in the classroom from his/her teachers.

A. Strongly Agree

B. Agree

C. Don't know

D. Disagree

E. Strongly Disagree

31. School rules and regulations affecting my child are reasonable.

A. Strongly Agree

B. Agree

C. Don't know

D. Disagree

E. Strongly Disagree

32. The electives offered at our school are sufficient to meet the needs of my child.

A. Strongly Agree

B. Agree

C. Don't know

D. Disagree

E. Strongly Disagree

33. I have children in the following grades:

☐ 7th Grade

☐ 8th Grade

☐ 9th Grade

☐ 10th Grade

☐ 11th Grade

☐ 12th Grade

34. Rate by placing a check mark (✓) in the column that best represents your opinion concerning the quality of each of the following programs at our school:

	Poor	Fair	Average	Good	Excellent	Don't Know
Art						
Music						
P.E.						
Reading						
Math						
Science						
Social Studies						
English						
Foreign Languages						
Drama						
Counseling						
Career/Technology Education						
Other: _____						

Source: *From School Management by Wandering Around*, by L. Frase and R. Hetzel, 2003, Lancaster, PA: Technomic Publishing Company. Copyright by Scarecrow Press, Inc. Reprinted with permission.

Resource C

Summative Teacher Performance Evaluation

Teacher's Name _____ Date _____

Grade/Subject _____

<table>
<tr><td colspan="4">PERFORMANCE AREA I: EFFECTIVE LESSON PLANNING</td></tr>
<tr><td>CRITERIA</td><td colspan="3">LEVELS OF PERFORMANCE</td></tr>
<tr>
<td>A. Demonstrates effective instructional planning skills

___ Not observed</td>
<td>___ Inadequate

Does not demonstrate evidence of effective planning.</td>
<td>___ Targeted for improvement

Needs to improve how the evidence of planning is demonstrated.</td>
<td>___ Professionally proficient

Demonstrates evidence of effective planning.</td>
</tr>
<tr><td colspan="4">Comments:

</td></tr>
<tr>
<td>B. Selects appropriate objectives.

___ Not observed</td>
<td>___ Inadequate

Does not select appropriate objectives.</td>
<td>___ Targeted for improvement</td>
<td>___ Professionally proficient</td>
</tr>
</table>

(Continued)

		Needs to select appropriate objectives more consistently.	Consistently selects objectives that are appropriate for the topic and students.
Comments:			
C. Assesses student learning. ___ Not observed	___ Inadequate Does not assess student learning.	___ Targeted for improvement Needs to improve upon assessing student learning.	___ Professionally proficient Systematically assesses student learning and uses the data for instructional planning.
Comments:			

PERFORMANCE AREA II: EFFECTIVE CLASSROOM MANAGEMENT			
CRITERIA	*LEVELS OF PERFORMANCE*		
A. Establishes and reinforces high standards for student discipline. ___ Not observed	___ Inadequate Does not establish/ reinforce high standards for student discipline.	___ Targeted for improvement Needs to improve how standards for student discipline are established/ reinforced.	___ Professionally proficient Establishes and reinforces high standards for student discipline in the classroom.

Comments:			

B. Maximizes student time-on-task. ___ Not observed	___ Inadequate Does not use techniques that maximize student time-on-task.	___ Targeted for improvement Needs to improve in using techniques that maximize student time-on-task.	___ Professionally proficient Uses techniques that maximize student time-on-task.

Comments:			

PERFORMANCE AREA III: EFFECTIVE TEACHING PRACTICES			
CRITERIA	*LEVELS OF PERFORMANCE*		
A. Teaches to the objective. ___ Not observed	___ Inadequate Does not teach to objective.	___ Targeted for improvement Needs to improve upon teaching to the objective.	___ Professionally proficient Teacher actions are congruent with the objective.

Comments:			

B. Monitors and adjusts instruction. ___ Not observed	___ Inadequate Does not monitor and	___ Targeted for improvement	___ Professionally proficient

(Continued)

	adjust instruction.	Needs to improve upon monitoring and adjusting instruction.	Consistently monitors and adjusts instruction.
Comments:			
C. Communicates and reinforces high expectations for student achievement. ___ Not observed	___ Inadequate Does not communicate and reinforce high expectations for student achievement.	___ Targeted for improvement Needs to improve upon communicating and reinforcing high expectations for student achievement.	___ Professionally proficient Consistently communicates and reinforces high expectations for student achievement.
Comments:			
D. Demonstrates the ability to motivate students. ___ Not observed	___ Inadequate Does not demonstrate ability to motivate students.	___ Targeted for improvement Needs to improve ability to motivate students.	___ Professionally proficient Demonstrates ability to motivate students.
Comments:			
E. Effectively reinforces learning through the use of	___ Inadequate	___ Targeted for improvement	___ Professionally proficient

appropriate practice. ___ Not observed	Does not effectively reinforce learning through appropriate practice.	Needs to improve effective reinforcement of learning through appropriate practice.	Effectively reinforces learning through the use of appropriate practice.
Comments:			
F. Demonstrates effective lesson presentation skills. ___ Not observed	___ Inadequate Does not demonstrate effective lesson presentation skills.	___Targeted for improvement Needs to improve lesson presentation skills.	___Professionally proficient Uses effective lesson presentation skills.
Comments:			

PERFORMANCE AREA IV: POSITIVE INTERPERSONAL RELATIONS			
CRITERIA	*LEVELS OF PERFORMANCE*		
A. Demonstrates effective interpersonal relations with parents. ___ Not observed	___ Inadequate Does not demonstrate effective interpersonal relations with parents.	___ Targeted for improvement Needs to improve interpersonal relations with parents.	___ Professionally proficient Demonstrates effective interpersonal relations with parents.
Comments:			

(Continued)

(Continued)

B. Demonstrates effective interpersonal relations with colleagues, administrators, and other support personnel. ___ Not observed	___ Inadequate Does not demonstrate effective interpersonal relations with colleagues, administration, and other support personnel.	___ Targeted for improvement Needs to improve interpersonal relations with colleagues, administration, and other support personnel.	___ Professionally proficient Demonstrates effective interpersonal relations with colleagues, administration, and other support personnel.
Comments:			
C. Demonstrates interpersonal skills in relating to students. ___ Not observed	___ Inadequate Does not Demonstrate effective interpersonal skills in relating to students.	___ Targeted for improvement Needs to improve interpersonal skills in relating to students.	___ Professionally proficient Demonstrates effective interpersonal skills in relating to students.
Comments:			
D. Actively uses techniques to build positive student self-esteem. ___ Not observed	___ Inadequate Does not use techniques to build positive student self-esteem.	___ Targeted for improvement Inconsistently uses techniques to build positive student self-esteem.	___ Professionally proficient Actively uses techniques to build positive student self-esteem.

Comments:			

PERFORMANCE AREA V: PROFESSIONAL RESPONSIBILITY

CRITERIA	LEVELS OF PERFORMANCE		
A. Demonstrates employee responsibility. ___ Not observed	___ Inadequate Does not demonstrate employee responsibility.	___ Targeted for improvement Needs to consistently demonstrate employee responsibility.	___ Professionally proficient Demonstrates employee responsibility.
Comments:			
B. Pursues professional growth. ___ Not observed	___ Inadequate Does not pursue professional growth.	___ Targeted for improvement Needs to improve upon how professional growth is pursued.	___ Professionally proficient Pursues professional growth.
Comments:			

TEACHER EVALUATION TIMELINE

Planning Conference	Observation _____ Post-conference _____

(Continued)

(Continued)

Formal Observations	Observation _____ Post-conference _____
Other Observations	_____
Summative Conference	_____
Professional Growth Plan Due	_____

Signature indicates that the teacher and evaluator have reviewed and discussed the evaluation report. (A summary statement from either the teacher or the evaluator is optional.)

Teacher's Signature _____	Date _____
Evaluator's Signature _____	Date _____

OPTIONAL COMMENTS:

White Copy—Personnel

Yellow Copy—Evaluator

Pink Copy—Teacher

Source: *From School Management by Wandering Around*, by L. Frase and R. Hetzel, 2003, Lancaster, PA: Technomic Publishing Company. Copyright by Scarecrow Press, Inc. Reprinted with permission.

Resource D

Teacher Self-Assessment Inventory of Skills and Interests

INTERPERSONAL COMMUNICATION

1. Learning strategies for communicating to the community

2. Communicating and interacting with parents

3. Knowing when and where to refer student problems

4. Developing strategies to successfully involve classroom assistants

5. Initiating and building professional relationships with colleagues

6. Resolving teacher–administrator differences in a positive and effective manner

7. Other

DEVELOPING PUPIL SELF-ESTEEM

8. Facilitating pupil self-concept and worth

9. Facilitating pupil social interaction

10. Instilling in the student the will to learn on his/her own initiative

11. Other

INDIVIDUALIZING INSTRUCTION

12. Assessing and selecting appropriate materials and activities for individualized instruction

13. Creating and developing materials and learning options

14. Implementing and supervising individualized instruction

15. Other

ASSESSMENT

16. Coping with the task of evaluating and communicating student progress

17. Selecting and specifying performance goals and objectives

18. Establishing appropriate performance standards

19. Constructing and using tests for evaluating academic progress

20. Involving students in self-evaluation

21. Diagnosing basic learning difficulties

22. Identifying students with disabilities who need referral or special remedial work

23. Other

DISCIPLINE

24. Using methods of classroom discipline at appropriate times

25. Maintaining classroom control without appearing as an ogre to students

26. Identifying student attitudes as an aid to solving problems in and out of the classroom

27. Other

DEVELOPING PERSONAL AND PROFESSIONAL HELP

28. Evaluating your instructional methods and procedures.

29. Developing or modifying instructional procedures to suit your own strengths

30. Developing a personal self-evaluation method

31. Developing a greater capacity for accepting others' feelings

32. Other

ORGANIZING FOR INSTRUCTION

33. Using alternative methods in school organization—multiage grouping, continuous progress, open classroom, minicourses

34. Utilizing staff resources—team teaching, aides, flexible scheduling

35. Deciding on appropriate pupil grouping procedures for instruction within the classroom

36. Creating an optimum physical environment for learning

37. Managing classrooms in order to get maximum learning

38. Presenting information and directions

39. Deciding which teaching technique is best suited for a specific purpose

40. Using questioning procedures that facilitate learning

41. Gearing instruction to problem solving

42. Using multimedia

43. Providing for reinforcement of basic skills

44. Other

FUTURE TRENDS AND ISSUES IN EDUCATION

45. Keeping abreast of developments in your own subject matter area

46. Year-round schools

47. Mainstreaming disabled children

48. Alternative education programs

49. Vocational and career education

50. Teacher centers

51. Professional retraining for future labor needs

52. Legislation affecting teachers

53. Other

Source: *From School Management by Wandering Around*, by L. Frase and R. Hetzel, 2003, Lancaster, PA: Technomic Publishing Company. Copyright by Scarecrow Press, Inc. Reprinted with permission.

References

Andelson, S. (2001). *FRISK documentation model.* Cerritos, CA: Atkinson, Andelson, Loya, Ruud & Romo.

Andrews, R., & Soder, R. (1987). Principal leadership and student achievement. *Educational Leadership, 44*(6), 9–11.

Annunziata, J. (1997). Linking teacher evaluation and professional development. In J. Stronge (Ed.), *Evaluating teaching: A guide to current thinking and best practice.* (pp. 288–301). Thousand Oaks, CA: Corwin.

Archer, J. (1998, February 18). Students' fortune rests with assigned teacher. *Education Week, 17*(23), 3.

Archer, J. (2003, January 9). Increasing the odds. *Quality Counts 2003: Education Week.* Retrieved September 17, 2010, from http://www.edcounts.org/archive/sreports/qc03/templates/article.cfm@slug=17odds.h22.html

Association of California School Administrators. (2010). *Walk'bout training.* Retrieved January 13, 2011, from http://www.acsa.org/MainMenuCategories/ProfessionalLearning/Quality-Solutions/WalkboutTraining.aspx

Basom, M. R., & Frase, L. (2004). Creating optimal work environments: Exploring teacher flow experiences. *Mentoring & Tutoring, 12*(2), 241–258.

Bennett, J. W. (1986). *What works: Research about teaching and learning.* Washington, DC: U.S. Department of Education.

Bennis, W. G. (1959, December). Leadership theory and administrative behavior: The problem of authority. *Administrative Science Quarterly, 4*(3), 259–260.

Bennis, W., & Nanus, B. (1985). *Leaders: The strategies for taking charge.* New York: Harper & Row.

Berliner, D. C. (1986). In pursuit of the expert pedagogue. *Educational Researcher, 15*(7), 5–13.

Blake, R. R., & Mouton, J. S. (1989). *The Managerial Grid III.* Houston, TX: Gulf.

Blase, J. (1987). Dimensions of effective school leadership: The teacher's perspective. *American Educational Research Journal, 24*(4), 589–610.

Blase, J., & Blase, J. (1998). *Handbook of instructional leadership.* Thousand Oaks, CA: Corwin.

Blase, J., & Kirby, P. C. (1992). The power of praise—A strategy for effective schools. *NASSP Bulletin, 76,* 69–77.

Bloom, B. (1956). *Taxonomy of educational objectives: The classification of educational objectives. Handbook I: The cognitive domain.* New York: Longman.

Board of Education v. Ingels, 394 N.E. 2d 69 (1979).

Boudett, K. P., City, E. A., & Murnane, R. J. (Eds.). (2007). *Data wise: A step-by-step guide to using assessment results to improve teaching and learning.* Cambridge, MA: Harvard Education Press.

Brandt, R. S. (1987). On leadership and student achievement: A conversation with Richard Andrews. *Educational Leadership, 44*(6), 9–16.

Bridges, E. (1990). *Managing the incompetent teacher.* Eugene: University of Oregon, Clearinghouse on Educational Management.

Brophy, J. E. (1996). *Teaching problem students.* New York: Guilford.

Buckingham, M., & Coffman, C. (1999). *First, break all the rules.* New York: Simon & Schuster.

Buckley, J., Schneider, M., & Shang, Y. (2004). *New structures and approaches for teacher preparation: Do they make a difference in teacher retention?* Retrieved September 13, 2010, from http://www.edfacilities.org/pubs/teacherretention.cfm

Burke, W. (1980). Developing and selecting leaders: What we know. In W. Eddy & W. Burke (Eds.), *Behavioral sciences and the manager's role* (pp. 173–186). San Diego, CA: University Associates.

Bushaw, W., & McNee, J. (2009, September). Phi Delta Kappa/Gallup Poll. Americans speak out: Are educators and policy makers listening? *Phi Delta Kappan, 91*(1), 9–23.

Businessballs.com. (n.d.). *People performance potential model: A simple group-profiling matrix tool for teams and organizations.* Retrieved October 8, 2011, from http://www.businessballs.com/people_performance_potential_model.htm

Camburn, E. M., Spillane, J. P., & Sebastian, J. (2010, December). Assessing the utility of a daily log for measuring principal leadership practice. *Educational Administration Quarterly, 46,* 707–737.

Caouette, A. (1995). *The phenomenon of flow as experienced by classroom teachers: Implications for leadership practice.* Unpublished doctoral dissertation, University of San Diego, California.

Chester, M. D., & Beaudin, B. Q. (1996, March). Efficacy beliefs of newly hired teachers in urban schools. *American Education Research, 33*(1), 233–257.

Cochran-Smith, M. (2006). *Policy, practice, and politics in teacher education.* Thousand Oaks, CA: Corwin.

Cohn, C. (2007, April 25). Empowering those at the bottom beats punishing them from the top. *Education Week, 26*(34), 32.

Collins, J. (2001). *Good to great: Why some companies make the leap . . . and others don't.* New York: HarperCollins.

Collins, J. (2005). *Good to great and the social sectors: Why business thinking is not the answer. A monograph to accompany Good to Great: Why Some Companies Make the Leap . . . and Others Don't.* New York: HarperCollins.

Colorado Statewide Systemic Initiative for Mathematics and Science (CONNECT). (1999). *Professional development criteria: A study guide for effective professional development.* Aurora, CO: Mid-continent Research for Education and Learning.

Commission on No Child Left Behind. (2007). *Beyond NCLB: Fulfilling the promise to our nation's children.* Washington, DC: The Aspen Institute.

Conway, W. (1992). *The quality secret: The right way to manage,* Nashua, NH: Conway Quality.

Cotton, K. (1995). *Effective school practices: A research synthesis. 1995 update* (School Improvement Research Series). Portland, OR: Northwest Regional Educational Laboratory.

Covey, S. (1992). *Principal-centered leadership.* New York: Fireside Press.

Creemers, B. P. (1994). *The effective classroom.* London: Cassell.

Csikszentmihalyi, M. (1990). *Flow: The psychology of optimal experience.* New York: Harper & Row.

Csikszentmihalyi, M., & Csikszentmihalyi, I. (1988). *Optimal experience.* Cambridge, UK: Cambridge University Press.

Darling-Hammond, L. (2000). Teacher quality and student achievement: A review of state policy evidence. *Education Policy Analysis Archives, 8*(1).

Darling-Hammond, L. (2003). Keeping good teachers. *Educational Leadership, 60*(8), 6–13.

Delehant, A. M. (2007). *Making meetings work: How to get started.* Thousand Oaks, CA: Corwin.

Deming, W. E. (1986). *Out of the crisis.* Cambridge: MIT Press/CAES.

Douglass, M., & Douglass, D. (1992). *Time management for teams.* New York: American Management Association, AMACOM Division.

Downey, C. J. (2004). *SchoolView: Gathering diagnostic trend data on curricular and instructional practices.* Huxley, IA: Curriculum Management Services.

Downey, C. J., & Frase L. E. (2003). *Participant's manual for conducting walk-throughs with reflective feedback to maximize student achievement: Basic seminar* (3rd ed.). Huxley, IA: Curriculum Management Services.

Downey, C. J., Frase, L., Poston, W., Steffy, B., English, F., & Melton, R. (2003). *Leaving no child behind: 50 ways to close the achievement gap.* Johnston, IA: Curriculum Management Systems.

Downey, C. J., Steffy, B., English, F., Frase, L., & Poston, W. (2004). *The three-minute classroom walk-through: Changing school supervisory practice one teacher at a time.* Thousand Oaks, CA: Corwin.

Downey, C. J., Steffy, B. E., Poston, W. K., & English, F. W. (2010). *Advancing the three-minute walk-through: Mastering reflective practice.* Thousand Oaks, CA: Corwin.

Doyle, M., & Straus, D. (1993). *How to make meetings work: The new interaction method.* New York: Berkley Trade. (Original work published 1976)

Doyle, W. (1985). Content representation in teachers' definitions of academic work. *Journal of Curriculum Studies, 18,* 365–379.

Drucker, P. (1974). *Management: Tasks, responsibilities, and practices.* New York: Harper & Row.

DuFour, R. (2004, May). What is a "professional learning community"? *Educational Leadership, 61*(8), 6–11.

DuFour, R., & Eaker, R. (1998). *Professional learning communities at work: Best practices for enhancing student achievement.* Bloomington, IN: Solution Tree.

DuFour, R., Eaker, R., & DuFour, R. (Eds.). (2005). *On common ground: The power of professional learning communities.* Bloomington, IN: Solution Tree.

Eisner, E. (2002). *The arts and the creation of mind.* New Haven, CT: Yale University Press.

English, F. W. (1992). *Deciding what to teach and test: Developing, aligning, and auditing the curriculum.* Thousand Oaks, CA: Corwin.

English, F. W. (2010). *Deciding what to teach and test: Developing, aligning and leading curriculum* (3rd ed.). Thousand Oaks, CA: Corwin.

English, F. W., & Poston, W. (1999, September). *GAAP: Generally accepted audit principles for curriculum management.* Huxley, IA: Curriculum Management Audit Centers.

English, F. W., & Steffy, B. (2001). *Deep curriculum alignment: Creating a level playing field for all children on high-stakes tests of educational accountability.* Lanham, MD: Scarecrow Press.

Erickson, H. L. (2007). *Concept-based curriculum and instruction for the thinking classroom.* Thousand Oaks, CA: Corwin.

Exstrom, M. (2009, September). Research into why teachers leave the profession is helping lawmakers craft better policies to hold onto them. *National Conference of State Legislatures.* Retrieved September 2, 2010, from http://www.ncsl.org/?tabid=18307

Farkas, S., Johnson, J., Foleno, T., Duffett, A., & Foley, P. (2000). A sense of calling: Who teaches and why. *Public Agenda.* Retrieved September 16, 2010, from http://www.publicagenda.org/reports/sense-calling

Feldusen v. Beach Pub. School Dist., 423 N.W. 2d 155 N.D. (1988).

Ferguson, R. F. (2006). Five challenges to effective teacher professional development. *Journal of Staff Development, 27*(4), 48–52.

Fernandez, C., & Yoshida, M. (2004). *Lesson study: A Japanese approach to improving mathematics teaching and learning.* Mahwah, NJ: Lawrence Erlbaum.

Fielder, F. (1967). *A theory of educational effectiveness.* New York: McGraw-Hill.

Firth, G. R., & Pajak, E. F. (Eds.). (1998). *Handbook of research on school supervision.* New York: Macmillan.

Floden, R. E., Porter, A. C., Schmidt, W. H., Freeman, D. J., & Schwille, J. R. (1981). Responses to curriculum pressures: A policy-capturing study of teacher decisions about content. *Journal of Educational Psychology, 73*(2), 129–141.

Frase, L. E. (2001, April). *A confirming study of the predictive power of principal classroom visits on efficacy and teacher flow experiences.* Paper presented at the Annual Meeting of the American Educational Research Association. Seattle, WA.

Frase, L. E. (2002, October). *Leadership and followership as "Flow Experience": Why and how attention to work environment and administrative practices matters.* Paper presented at the annual conference of the University Council for Educational Administration, Cincinnati, OH.

Frase, L. E. (2003, April). *Policy implications for school work environments: Implications from three research studies regarding frequency of teacher flow experiences, school principal classroom walk-throughs, teacher evaluation, professional development, and three efficacy measures.* Paper presented at the annual meeting of the American Education Research Association, Chicago.

Frase, L. E. (2005). Refocusing the purposes of teacher supervision. In F. English (Ed.), *The SAGE handbook of educational leadership.* Thousand Oaks, CA: Sage.

Frase, L. E., & Hetzel, R. (1990). *School management by wandering around.* Lanham, MD: Scarecrow Press.

Fraser, B. J., Williamson, J. C., & Tobin, K. (1987). Use of classroom and school climate scales in evaluating alternative high schools. *Teaching and Teacher Education, 3*(3), 219–231.

Freedman, B., & Lafleur, C. (2003, January). *Making leadership visible and practical: Walking for improvement.* Paper presented at the annual meeting of the International Congress of School Effectiveness and School Improvement, Sydney, Australia.

Freeman, D., Kuhs, T., Porter, A., Knappen, L., Floden, R., Schmidt, W., et al. (1980). *The fourth-grade mathematics curriculum as inferred from textbooks and tests* (Research Series No. 82). East Lansing: Michigan State University, Institute for Research on Teaching.

Freeston, K. R., & Costa, J. P. (1998). Making time for valuable work. *Educational Bulletin, 84,* 6–12.

Fruth, M., Bredeson, P., & Kasten, K. (1982, February). *Commitment to teaching: Teachers' responses to organization incentives.* Madison: Wisconsin Center for Education Research, University of Wisconsin-Madison.

Fullan, M. (2003). *The moral imperative of school leadership.* Thousand Oaks, CA: Corwin, and Toronto: Ontario Principals' Council.

Fullan, M., & Hargreaves, A. (1991). *What's worth fighting for? Working together for your school.* Toronto: Ontario Public School Teachers' Federation.

Futernick, K. (2007). *A possible dream: Retaining California teachers so all students learn.* Sacramento: California State University.

Galloway, F., & Frase, L. (2003, April). *A methodological primer for estimating the effects of flow in the classroom and the factors that foster them.* Paper presented at the annual meeting of the American Education Research Association, Chicago.

Garet, M., Porter, A., Desimone, L., Birman, B., & Kwang, S. Y. (2001). What makes professional development effective? Results from a national sample of teachers. *American Educational Research Journal, 38*(4), 915–945.

Gilson, T. (2008, Summer). Educational leadership: Are we busy yet? *American Secondary Education, 36*(3), 84–97.

Glanz, J. (2001, April 3). Pluto gives weight to Einstein's thesis of negative gravity. *New York Times,* pp. 51, 712.

Glatthorn, A. (2009). *The principal as curriculum leader: Shaping what is taught and tested.* Thousand Oaks, CA: Corwin.

Glickman C. D. (2002). *Leadership for learning: How to help teachers succeed.* Alexandria, VA: Association for Supervision and Curriculum Development.

Glickman, C. D., Gordon, S. P., & Ross-Gordon, J. M. (2005). *The basic guide to supervision and instructional leadership.* Boston: Pearson Education.

Good, T. L. (1982). How teachers' expectations affect results. *American Education, 18*(10), 25–32.

Goodman, K., Shannon, P., Freeman, Y., & Murphy, S. (1988). *Report card on basal readers.* New York: Richard C. Owen.

Gostick, A., & Elton, C. (2009). *The carrot principle: How the best managers use recognition to engage their people, retain talent, and accelerate performance.* New York: Free Press.

Gottesman, B. (2000). *Peer coaching for educators.* Lanham, MD: Scarecrow Press.

Gray, P. (2003). *An exploratory study of the relationship between principal walk-throughs and the work of teachers and principals.* Research toward doctoral dissertation, Claremont Graduate University and San Diego State University.

Gray, P., & Frase, L. E. (2003). *Analysis of teacher flow experiences as they relate to principal classroom walk-throughs.* Unpublished raw data from report to Shawnee Mission School Board, Shawnee Mission, KS.

Gray, S. P. (2005). *Good to great: A qualitative study of school principals who made the leap.* Unpublished doctoral dissertation, Claremont Graduate University and San Diego State University.

Gray, S. P., & Streshly, W. A. (2008). *From good schools to great schools: What their principals do well.* Thousand Oaks, CA: Corwin.

Gray, S. P., & Streshly, W. A. (2010). *Leading good schools to greatness: Mastering what great principals do well.* Thousand Oaks, CA: Corwin.

Griffin, M., & Tantiwong, T. (1989). *A six-year view of why women students want to become teachers.* Presented at the annual meeting of the American Educational Research Association, San Francisco.

Guarino, C., Santibañez, L., & Daley, G. (2006). Teacher recruitment and retention: A review of the recent empirical literature. *Review of Educational Research, 76*(2), 173–208.

Hager, J. L., & Scarr, L. E. (1983). Effective schools-effective principals: How to develop both. *Educational Leadership, 40*(5), 38–40.

Hall, G. E., & Hord, S. M. (2006). *Implementing change: Patterns, principles, and potholes* (2nd ed.). Boston: Allyn & Bacon.

Hallinger, P. (2005). Instructional leadership and the school principal: A passing fancy that refuses to fade away. *Leadership and Policy in Schools, 4,* 1–20.

Hallinger, P., & Heck, R. (1997). Exploring the principal's contribution to school effectiveness: 1980–1995. *School Effectiveness and School Improvement, 9*(2), 157–191.

Harutunian, A. T., III. (1980, July). Hoyem v. Manhattan Beach City School District: School district liability for injuries to truants. *California Law Review, 68*(4), 881–894.

Hattie, J. A. (1992). Measuring the effects of schooling. *Australian Journal of Education, 36*(1), 5–13.

Hawkins, C. (1997). *First aid for meetings.* Wilsonville, OR: BookPartners.

Haycock, K. (1998, Summer). Good teaching matters . . . a lot. *Thinking K–16, 3*(2).

Heck, R. (1991, April). *The effects of school context and principal leadership on school climate and school achievement.* Paper presented at the annual meeting of the American Educational Research Association, San Francisco.

Heck, R. (1992). Principals' instructional leadership and school performance: Implications for policy development. *Educational Evaluation and Policy Analysis, 14,* 21–34.

Heck, R., Larsen, T., & Marcoulides, G. (1990). Instructional leadership and school achievement: Validation of a causal model. *Educational Administration Quarterly, 26,* 94–125.

Hersey, P., & Blanchard, H. (1982). *Management of organizational behaviors: Utilizing human resources.* Englewood Cliffs, NJ: Prentice Hall.

Howell, B. (1981, January). Profile of the principalship. *Educational Leadership, 38,* 333–336.

Inman, D., & Marlow, L. (2004, Summer). Teacher retention: Why do beginning teachers remain in the profession? *The CBS Interactive Business Network.* Retrieved September 8, 2010, from http://findarticles.com/p/articles/mi_qa3673/is_4_124/ai_n29117808/

Jennings, M. (2007). *Leading effective meetings, teams, and work groups in districts and schools.* Alexandria, VA: Association for Supervision and Curriculum Development.

Johnson, J. (2008). The principal's priority 1. *Educational Leadership, 66*(1), 72–76.

Joseph, P., & Green, N. (1986). Perspectives on reasons for becoming teachers. *Journal of Teacher Education, 37*(6) 28–33.

Kachur, D., Stout, J., & Edwards, C. (2010). *Classroom walk-throughs to improve teaching and learning.* Larchmont, NY: Eye on Education.

Kane, P. (1989). *Attraction to teaching: A study of graduating seniors at Columbia and Barnard College.* Presented at the 1989 annual meeting of the American Educational Research Association, San Francisco.

Keigher, A. (2010). *Teacher attrition and mobility: Results from the 2008–09 Teacher Follow-Up Survey* (NCES 2010–353). Washington, DC: National Center for Education Statistics, U.S. Department of Education. Retrieved August 31, 2010, from http://nces.ed.gov/pubsearch/pubsinfo.asp?pubid=2010353

Keller, B. (2003, January 9). Hiring headway. *Quality Counts 2003: Education Week, 22*(17), 43–44.

Keruskin, T. (2005). *The perceptions of high school principals on student achievement by conducting walk-throughs.* Unpublished doctoral dissertation, University of Pittsburgh, PA.

Kmetz, J. T., & Willower, D. J. (1982). Elementary school principals' work behavior. *Educational Administration Quarterly, 18*(4), 62–78.

Kohn, A. (1999). *Punished by rewards: The trouble with gold stars, incentive plans, A's, praise, and other bribes* (2nd ed.). New York: Houghton Mifflin.

Kottkamp, R., Provenzo, E., & Cohn, M. (1986, April). Stability and change in a profession: Two decades of teacher attitudes, 1964–1984. *Phi Delta Kappan, 67*(8), 559–567.

Kouzes, J. M., & Posner, B. Z. (1993). *Credibility: How leaders gain and lose it, why people demand it.* San Francisco: Jossey-Bass.

Kouzes, J. M., & Posner, B. Z. (2010). *The truth about leadership: The no-fads, heart-of-the-matter facts you need to know.* San Francisco: Jossey-Bass.

Kulm, G., Roseman, J., & Treistman, M. (1999). A benchmarks-based approach to textbook evaluation. *Science Books & Films, 35*(4), 147–153.

Lawrance, C., Vachon, M., Leake, D., & Leake, B. (2001). *The marginal teacher: A step-by-step guide to fair procedures for identification and dismissal* (2nd ed.). Thousand Oaks, CA: Corwin.

Lebeis, C. (1939). Teacher tenure legislation. *Michigan Law Review, 37,* 430.

Leithwood, K., & Mascall, B. (2008). Collective leadership effects on student achievement. *Educational Administration Quarterly, 44*(4), 529–561.

Lencioni, P. (2004). *Death by meeting: A leadership fable . . . about solving the most painful problem in business.* San Francisco: Jossey-Bass.

Lewin, T. (1997). New methods tested in response to teachers who fail to teach. *New York Times, 146*(50,875), Section A, p. 1.

Louis, K., & Miles, M. (1991). Managing reform: Lessons from urban high schools. *School Effectiveness and School Management, 2*(2), 75–96.

Mackenzie, A., & Nickerson, P. (2009). *The time trap: The classic book on time management.* New York: AMACOM.

Mackenzie, R. A. (1997). *The time trap.* New York: American Management Association. (Original work published 1972)

Marquand, L. (1997). *Dealing with the less-than-effective employee.* Compton, CA: Compton Unified School District.

Marshall, K. (2009). *Rethinking teacher supervision and evaluation: How to work smart, build collaboration, and close the achievement gap.* San Francisco: Jossey-Bass.

Martin, W., & Willower, D. (1981). The managerial behavior of high school principals. *Educational Administration Quarterly, 17*(1), 69–90.

Marzano, R. J. (2003). *What works in schools: Translating research into action.* Alexandria, VA: Association for Supervision and Curriculum Development.

Marzano, R. J. (2007). *The art and science of teaching.* Alexandria, VA: Association for Supervision and Curriculum Development.

Marzano, R. J., Pickering, D., & Pollock, J. (2004). *Classroom instruction that works: Research-based strategies for increasing student achievement.* Englewood Cliffs, NJ: Prentice Hall. (Original work published 2001)

McBer, H. (2000). *Research into teacher effectiveness: A model of teacher effectiveness* (Research Report #216). London: Department for Education and Employment.

McCall, J. (1997). *The principal as steward.* Larchmont, NY: Eye On Education.

McEwan, E. K. (2003). *Ten traits of highly effective principals: From good to great performance.* Thousand Oaks, CA: Corwin.

McEwan, E. K., & McEwan, P. J. (2003). *Making sense of research.* Thousand Oaks, CA: Corwin.

McGregor, D. (1960). *The human side of enterprise.* New York: McGraw-Hill.

McKenna, J. (1993). Close encounter of the executive kind: Regrettably, for boss and subordinates alike, they're few in number. *Industry Week,* Features Section, p. 13.

McPeake, J. A. (2007). *The principalship: A study of the principal's time on task from 1960 to the twenty-first century.* Unpublished doctoral dissertation, Marshall University Graduate College, Huntington, WV. Retrieved January 1, 2011, from http://www.marshall .edu/etd/descript.asp?ref=767

MetLife. (2006). *Survey of America's teachers: Expectations and experiences.* Retrieved September 10, 2010, from http://www.metlife .com/about/corporate-profile/citizenship/metlife-foundation/ metlife-survey-of-the-american-teacher.html?WT.mc_id=vu1101

Microsoft Corporation. (2005, March). *Survey finds workers average only three productive days per week.* Retrieved December 13, 2010, from http://www.microsoft.com/presspass/press/2005/ mar05/03–15ThreeProductiveDaysPR.mspx

Miller, A., Ferguson, E., & Simpson, R. (1998). The perceived effectiveness of rewards and sanctions in primary schools: Adding in the parental perspective. *Educational Psychology, 18*(1), 55–64.

Miller, J. E., McKenna, M. C., & McKenna, B. A. (1998). A comparison of alternatively and traditionally prepared teachers. *Journal of Teacher Education, 49*(3), 165–176.

Mind Tools. (2011). Blake Mouton managerial grid: Balancing task- and people-oriented leadership. Retrieved July 5, 2011, from http://www.mindtools.com/pages/article/newLDR_73.htm

Molinaro, V., & Drake, S. (1998). Successful educational reform: Lessons for leaders. *International Electronic Journal for Leadership in Learning, 2*(9). Retrieved August 15, 2010, from http://www.ucalgary.ca/iejll/molinaro_drake

Moran, C. (2009, September 26). Principal gets credit for turning schools around: Chula Vista's Tessier got one out of U.S. sanctions. *San Diego Union Tribune,* p. A1.

Morris, V. C. (1981). *The urban principal: Discretionary decision-making in a large educational organization.* Washington, DC: National Institute of Education. (ERIC Document Reproduction Service No. ED207178)

Morris, V. C., Crowson, R. L., Nicherson, N. C., & Keefe, J. W. (1984). *Principals in action: The reality of managing schools.* Columbus, OH: Charles Merrill.

Mundry, S., Britton, E., Raizin, S., & Loucks-Horsley, S. (2000). *Designing successful professional meetings and conferences in education: Planning, implementation, and evaluation.* Thousand Oaks, CA: Corwin.

National Association of Secondary School Principals (NAASP). (1997). Students say: What makes a good teacher? *NASSP Bulletin, 6*(5), 15–17.

National Staff Development Council. (2001). *NSDC's standards for staff development.* Retrieved August 19, 2010, from http://www.nsdc.org/standards/index.cfm

Newman, T., Smith, B., Allensworth, E., & Bryk, A. (2001, Winter). Instructional program coherence: What it is and why it should guide school improvement policy. *Educational Evaluation and Analysis, 23*(4), 297–321.

North Carolina's Teacher Working Conditions Initiative. (2010, June). *2010 North Carolina North Carolina Teacher Work Conditions Survey: Analyses of current trends.* Retrieved August 31, 2010, from http://ncteachingconditions.org/research2010

Obama, B. A. (2010, March). A blueprint for reform: The reauthorization of the Elementary and Secondary Education Act. *ESEA Blueprint for Reform.* Washington, DC: U.S. Department of Education, Office of Planning, Evaluation and Policy Development.

Odiorne, G. (1983). *Management decisions by objective.* Englewood Cliffs, NJ: Prentice Hall Trade.

Olsen, B., & Anderson, L. (2007, January). Courses of action: A qualitative investigation into urban teacher retention and career development. *Urban Education, 42*(1), 5–29.

Olson, L. (2003, January 9). Swimming upstream. *Quality Counts 2003: Education Week, 22*(17), 43–44.

Peters, T. (1987). *Thriving on chaos.* New York: Knopf.

Peters, T., & Austin, N. (1984). *A passion for excellence.* New York: Random House.

Peters, T., & Waterman, R. (2004). *In search of excellence: Lessons from America's best-run companies.* New York: HarperBusiness Essentials. (Original work published 1982)

Peterson, K. D. (1977–1978). The principal's tasks. *Administrator's Notebook, 26*(8), 4.

Peterson, K. D. (2001, Winter). The roar of complexity. *Journal of Staff Development, 22*(1), 18–21.

Phillips, D. (1992). *Lincoln on leadership: Executive strategies for tough times.* New York: Warner Books.

Pitler, H., & Goodwin, B. (2008, Summer). Classroom walkthroughs: Learning to see the trees and the forest. *Mid-continent Research for Education and Learning (McREL).* Retrieved November 10, 2010, from http://www.mcrel.org/pdf/teacherprepretention/0125NL_ChangingSchools_58_4.pdf

Powell, C. (1995). *My American journey.* New York: Ballantine Books.

Price-Baugh, R. (1997). Correlation of textbook alignment with student achievement scores. *Dissertation Abstracts International, 58–05A*, 1529.

PriceWaterhouseCoopers LLP. (2007, January). *An independent study into school leadership.* Retrieved October 8, 2011, from http://www.cfbt.com/lincolnshire/pdf/latest%20summary%20of%20pcw%20Jan%2007.pdf

Ravitch, D. (2010). *The death and life of the great American school system: How testing and choice are undermining education.* New York: Basic Books.

Redfern, G. (1983). Dismissing unsatisfactory teachers. *ERS Spectrum, 1*(2), 17–21.

Reeder, S. (2005). *The hidden costs of tenure. Why are failing teachers getting a passing grade?* Retrieved February 11, 2011, from http://Thehiddencostsoftenure.com

Reeves, D. B. (2006). *The learning leader: How to focus school improvement for better results.* Alexandria, VA: Association for Supervision and Curriculum Development.

Reinbach, A. (2010, February 19). Why teachers teach. *Huffington Post.* Retrieved August 31, 2010, from http://www.huffingtonpost.com/andrew-reinbach/why-teachers-teach_b_468012.html

Ritsch, M. (2001, August 24). Principals urged to visit more classrooms. *Los Angeles Times,* Editorial Section. Retrieved May 10, 2010, from http://articles.latimes.com/2001/aug/24/local/me-37704

Robinson, V. (2007). *School leadership and student outcomes: Identifying what works and why* (ACEL Monograph Series No. 41). Winmalee, NSW: Australian Council for Educational Leaders.

Rosenshine, B. (1983). Teaching functions in instructional programs. *Elementary School Journal, 83*(4), 335–351.

Rossi, G. A. (2007). *The classroom walk-through: The perceptions of elementary school principals on its impact on student achievement.* Unpublished doctoral dissertation, University of Pittsburgh, PA. Retrieved October 8, 2011, from http://etd.library.pitt.edu/ETD/available/etd-07292007–140309/unrestricted/Rossi_ETD_7–29–07.pdf

Rotter, J. B. (1966). Generalized expectancies for internal versus external control of reinforcement. *Psychological Monographs, 80*(609).

Rotter, J. B. (1971). External control and internal control. *Psychology Today, 5,* 37–47.

Sager, R. (1992). Three principals who make a difference. *Educational Leadership, 40*(5).

Sanders, N. M., & Simpson, J. (2005). *State policy framework to develop highly qualified administrators.* Washington, DC: Council of Chief State School Officers.

Sarason, S. (1990). *The predictable failure of school reform.* San Francisco: Jossey-Bass.

Sather, S. (2009). *Leading professional learning teams: A start-up guide for improving instruction.* Thousand Oaks, CA: Corwin.

Schalock, D., Schalock, M., & Myton, D. (1998). Effectiveness—along with quality—should be the focus. *Phi Delta Kappan, 79*(6), 468.

Scholastic and the Bill & Melinda Gates Foundation. (2010). *Primary sources: America's teachers on America's schools.* Retrieved September 1, 2010, from www.scholastic.com/primarysources/pdfs/100646_ScholasticGates.pdf

Scott, S. S. (1991). *The critical role of the superintendent in the induced exits of tenured certificated staff.* Unpublished doctoral dissertation, University of La Verne, La Verne, CA.

Shipman, N. J. (1983). *Effective time-management techniques for school administrators.* Englewood Cliffs, NJ: Prentice Hall.

Simons, T. L., & Peterson, R. S. (2000). Task conflict and relationship conflict in top management teams: The pivotal role of intragroup trust. *Journal of Applied Psychology, 85,* 102–111.

Smylie, M. A., Allensworth, E., Greenberg, R. C., Harris, R., & Luppescu, S. (2001). *Teacher professional development in Chicago: Supporting effective practice.* Chicago: Consortium on Chicago School Research.

Sparks, K., & Keiler, L. (2003). Why teachers leave. In M. Scherer (Ed.), *Keeping good teachers* (pp. 213–218). Alexandria, VA: Association for Supervision and Curriculum Development.

Sproul, L. (1976, November). *Managerial attention in new educational systems.* Seminar on Organizations as Loosely Coupled Systems, Urbana, Illinois.

Stamper v. Board of Education, 491 N.E. 2d 36, IL. App. Ct. (1986).

Stage, S. A., & Quiroz, D. R. (1997). A meta-analysis of interventions to decrease disruptive classroom behavior in public education settings. *School Psychology Review, 26*(3), 333–368.

Steffy, B. (1989). *Career stages of classroom teachers: Maintaining excellence for a lifetime.* Lancaster, PA: Technomic.

Stiggins, R. D., & Duke, D. L. (1988). *The case for commitment to teacher growth.* Albany: State University of New York.

Stigler, J. W., & Hiebert, J. (1999). *The teaching gap: Best ideas from world's teachers for improving education in the classroom.* New York: The Free Press.

Stronge, J. H. (1988, May). The elementary school principalship: A position in transition? *Principal, 67*(5), 32–33.

Stronge, J. H., Richard, H. B., & Catano, N. (2008). *Qualities of effective principals.* Alexandria, VA: Association for Supervision and Curriculum Development.

Supovitz, J. A., & Weathers, J. (2004). *Dashboard lights: Monitoring implementation of district instructional reform strategies.* Philadelphia: Consortium for Policy Research in Education, University of Pennsylvania.

Taylor, F. (1911). *The principles of scientific management.* New York: Harper & Row.

Teddlie, C., Kirby, P., & Springfield, S. (1989). Effective versus ineffective schools: Observable differences in the classroom. *American Journal of Education, 97,* 221–236.

Thorndike, R. (1951). Community variables as predictors of intelligence and academic achievement. *Journal of Educational Psychology, 42,* 321–338.

Tienken, C. H., & Stonaker, L. (2007). When every day is professional development day. *Journal of Staff Development, 24*(2), 24–29.

Togneri, W., & Anderson, S. E. (2003). *Beyond islands of excellence: What districts can do to improve instruction and achievement in all schools.* Washington, DC: Learning First Alliance. Retrieved September 5, 2010, from http://learningfirst.org/publications/districts/

Tschannen-Moran, M. (2004). *Trust matters: Leadership for successful schools.* San Francisco: Jossey-Bass.

U.S. Department of Education. (2010). *ESEA blueprint for reform: The reauthorization of the Elementary and Secondary Education Act.* Washington, DC: Author.

Valentine, J., Clark, D., Nickerson, N., & Keefe, J. (1981). *The middle school principal.* Reston, VA: National Association of Secondary School Principals.

Van Horn, R. (1999). Inner-city schools: A multiple-variable discussion. *Phi Delta Kappan, 81*(4), 291.

Varrati, A., & Smith, A. (2008). Principals as mentors in teacher education: How preservice teachers' voices informed practice. *Academic Leadership Live, 6*(4).

Walberg, H. J., & Waxman, H. C. (1983). Teaching, learning, and the management of instruction. In D. C. Smith (Ed.), *Essential knowledge for beginning educators* (pp. 38–54). Washington, DC: American Association of Colleges for Teacher Education. (ERIC Document Reproduction Service No. ED237458)

Wang, M. C., Haertel, G. D., & Walberg, H. J. (1993). Toward a knowledge base for school learning. *Review of Educational Research, 63*(3), 249–294.

Wells, H. G. (1920). *The outline of history.* Garden City, NY: Doubleday. (Original work published 1961)

Western Regional Educational Laboratory. (2000). *Teachers who learn, kids who achieve: A look at schools with model professional development.* Retrieved September 14, 2010, from http://www.wested.org/cs/we/view/rs/179

Whitefield, D. (1981, February 2). Gutenberg writing the Bible on how to select management teams that mesh. *Los Angeles Times,* part VI, pp. 3–5.

Wiggins, G., & McTighe, J. (2005). *Understanding by design.* Alexandria, VA: Association for Supervision and Curriculum Development.

Wimpelberg, R., Teddlie, C., & Stringfield, S. (1989). Sensitivity to context: The past and future of effective school research. *Educational Administration Quarterly, 25*(1), 82–107.

York v. Bd. of School Com. of Mobile County, 460 S. 2d 857, AL (1884).

Zepeda, S. (2008). *Professional development: What works.* Larchmont, NY: Eye On Education.

Zhu, N. (2001). *The effects of teachers' flow experiences on the cognitive engagement of students.* Unpublished doctoral dissertation, San Diego State University/University of San Diego Joint Doctoral Program, San Diego, CA.

Index

CORWIN

A SAGE Company

The Corwin logo—a raven striding across an open book—represents the union of courage and learning. Corwin is committed to improving education for all learners by publishing books and other professional development resources for those serving the field of PreK–12 education. By providing practical, hands-on materials, Corwin continues to carry out the promise of its motto: **"Helping Educators Do Their Work Better."**